TEACHING MITZVOT

CONCEPTS, VALUES, and ACTIVITIES

by Barbara Binder Kadden and Bruce Kadden

A.R.E. Publishing, Inc.
Denver, Colorado

Published by:
A.R.E. Publishing, Inc.
Denver, Colorado

Library of Congress Catalog Card Number 88-70869
ISBN 0-86705-021-7

Printed in the United States of America
10   9   8   7   6   5   4   3   2

DEDICATION

To our parents Alan and Shirley Binder,
may their memories be for a blessing,
and Paul and Shirley Kadden;
and to our children,
Alana Sharon and Micah Benjamin.

CONTENTS

AHAVAH

ACKNOWLEDGEMENTS

If we had only been blessed by having such
wonderful editors and publishers as Audrey
Friedman Marcus and Rabbi Raymond A.
Zwerin

. . . **Dayenu!**

If we had only received inspiration when it
was greatly needed from Judy Drueding and
Carol Brown

. . . **Dayenu!**

If we had only been offered answers to many
of our research questions by the staff of the
John Steinbeck Public Library

. . . **Dayenu!**

Had we only received suggestions for
audiovisual resources from Eric Goldman of
Ergo Media Inc.

. . . **Dayenu!**

And if we had only been given permission by
Temple Emanuel in Denver to photograph the
beautiful Shabbat lamp which is on the cover
of this book

. . . **Dayenu!**

We appreciate the help of all these people and
institutions who came through for us whenever
called upon.

Cover: Antique brass Sabbath lamp, nine-
teenth century Europe. Donated to Temple
Emanuel of Denver, Colorado by Dr. Byron
Cohn in memory of Dr. Essie White Cohn.

ABOUT MITZVOT

The word Mitzvah (plural Mitzvot) means commandment, specifically a divine commandment. Through common usage, sometimes misusage, the word has also come to mean a good deed. These definitions are probably not so diverse as they may appear to be, especially since many of the Mitzvot described in this book seem to fall under both definitions.

The most common associations with the word Mitzvah are Bar Mitzvah and Bat Mitzvah, the ceremonies which mark the passage from childhood to religious maturity. A Jewish boy becomes a Bar Mitzvah at age 13, a girl a Bat Mitzvah at age 12½. But these terms refer to something far more significant than ceremonies. They refer to young persons coming of age, taking on the *Ol HaTorah* — the obligation to participate in the Jewish community and to observe the commandments.

The original source of Mitzvot is the Torah. Yet, though the commandments are in the Torah, they are neither specified nor enumerated there. One must go to the Talmud to find the tradition that Torah contains 613 Mitzvot (*Makkot* 23b). The number 613 is not, in and of itself, significant. Rather, it is the sum of 248 positive Mitzvot (which, according to the Rabbis, corresponds to the bones in the human body), and 365 negative Mitzvot (corresponding to the number of days in a solar year).

We might ask why the number of Mitzvot is 613 and not 611, which is the numerical value (*gematria*) of the four Hebrew letters (400 + 6 + 200 + 5) in the word Torah. To resolve this puzzlement, the Rabbis said that the first two of the Ten Commandments ("I am the Lord, your God . . ." and "You shall have no other gods beside me") were given directly to the people by God, while the other 611 Mitzvot were given by God to Moses. Another explanation is that 613 is equal to the value of the word *baTorah* — "in the Torah."

The 613 Mitzvot are also referred to as the *Taryag Mitzvot*. In *gematria*, *taryag* is the pronunciation of the four Hebrew letters whose sum is 613. Just as they are not enumerated in the Torah itself, the 613 are also not enumerated in the Talmud. The first systematic attempt to list the Mitzvot was done by

Simon Kairo in the eighth century. Curiously, his work contains 265 positive Mitzvot and 348 negative Mitzvot.

The most significant enumeration of the commandments is *Sefer HaMitzvot*, written by Maimonides in about 1170 C.E. In it Maimonides cites the biblical source of each Mitzvah, and discusses certain aspects of its observance. While some medieval authorities criticized Maimonides' list, it became the definitive list of Mitzvot. *Sefer HaChinuch*, a thirteenth century work written by the Spanish Talmudist Aaron Ha-Levi of Barcelona, utilizing Maimonides' work, lists the Mitzvot in the order they are found in the Torah, and discusses each one.

In addition to the 613 Mitzvot of the Torah (called *Mitzvot De'Oraita*), the Rabbis ordained seven Mitzvot (*Mitzvot De'Rabbanan*) which were not based on Torah. They are: Reciting a blessing for anything that is enjoyed (fruit, wine, etc), washing one's hands before eating, lighting Shabbat candles, making an *eruv* (which permits a wider interpretation of Sabbath laws), reciting the *Hallel* (Psalms 113-118) on festivals, lighting Chanukah candles, and reading the scroll of Esther on Purim (Maimonides, *The Commandments*, vol. 1, p. 265).

Besides the division into positive and negative Mitzvot, there are other significant divisions of the Mitzvot:

1. Time-bound and non-time bound:

   Time-bound Mitzvot are those which are observed at a particular time each day (e.g., reciting the *Sh'ma*, putting on *Tefillin*) or at a specific time during the year (e.g., hearing the *Shofar* on Rosh Hashanah). This distinction is important because, since Talmudic times, the primary responsibilities of a woman (being a wife and mother, and bearing and caring for children and the home) removes her from a predictable schedule. Therefore, women are deemed exempt from performing most positive time-bound Mitzvot. In many traditional Jewish communities, this exemption has been tantamount to a prohibition. For instance, a person who is exempt from performing a Mitzvah may not perform the Mitzvah on behalf of someone who is obligated to perform it. A woman, therefore, may not lead a worship service if men are present, since she is exempt from the Mitzvah, while the men are obligated. As if to obviate this exclusion, in some traditional communities, women have created and serve as leaders of women's service. Liberal congregations, for the most part, have no objection to women leading worship services or serving as Rabbis or Cantors.

Women are, however, obligated to observe certain positive time-bound Mitzvot including lighting Shabbat candles and fasting on Yom Kippur, eating *matzah* on Pesach, and going to the *Mikvah* each month.

2. *Mitzvot Kallot* and *Mitzvot Chamurot*:

Some sources distinguish between "light" (less important) and "serious" (more important) Mitzvot. However, the general consensus has been that one should observe all of the Mitzvot, and that violating any Mitzvah is a serious transgression.

3. *Mitzvot sheh'bein adam lachaveiro/Mitzvot sheh'bein adam laMakom*:

Mitzvot can also be divided into those that are between one person and another (you shall not covet, steal, murder, etc.) and those that are between a person and God (dwelling in a *Sukkah*, affixing a *Mezuzah*, etc.). It should be pointed out that *all* transgressions against another person are also transgressions against God. This distinction is particularly important with regard to asking forgiveness for a sin. If one has sinned against another, one must ask his or her forgiveness first. Only then is it permitted to ask God's forgiveness.

4. *Mishpatim/Chukim*:

The Rabbis distinguished between *Mishpatim*, those laws that would have been apparent even if they were not in the Torah (e.g., not to murder, steal, slander, etc.), and *Chukim*, those laws that are divine decrees (e.g., *Kashrut*, *sha'atnez*, etc.). During the medieval period, some Rabbis saw *Mishpatim* as laws based on reason, and *Chukim* as laws to be observed for no apparent logical reason, but because they were commanded by the Almighty.

Positing reasons for the Mitzvot (*Ta'amei Mitzvot*) has often led to controversy. Some Rabbis insisted

that the *Ta'amei Mitzvot* were purposely left unclear in order to encourage our speculation. Others argued that the reasons are in the Torah, we must simply persist in searching them out. To Maimonides every Mitzvah in the Torah has a reason that is known to God, if not to human beings. Ultimately, he said, every Mitzvah is intended for the welfare of the body and/or of the soul.

Debate about the *Ta'amei Mitzvot* is due in part to the sparseness of explication in the Torah. Very few of the Mitzvot include a reason for their observance, and whatever reasons are included seem more like a promise of reward than a reason — e.g., "Honor your father and your mother, that you may long endure on the land that the Eternal One, your God, is giving you" (Exodus 20:12). The Torah also implies that the reason for the dietary laws is to make us holy, which is usually interpreted to mean set apart from other peoples (Leviticus 11:44-45, 20:26).

Any reluctance to search for the *Ta'amei Mitzvot* is in part an effort to emphasize that one observes the Mitzvot not just because they make sense, but because they are divine commands. Even those Rabbis who would encourage speculation agree on this point.

Doing Mitzvot carries an implied reward — life in the world to come. However, what this means is never made clear. We are taught to do Mitzvot, not for a promised reward, but simply because they are Mitzvot — God's commandments. Furthermore, the *kavanah* (intention) with which we approach Mitzvot is also considered important. Simply going through the motions to fulfill the law, while acceptable, is discouraged. Rather, Mitzvot are to be performed with joy and devotion.

The Mitzvot are the foundation of Jewish practice, but have required much interpretation throughout the ages. This process of interpreting the Mitzvot as they apply to specific situations is called *halachah* (literally, "the way"). The process of *halachah* has been carried out by the leading Rabbis of each generation, first through their teachings, which became a part of the *Mishnah* and Talmud, then through the Codes, such as the *Mishneh Torah* of Maimonides and the *Shulchan Aruch* of Joseph Karo, and through the *Responsa*, which are the Rabbis' answers to questions of Jewish practice.

The Conservative movement considers the Mitzvot to be binding, and follows the practice of preserving and enhancing *halachah* through

Rabbinic decisions. These decisions sometimes differ significantly from the tradition. For example, driving to synagogue on Shabbat is permitted. Women are permitted to lead services, and now to perform the duties of Rabbi and *Chazan*.

The Reform Movement has taken a different approach to the Mitzvot. Because of its emphasis upon personal autonomy, Reform Judaism places responsibility on the individual (guided by the tradition) to decide which Mitzvot to observe. Historically, Reform has put great emphasis on the ethical Mitzvot, and has de-emphasized the ritual Mitzvot. However, each person has a responsibility to learn about the Mitzvot and to make a decision based upon knowledge.

ABOUT THIS BOOK

Contents

Teaching Mitzvot: Concepts, Values, and Activities consists of 36 units, each dealing with one Mitzvah or a number of related Mitzvot. Each unit contains four sections: Overview, Activities, All-school Programs, and Resources. The Overview consists of the historical development of the Mitzvah or Mitzvot, concepts derived by extension of the basic principles, and ramifications and implications of the Mitzvah for today. The historical development usually begins with citation of the appropriate biblical verses followed by pertinent material from later Jewish sources. This section is intended to provide sufficient background on a Mitzvah to enable either an experienced or beginning teacher to feel comfortable with the subject.

The Activities section in each unit contains a wide variety of teaching ideas listed by grade levels: Primary (Grades K-3), Intermediate (Grades 4-6), and Secondary (Grades 7-up).

The sections on All-school Programs contain ideas for learning activities involving the entire school.

At the end of each unit, there is an extensive Resources section. Some of the listings are specifically "For the Teacher" who wishes to do further reading and research in order to expand his or her own knowledge prior to teaching a particular Mitzvah. The "For the Student" list contains materials available to supplement information about the Mitzvah. An annotated listing of appropriate audiovisual materials completes the Resources section. Grade levels are specified on all student and audiovisual entries.

Preparing to Teach

When preparing to teach a particular unit or a specific Mitzvah, it is suggested that the teacher first read the Overview and then examine the instructional activities, choosing those that best suit his or her teaching objectives and the abilities of the students. The teacher should then decide what, if any, additional information might be needed in order to proceed with the lesson. Utilize the "For the Teacher" resources for that purpose. Then, select activities which are judged to be most suitable to provide a dynamic and challenging lesson.

Creative Uses of This Material

The contents of *Teaching Mitzvot* can provide the basis for an entire curriculum on Mitzvot for a grade, several grades, and for an entire school. Or, teachers may choose to utilize the background material and activities in those units which relate to the subject matter of the existing curriculum, such as life cycle, holidays, ethics, and the Ten Commandments. The book is an essential reference on the subject of Mitzvot and belongs in every teacher's library. Furthermore, substitute teachers will benefit by having over 600 ready-made teaching activities available to them.

Teaching Mitzvot is also designed for use as a "Mitzvah of the Week" or "Mitzvah of the Month" program for any grade of the religious school, or for all grades simultaneously. Each week, for 36 weeks, a grade or grades can study a different Mitzvah. Some grades might allot one or two hours for their study; others might allot a 20 minute period of each session throughout the year. The unusual All-school Programs provide many ideas for a stimulating and educational introduction or conclusion to each unit of study. Such programs might coincide with the observance of a particular holiday, or they can stand on their own as an opportunity for the entire school to participate together in a learning experience.

If a decision is made to involve the whole school in the study of Mitzvot, the entire congregation can participate in related programs. For example, Shabbat sermons can focus on the Mitzvah of the Week or Month. Bulletin articles by the Rabbi, Director of Education, teachers, or students, can further illuminate the Mitzvah or Mitzvot under consideration. Adult classes can study the same material. Parents and other congregants can join the school for the all-school events.

CONCLUSION

The Mitzvot are not always understood by Jews, let alone by non-Jews. This book can serve as a reference and a resource providing Jews and non-Jews alike with insights into Jewish law and practice.

Mitzvot are at the very core of Judaism. The observance of the Mitzvot has preserved the vitality and traditions of the Jewish people from generation to generation. *Teaching Mitzvot* provides teachers with the tools for transmitting the essence of Jewish values and practices to their students.

UNIT 1

Observing/Remembering Shabbat
שָׁמוֹר וְזָכוֹר שַׁבָּת

OVERVIEW

The only holiday mentioned in the Ten Commandments pertains to Shabbat: "Remember (*zachor*) the Sabbath day to keep it holy. Six days you shall labor and do all your work, but the seventh day is a Sabbath of the Lord your God: you shall not do any work, you, your son or daughter, your male or female servant, or your cattle, or the stranger who is within your settlements. For in six days the Eternal One made heaven and earth and sea, and all that is in them, and God rested on the seventh day; therefore, the Eternal One blessed the seventh day and hallowed it" (Exodus 20:8-11). When the Ten Commandments are repeated in Deuteronomy 5:15, the Sabbath is to be observed (*shamor*) as a remembrance "that you were a slave in the land of Egypt and the Lord your God freed you from there with a mighty hand and an outstretched arm."

The Torah does not specify what constitutes work. The Rabbis, however, noted that Leviticus 19:30 states: "You shall keep My Sabbaths and venerate My sanctuary: I am the Lord." Since Shabbat and the sanctuary are mentioned in the same verse, they concluded that those labors which were required for constructing the Tabernacle were the very work prohibited on the Sabbath. The *Mishnah* enumerates 39 categories of work (*muktzah*) that are forbidden: plowing, sowing, reaping, sheaf-making, threshing, winnowing, selecting, sifting, grinding, kneading, baking, sheep-shearing, bleaching, combining raw materials, dying, spinning, separation into threads, tying a knot, untying a knot, sewing, tearing, trapping, slaughtering, skinning, tanning, scraping pelts, marking out, cutting to shape, writing, erasing, building, demolishing, kindling a fire, extinguishing a fire, the final hammer blow (of a new article), carrying from the private to the public domain or vice versa (*Shabbat* 7:2).

Some of these activities relate to the manufacture and preparation of fabrics, hides, and poles used to build the Tabernacle. Others relate to preparing dyes that were used, or to baking bread used for sacrifices.

While these activities reflect the day-to-day life of the ancient Jewish community, Rabbis throughout history have used them as a basis for deciding whether new activities are permitted or forbidden on Shabbat. For example, it is forbidden to turn electricity on or off, since such acts are analogous to kindling or extinguishing a fire. It is permitted, however, to leave an electrical appliance running during Shabbat, or to use a timer to turn an appliance on and off, as long as the timer is set before Shabbat. It is also forbidden to drive or ride in a motor driven vehicle on Shabbat.

All of these restrictions may be lifted in order to save a human life. "The commandment of the Sabbath, like all other commandments, may be set aside if human life is in danger" (*Mishneh Torah, Hilchot Shabbat* 1). Saving a life takes precedence because the Torah states: "You shall keep My laws and My rules, by the pursuit of which human beings shall live" (Leviticus 18:5), i.e., shall live and not die. Even if there is doubt about whether a life will be saved, one may violate the Sabbath "for the mere possibility of danger to human life overrides the Sabbath" (*Mishneh Torah, Hilchot Shabbat* 1).

Many find the numerous restrictions of activities on Shabbat liberating. Rabbi Samuel Dresner has called keeping Shabbat "one of the surest means of finding peace in the war-torn realm of the soul" (*The Sabbath*, p. 14). Erich Fromm has written: "The Sabbath symbolizes a state of union between a man and nature and between man and man. By not working — that is to say, by not participating in the process of natural and social change — man is free from the chains of time" (*You Shall Be As Gods*, p. 198).

Not only is it a Mitzvah to refrain from working on Shabbat, it is a positive Mitzvah to rest on Shabbat. Some Jews take a nap on Shabbat afternoon to observe this Mitzvah.

The second positive Mitzvah pertaining to Shabbat is to proclaim the sanctity of the Sabbath, based on the phrase "Remember the Sabbath day to keep it holy" (Exodus 20:8). This Mitzvah is fulfilled by reciting the Shabbat *Kiddush* on Friday evening, and by the Havdalah ceremony at the end of Shabbat. In addition, one honors Shabbat by bathing, by the way that one prepares for it by wearing one's finest clothes, and by eating the finest food one can afford. According to Maimonides the lighting of the Shabbat candles also falls under the Mitzvah to sanctify the Sabbath, although some Rabbis list it as a separate Mitzvah.

Besides the prohibition of work on Shabbat, there are two other negative Mitzvot: prohibiting both traveling and punishing. It is forbidden to walk more than 2,000 cubits beyond the boundary of town, although in order to hear a noted sage in a neighboring town, one can go twice as far. It is also forbidden to carry out punishment against a criminal on Shabbat. It was further deduced from this prohibition that Jewish courts are not to meet on the Sabbath (*Palestinian Talmud, Sanhedrin* 4:6).

The importance of these Mitzvot has been stressed throughout Jewish history. Profaning the Sabbath is similar to testifying in the presence of God, by whose word the universe came into being, that God did not create the world in six days and did not rest on the Sabbath (*Mechilta* to Exodus 20:14).

Maimonides considered these Mitzvot as being equal to all of the other Mitzvot of the Torah (*Mishneh Torah Hilchot Shabbat* 30:15). Ahad Ha-am summarized the importance of the Sabbath to the people Israel in his famous phrase: "More than Israel has kept the Sabbath, the Sabbath has kept Israel."

ACTIVITIES

Primary

1. Read the story of Creation to your students (Genesis 1:1-2:3). Ask your class: Which day of the week is the seventh day? What happened on the seventh day of creation? What do you do on the seventh day? Point out that evening is mentioned first, and then morning at the end of each day of creation, which reflects the Jewish custom of beginning Shabbat and holidays in the evening. Discuss how often Shabbat occurs, how long it lasts, and the customs and ceremonies with which they are familiar.

2. Very often young children learn the Shabbat blessings for candles, wine, and *challah* by rote without understanding their meaning. To help them learn the meaning of these blessings, create an illustrated poster series. Identify key words for the students to know (*baruch* means blessed, *ner* means candle, *lechem* means bread, *boray*

means creator, *p'ri hagafen* means fruit of the vine). With children this age, follow the Hebrew recitation of each blessing with the English translation.

3. Gather together the ritual objects associated with Shabbat (candlestick holders, *challah* board, *challah* cover, *Kiddush* cup, Havdalah candle, spice box, *challah*, wine). Display and discuss each one with students. Afterward, place all the objects on a table, assemble students around it, then cover the objects with a cloth. Direct the children to shut their eyes. While they do this, remove one object. Uncover the objects. Ask the students to open their eyes and guess which object is missing.

4. With your students practice setting a Shabbat table. Spread a white cloth and then set the table with plates, flatware, ritual objects, and flowers.

5. Have each student create a scrapbook. Each Shabbat he/she puts something into it which connects the child to the spirit of Shabbat. These items could be something from their home ritual, from attending services, or from a special experience.

6. Bake *challah* with your students. In addition to simply baking it, observe the Mitzvah of taking *Challah*. A small amount of dough, at least the size of an olive, is removed. It is then burned, and the following prayer is recited:

בָּרוּךְ אַתָּה, יְיָ אֱלֹהֵינוּ, מֶלֶךְ הָעוֹלָם, אֲשֶׁר קִדְּשָׁנוּ בְּמִצְוֹתָיו וְצִוָּנוּ לְהַפְרִישׁ חַלָּה.

Blessed are You, O Eternal our God, Ruler of the Universe, Who has made us holy with Mitzvot and commanded us to separate *challah*.

This Mitzvah is in remembrance of that part of a sacrifice which was given to the priests during the time of the Temple in Jerusalem.

Recipes for *challah* are available in nearly any Jewish cookbook.

Reference: *In Search of Plenty: The History of Jewish Food* by Oded Schwartz.

7. Ask students to imagine that they are to be the first Jewish space station residents. Ask: What will you have to bring with you in order to observe Shabbat on board?

Intermediate

1. Have students write metaphors for Shabbat using the following: Shabbat is like _____. Have them each write a poem based on their sentences. Read the poems as an introduction to a Shabbat celebration.

2. Shabbat involves the use of all our senses. Create five dittos. On each ditto draw a representation of one of our physical senses (a nose, ear, mouth, eyes, and a hand to represent touch). Each student receives a set of five dittos and is asked to list or draw Shabbat experiences which correlate to each of the senses. Some experiences can be added to more than one ditto.

3. Prepare a variety of Jewish foods which are typically served on Shabbat. These might include *challah*, chicken soup with *matzah* balls, *cholent*. Serve each food and encourage students to shut their eyes and let all their senses communicate to them. Ask the following questions: How do the foods smell? How do your other senses react when they smell these foods? How can the memory of the smell or taste or texture of a particular food remind us of the feeling of a Jewish holiday or of another special time?

4. Extend activities #2 and/or #3 by reading or putting on the play "Shabbat Recipe" from *Jewish Plays for Jewish Days* by Michelle Gabriel.

5. Share the following *midrash* with your class:

The Journey

Three men were traveling in the forest. It was getting late and Shabbat was approaching. Concerned about robbers, they debated whether or not to continue their journey. Two went on, but the third, not wanting to violate the Sabbath, camped in the forest. A large, tame bear came to the man. The man shared his meals with the bear.

After the Sabbath, the man continued on his journey, with the bear following along. Robbers approached the man and demanded to know who he was. He told them, "I am a Jew."

"From where do you come?" they asked.

"From the king's palace," he replied.

"Who gave you this bear?" they asked.

He answered that the king gave him the bear for protection and company. So that the man would not reveal the robbers to the king, they gave the man all their money and accompanied him home.

Ask the following questions: Who is the king in this story? What is the palace? Why did the man receive the money? Did the man deserve a reward? Do you think this could really happen? Do you expect a reward for observing the Sabbath? If so, what would the reward be?

6. The opening paragraph of the *Kiddush* for Erev Shabbat comes from Genesis 2:1-3. Have students do the activity sheet on this blessing in *Hebrew Blessings Ditto Pak*, pp. 12 and 13.

7. Since many children do not have an opportunity to participate in Havdalah, spend a few sessions creating the ritual items for this ceremony. Instructions follow for making a Havdalah candle, a spice box, and a *Kiddush* cup.

Havdalah Candle

Materials needed: Candle wicking, paraffin, and coloring for the wax (obtain at a crafts store); at least four metal tennis ball cans; four large coffee cans for melting the wax.

Procedure: Melt chunks of paraffin in the tennis ball cans and add coloring. These are then placed inside the coffee cans which are filled half way up with water. The coffee can is then placed on a heat source set on low. Give each student three or four equal lengths of wicking. Each wick is then dipped in the wax over and over again until the desired thickness is created. The three or four strands are then braided.

Spice Box

Materials needed: A small jar or box, paint, or fabric.

Procedure: Fill the container with a variety of sweet smelling spices. Punch holes in the lid and decorate with paint or fabric. Then place the lid on the container.

Kiddush Cup

Materials needed: Greenware cups (unfinished pottery that can be obtained at a ceramic shop), paints and glazes as recommended by the shop.

Procedure: Decorate the cups and return them to the ceramic shop for firing and then glazing. This *Kiddush* cup will be a long lasting ritual object for the students to use at home.

Secondary

1. Utilizing information from the Overview for this unit, synthesize the Jewish concept of an ideal Shabbat. Then ask each student to come up with his/her own personal version of an ideal Shabbat. Compare and discuss.

2. With your students listen to the song "Sabbath Prayer" from the musical *Fiddler on the Roof*. Discuss the content of the song. Does it reflect an outmoded life style or can we derive meaning from it for today? Using a melody of a contemporary song, write new lyrics to create the students' own "Sabbath Prayer."

3. The Rabbis have taught that nothing is repeated in the Torah without reason. The commandment to observe Shabbat appears twice: Exodus 20:8-11 and Deuteronomy 5:12-15. With your students compare these two versions. Questions to consider: In the Exodus passage, the initial word is "remember" and in Deuteronomy, it is "observe." How are these words different? Which is the more important concept for Jewish survival — to remember the Sabbath or to observe it? What important event is mentioned in the Exodus passage? Is it mentioned in Deuteronomy? If not, what event is singled out? Compare these passages with the *Kiddush* for Erev Shabbat.

4. Ask students if they think they will observe Shabbat in different ways at different stages in their lives. How do they think they will observe Shabbat when they are in college? When they are married? When they have children? When they have grandchildren?

5. Have students do research in order to formulate a Shabbat celebration for the class. The excellent sources below deal with Shabbat celebrations.

References: *A Shabbat Haggadah for Celebration*

and Study compiled by Michael Strassfeld; *The Art of Jewish Living: The Shabbat Seder* by Dr. Ron Wolfson; *Sabbath: The Day of Delight* by Abraham E. Millgram; *The First Jewish Catalog* by Richard Siegel, Michael Strassfeld, and Sharon Strassfeld; *The Sabbath: Time & Existence* by David Zisenwine and Karen Abramovitz; *The Sabbath: Its Meaning for Modern Man* by Abraham Joshua Heschel.

6. Create a Shabbat table display for the class. Announce that students are to be guides for the display for non-Jewish groups. Have them write monologues which explain the history, special features, and significance of the objects to the visitors. If students desire, they can prepare similar tables for all the holidays and festivals, write scripts for each, and lead an invited church group or groups through the display.

ALL-SCHOOL PROGRAMS

1. Hold an all-school Erev Shabbat dinner, service, and Oneg Shabbat. The dinner may be organized in several different ways: Each class could cook a part of the meal, the meal could be potluck, a committee of parents and students could prepare the meal, or it could be catered. The meal should include the recitation of the Shabbat blessings, *zemirot*, and the *Birkat HaMazon*. Continue the communal nature of this Shabbat by encouraging each class to participate in the worship service. They might lead a song, recite a prayer or special reading, or perform a dance or a skit with a Shabbat theme. Conclude the evening with an *Oneg Shabbat* and, if possible, Israeli dancing.

2. Hold an all-school Shabbat Quiz. Depending on the size of your school, divide into teams of eight to ten students each. A few examples of questions follow:
   a.   Shabbat is our day of _____.
   b.   Name three items found on the Shabbat table.
   c.   Give an example of a Shabbat greeting.
   d.   When was the first Shabbat celebrated?
   e.   Traditionally, how many *challot* are placed on the table?
   f.   Where can we find the commandment telling us to keep Shabbat?
   g.   Recite the blessing for the Shabbat candles.
   h.   Recite the blessing for the *challah*.

i.   Recite the blessing for the wine.

j.   What is the Hebrew name for the blessing over the wine?

k.   What is the ceremony for the close of Shabbat called?

l.   What three objects do we use during the Havdalah ceremony?

Add questions based on what your students have studied.

3. At a retreat or Shabbaton, prepare a booklet about the home observance of Shabbat for members of your congregation. First, study material about Shabbat. Then divide into task forces, each of which will prepare one part of the booklet. Chapters might include: historical background, Shabbat home ritual for Friday evening, Shabbat songs, a Havdalah ceremony, resources.

4. For this activity you will need a real or symbolic bridge. Gather the students (this is best done with grades K-6) on one side of the bridge, which represents the weekdays. There should be loud music blaring, people yelling, loud machines running (e.g., a vacuum cleaner, hair dryer, etc.). and general chaos. In small groups dismiss students to walk across the bridge and "enter" Shabbat. There should be a sign that says "Shabbat Shalom," and general peace and calm on the Shabbat side of the bridge. A song leader or Cantor could be leading mellow Shabbat songs. After all the students have crossed over the bridge, discuss the difference between the two sides, and the importance of Shabbat as an escape from the clamor of the weekday world.

RESOURCES

For the Teacher

Gold-Vukson, Marji. *Shabbat Shalom Copy Pak™ 1-4.* Denver: A.R.E. Publishing, Inc., 1993.

Goodman, Robert. *A Teachers Guide to Jewish Holidays.* Denver: A.R.E. Publishing, Inc., 1983.

Heschel, Abraham Joshua. *The Sabbath: Its Meaning for Modern Man.* New York: Farrar, Straus and Giroux, 1975.

Holman, Marilyn. *Using Our Senses.* Denver: A.R.E. Publishing, 1984.

Millgram, Abraham E. *Sabbath: The Day of Delight.* Philadelphia: The Jewish Publication Society of America, 1965.

Schwartz, Oded. *In Search of Plenty: The History of Jewish Food.* North Pomfret, VT: Trafalgar Square, 1993.

Siegel, Richard; Michael Strassfeld; and Sharon Strassfeld, comps. and eds.. *The First Jewish Catalog.* Philadelphia: The Jewish Publication Society of America, 1973.

Strassfeld, Michael, comp. *A Shabbat Haggadah for Celebration and Study.* New York: Institute of Human Relations Press of the American Jewish Committee, 1981.

Wolfson, Dr. Ron. *The Art of Jewish Living: The Shabbat Seder.* New York: The Federation of Jewish Men's Clubs and the University of Judaism, 1985.

For the Students

Abrams, Judith Z. *Shabbat A Family Service.* Rockville, MD: Kar-Ben Copies, Inc., 1991. (Grades K-4)

Artson, Bradley Shavit. *It's a Mitzvah: Step-by-Step to Jewish Living.* West Orange, NJ: Behrman House and New York: The Rabbinical Assembly, 1995, pp. 130-146. (Grades 8-adult)

Belf, Judith. *Hebrew Shabbat Lotto.* Denver: A.R.E. Publishing, Inc., 1976. (Grades 3-6)

Borovetz, Frances. *Hebrew Blessings Ditto Pak.* Denver: A.R.E. Publishing, Inc., 1980. (Grades 3-6)

Brody, David, and Dena Thaler. *Ani Tefilati. A Project of the Israel Movement for Progressive Judaism.* New York: UAHC Press, 1996. (Grades K-3)

Cohen, Floreva G. *Before Shabbat Begins.* New York: Board of Jewish Education, Inc., 1985. (Grades K-3)

Golub, Jane. *Mastering the Shabbat Table. Instant Lesson.* Los Angeles: Torah Aura Productions. (Grades 3-6)

Isaacs, Ronald H., and Kerry M. Olitzky. *Doing Mitzvot: Mitzvah Projects for Bar/Bat Mitzvah.* Hoboken, NJ: KTAV Publishing House, Inc., 1994, pp. 135-145. (Grades 6 and up)

Marcovic, Debra, and Lisa Rauchwerger. *Symbols of Shabbat.* Instant Lesson. Los Angeles: Torah Aura Productions. (Grades K-2)

Schwartz, Amy. *Mrs. Moskowitz and the Sabbath Candlesticks.* Philadelphia: The Jewish Publication Society of America, 1983. (Grades K-4)

Zwerin, Raymond A., and Audrey Friedman Marcus. *Shabbat Can Be.* New York: UAHC Press, 1979. (Grades PK-3)

Audiovisual

Because We Love Shabbat. Songbook and sound recording by Leah Abrams containing original and traditional songs, stories, and activities for young children and parents. Tara Publications. (Grades 4-6)

The Seventh Day. Audiocassette by Fran Avni that is a musical celebration of the beauty of Shabbat. Lemonstone Records. Available from A.R.E. Publishing, Inc. (Grades PK-3)

Celebrate with Us: Shabbat. Contains a joyful approach to Shabbat through engaging stories and charming songs told and sung by professional actors and singers. Jewish Family Productions. Available from A.R.E. Publishing, Inc. (Grades PK-3)

Fiddler on the Roof. The popular 169 minute feature film on video, based on the stories of Sholem Aleichem. Facets Multimedia, Inc. and local video stores. (Grades 5 and up)

Fiddler on the Roof. Sound recording of the musical, contains the song "Sabbath Prayer." RCA Records LSO-1093. (Grades 3 and up)

The Legend of Chanale's Shabbat Dress. A 10 minute video about Chanale, who takes a pre-Shabbat walk and receives a miraculous reward for her kind deeds. Board of Jewish Education of Greater New York. (Grades PK-6)

Around Our Sabbath Table by Margie Rosenthal and Ilene Safyan is an audiocassette featuring Shabbat songs in Hebrew and English from around the world. Sheera Recordings. Available from A.R.E. Publishing, Inc. (All ages)

The Sabbath. An 18 minute video that includes four separate animated and live action discussion starters. Ergo Media, Inc. (Grades K-2)

"Shababat Shalom." On the recording *My Jewish Discovery* by Craig Taubman/Craig 'n Co. A fun doo-wop style song about the symbols and observance of Shabbat. Sweet Louise Music. Available from A.R.E. Publishing, Inc. (All ages)

T.G.I.S. (Thank God It's Shabbat). A 28 minute video about a man going home on a train on a Friday afternoon. When the train is delayed, he recalls his visits to an aunt and uncle for Shabbat. Includes study guide. Ergo Media, Inc. (Grades 4 and up)

UNIT 2

Hearing the Shofar
לִשְׁמֹעַ קוֹל שׁוֹפָר

OVERVIEW

One of the most significant symbols of the High Holy Days is the Shofar, which is sounded during the *Shacharit* and *Musaf* services on both the first and second days of Rosh Hashanah and at the conclusion of Yom Kippur. In some communities the Shofar is also sounded daily during Elul, beginning with the second day of that month, to usher in the penitential season. However, it is not sounded on the day before Rosh Hashanah so as to distinguish between the daily sounding and the sounding on Rosh Hashanah.

The Shofar is one of the oldest musical instruments still in use. Its association with the Jewish people is long and varied. From Torah we learn that it was sounded at the moment of revelation on Mt. Sinai (Exodus 19:16, 19), that it was used to proclaim the Jubilee (50th) year (Leviticus 25:9-10), and, of course, that it was integral to Rosh Hashanah, which is called *Yom Teruah*, the day of sounding (Numbers 29:1).

In biblical times it was also used in processionals, as a call to war, to induce fear in an enemy, and as a signal to assemble the people, and on every Rosh Chodesh, not just the first of Tishri.

Through the ages, the Shofar has also been used to announce a death, to proclaim fasts, at funerals, and to proclaim an excommunication. In some communities during the Middle Ages, the Shofar would be blown six times on Friday afternoons, marking the approach of Shabbat.

In Israel the Shofar is sounded at the inauguration of a new president, and it was sounded when Israeli troops reached the Western Wall during the Six Day War.

Traditionally, the Shofar is not sounded on Shabbat, lest one forget the Shofar at home and carry it to the synagogue, or lest one hire someone for a lesson prior to the sounding. The sounding itself is not forbidden on the Sabbath. In most Reform synagogues, the Shofar is sounded when Rosh Hashanah falls on Shabbat.

The *Musaf* Shofar Service consists of three parts: *Zichronot* (remembrances), *Malchuyot* (God's Sovereignty), and *Shofarot* (Shofar soundings).

Each part includes a number of biblical verses and other readings related to the theme.

It is a Mitzvah to hear the sounding of the Shofar. While women and children are exempt from this obligation, according to some sources, women may take this precept upon themselves if they wish.

Two blessings are recited prior to the sounding of the Shofar. They are:

בָּרוּךְ אַתָּה, יְיָ אֱלֹהֵינוּ, מֶלֶךְ הָעוֹלָם, אֲשֶׁר קִדְּשָׁנוּ בְּמִצְוֹתָיו וְצִוָּנוּ לִשְׁמוֹעַ קוֹל שׁוֹפָר.

Blessed are You, O Eternal our God, Ruler of the universe, Who has made us holy with Mitzvot and commanded us to hear the sound of the Shofar.

בָּרוּךְ אַתָּה, יְיָ אֱלֹהֵינוּ, מֶלֶךְ הָעוֹלָם, שֶׁהֶחֱיָנוּ וְקִיְּמָנוּ וְהִגִּיעָנוּ לַזְּמַן הַזֶּה.

Blessed are You, O Eternal our God, Ruler of the universe, Who has given us life, has sustained us, and has enabled us to reach this season.

There are three distinct sounds which are made with the Shofar on Rosh Hashanah: *tekiah* — a long blast with a short higher note at the end, *teruah* — nine short blasts, and *shevarim* — three blasts, each composed of a low note followed by a higher note. The final sounding on Rosh Hashanah and at the end of Yom Kippur is the sustained *tekiah gedolah*. The person who sounds the Shofar is called the *ba'al tekiah* (master of sounding) and the person who calls the notes is a *makri* (caller).

The Shofar is sounded at the New Year for a number of reasons. According to the Talmud (*Rosh Hashanah* 16a), when the Shofar is sounded God recalls the *Akedat Yitzchak* (the binding of Isaac, which is the Torah portion traditionally read on the second day of Rosh Hashanah). At that time, it is considered as if each Jew is actually bound before God. Instead of sacrificing Isaac, Abraham offered up a ram "caught in the thicket by its horns" (Genesis 22:13). Although the Hebrew word used in the *akedah* for horn is *keren*, and not Shofar, the Rabbis consider this event to be the basis for sounding the Shofar on Rosh Hashanah.

Saadia Gaon, a ninth century Jewish sage, listed ten reasons for sounding the Shofar at the New Year. They are:

1. Because Rosh Hashanah marks the beginning of Creation.
2. To announce the beginning of the Ten Days of Repentance.
3. To remind us of standing at Mt. Sinai when the Shofar was sounded (Exodus 19:19).
4. To remind us that the words of the prophets were compared to a ram's horn.
5. To remind us of the destruction of the Temple.
6. To remind us of the binding of Isaac.
7. Because when we hear the sound of the Shofar we fear and tremble (*Amos* 3:6).
8. To remind us of the Day of Judgment.
9. To remind us of the gathering of the dispersed of Israel.
10. To remind us of the revival of the dead.

The Shofar is usually a ram's horn because of the *akedah*, but it may be the horn of any kosher animal except a cow, which is excluded due to the sin of the golden calf. A Shofar may be gilded or carved, but it may not have a hole in the side, nor may it be painted.

ACTIVITIES

Primary

1. To introduce the children to the Shofar, make a surprise box of Jewish ritual objects. In addition to a Shofar, some suggested items to include are Shabbat candlestick holders, a *challah* cover, a *Seder* plate, a *chanukiyah*, a *Mezuzah*. Try to have at least one object for each child. Use a large carton with an easily removable lid or a cloth to cover the top. Have each child reach in and choose an object. As each object is shown, have the students discuss what it is, what its uses are, how and when it is used.

2. Make Rosh Hashanah greeting cards or mounted pictures utilizing the Shofar motif. Into linoleum or into a large raw potato, carve a Shofar shape. Cut in half lengthwise. Using water based acrylic paint, start printing.

3. Try a variation of activity #2 by carving a tiny Shofar on the flat end of a carrot. Using this small image, create a picture or outline of something larger. This can be called picture micrography.

4. Have children try to sound the Shofar. Remember to have some cleaning material available to prepare the Shofar for each *"ba'al tekiah."* Invite a real *ba'al tekiah* to the classroom to instruct the students.

5. The Shofar is sounded for many reasons, some of which are listed and discussed in the Overview section above. Share these reasons with the students. Tell each of them to imagine that he or she is a Shofar. Ask them what message or wish they would "sound" for the Jewish people. On streamers of paper, write each student's statement. Attach these to a giant pre-cut Shofar shape (use light cardboard or posterboard to make this). Tack the whole thing to a wall or hang it from the ceiling.

6. To reinforce the motif of Shofar during the High Holy Days, each student can construct a stuffed Shofar which may then be hung from the ceiling.

   Materials needed: Pencils; stapler with staples; paper or fabric scraps; heavy duty string or yarn; scissors; and, for each student, a large sheet of brown wrapping paper folded in half and measuring 12″ x 24″ after it is folded.

   Procedure: Draw a large Shofar shape on the wrapping paper. Younger students may need a pattern to trace and help from the teacher or an aide. Then cut through both layers of paper. Staple the two halves together, leaving an opening to allow for the stuffing. Stuff the Shofar with scraps of paper or fabric. Finish by stapling the Shofar shut. Attach yarn or string to each Shofar and hang from the ceiling.

Intermediate

1. Display several different Shofarot and various wind instruments (flute, coronet, tuba, trombone, etc.). Each instrument should be sounded by a competent player. Discuss with the students the similarities and differences. Also discuss what makes the Shofar unique. You might consider inviting a musicologist into your class who could provide background information on the instruments.

2. Teach each student to become a *baal tekiah* or a *marki*. Those students who have trouble sounding the Shofar can call the notes for others. The educator, Cantor, Rabbi or *baal*

tekiah could serve as a resource person for this activity.

3. Direct each student to complete the following sentences:
    a. When I touch the Shofar, I feel _____.
    b. When I try to blow the Shofar, I am _____.
    c. When I hear the Shofar sounded, I think _____.

4. To extend activity #3 have the students write a cinquain about the Shofar. A cinquain is a five line poem with each line having a particular structure:

    Line One: A noun or the name of a person.
    Line Two: Two adjectives.
    Line Three: Three verbs ending in "ing."
    Line Four: Four more adjectives.
    Line Five: A synonym for the noun or person in Line One.

5. Have the students learn to read in Hebrew the two blessings for the Shofar ritual. They may be found in the Overview section above, and also in any *Machzor* (High Holy Day prayerbook).

6. Read and discuss the story *The Shofar That Lost Its Voice* by David E. Fass. Consider these questions: How does Avi react when the Rabbi asks him to blow the Shofar on the High Holy Days? What does Avi do when the Shofar won't sound? What does Avi find when he goes inside the Shofar? How does he "retrieve" the Shofar sounds? In your own words, explain why Shimone did not want to share the sound of the Shofar. What does the sound of the Shofar mean to you?

Secondary

1. Provide each student with a list of Saadia Gaon's reasons for sounding the Shofar (see Overview above). Ask students to rank the reasons from 1 (most important) to 10 (least important), according to their opinion. As a class discuss the rankings and attempt to come to a consensus. Then ask the students which reasons are most important for the survival of Judaism. Compare this ranking to the first one.

2. Saadia Gaon stated that the words of the prophets are like the ram's horn. Assign each student a different prophet. They should read all or part of their assigned prophet's book in the Bible and research additional material about their subject. Have students do one or more of the following activities with the information they have gathered:
    a. Write a biographical sketch of the prophet.
    b. Compose a Rosh Hashanah message to modern day Jews reflecting the character and personality of the prophet.
    c. Stage a "Meet the Prophet" interview along the lines of the television show "Meet the Press."
    d. Create a bulletin board display of the prophet.

3. It is traditional to blow the Shofar at morning services during the month of Elul preceding Rosh Hashanah in order to usher in the penitential season. Think about why the Rabbis instituted this daily sounding of the Shofar. Ask students how they prepare themselves for the High Holy Days.

4. View and discuss the movie *The Dybbuk* with your students. Note particularly the use of the Shofar during the exorcism. Questions to discuss after the film: How is the Shofar used in the movie? Were you surprised that it was used this way? In what ways does the Shofar serve a similar function on Rosh Hashanah? (It awakens us to our responsibility of avoiding evil.)

5. Saul Lieberman has called the Shofar sounds "a prayer without words."
    a. Brainstorm with the students other examples of prayers without words, such as a *nigun*, a dance, a work of art, a mime, etc.
    b. Divide the students into groups. Assign each of the groups one of the wordless prayer forms listed above. Each group is to use this form to create a wordless prayer expressing an emotion, such as joy, anger, repentance, tranquility, etc.
    c. Compose a creative Shofar service for Rosh Hashanah.

References: *Mahzor for Rosh Hashanah and Yom Kippur: A Prayer Book for the Days of Awe; The New Mahzor for Rosh Hashanah and Yom Kippur; On Wings of Awe: A Machzor for Rosh Hashanah and Yom Kippur; Gates of Repentance: The New Union Prayerbook for the Days of Awe.*

ALL-SCHOOL PROGRAMS

1. Plan a *Shabbaton* prior to the High Holy Days. Suggested activities:
   a. Hold a group discussion on "What the call of the Shofar means to me."
   b. Have a study session on Saadiah Gaon's ten reasons for sounding the Shofar (found in the Overview above).
   c. Divide the group into three smaller groups. Assign each group one of the three parts of the Shofar service. Each group is to give a creative interpretation of their assigned section using art, drama, dance, or a combination of these.

2. Establish a "Shofar Corps" at your synagogue. Recruit adults and youth and teach them how to sound the Shofar properly.

3. Divide the students into three groups of mixed grade levels. Assign each group one of the parts of the Shofar service. Appoint a teacher or resource person in each group to explain the theme of the assigned part and discuss it (he or she should be familiar with that section in the congregation's *Machzor*).

RESOURCES

For the Teacher

Goodman, Philip. *The Rosh Hashanah Anthology.* Philadelphia: The Jewish Publication Society of America, 1973.

Goodman, Robert. *A Teachers Guide to Jewish Holidays.* Denver: A.R.E. Publishing, Inc., 1983.

Greenberg, Sidney, and Jonathan D. Levine, eds. *Mahzor Hadash: A New High Holiday Prayer Book.* rev. ed. Bridgeport, CT: The Prayer Book Press, 1992.

Harlow, Jules, ed. *Mahzor for Rosh Hashanah and Yom Kippur: A Prayer Book for the Days of Awe.* New York: The Rabbinical Assembly, 1972.

Levy, Richard N., ed. *On Wings of Awe: A Machzor for Rosh Hashanah and Yom Kippur.* Washington, DC: B'nai B'rith Hillel Foundation, 1985.

Maimonides, Moses. *The Commandments.* New York: The Soncino Press, 1967, vol. 1, pp. 179-180.

"Shofar." In *Encyclopaedia Judaica.* Jerusalem: Keter Publishing House Jerusalem Ltd, 1972, vol. 14, cols. 1442-1447.

Stern, Chaim, ed. *Gates of Repentance: The New Union Prayerbook for the Days of Awe.* New York: Central Conference of American Rabbis, 1978

Strassfeld, Michael. *The Jewish Holidays: A Guide and Commentary.* New York: Harper and Row Publishers, 1985.

For the Students

Abrams, Judith Z. *Rosh Hashanah: A Family Service.* Rockville, MD: Kar-Ben Copies, Inc., 1990. (Grades PK-2)

Bin-Nun, Judy, with Fran Einhorn. *Rosh Hashanah: A Holiday Funtext.* New York: UAHC Press, 1979. (Grades K-4)

Chaikin, Miriam. *Sound the Shofar: The Story and Meaning of Rosh Hashanah and Yom Kippur.* New York: Clarion Books, 1986. (Grades 3-6)

Fass, David. *The Shofar That Lost Its Voice.* New York: UAHC Press, 1982. (Grades 4-6)

Grishaver, Joel Lurie. *Building Jewish Life/Rosh Ha-Shanah & Yom Kippur.* Los Angeles: Torah Aura Productions, 1987. (Grades 2-5)

Holiday Stamp Sets — Shofar. West Palm Beach, FL: The Learning Plant. (Grades K-3)

Marcus, Audrey Friedman, and Raymond A. Zwerin. *High Holy Day Do-It-Yourself Dictionary.* New York: UAHC Press, 1983. (Grades 3-6)

Saypol, Judyth Robbins, and Madeline Wikler. *My Very Own Rosh Hashanah.* Rockville, MD: Kar-Ben Copies, Inc., 1978. (Grades K-4)

Audiovisual

Back to Tishri. In this 23 minute video, a girl gets lost in a magical Jewish calendar. She reunites with her mother after she has gone through all the months of the year. Bureau of Jewish Education of Boston. (Grades K-2)

High Holidays in Song. An audiocassette featuring four original songs that supplement traditional high holiday melodies. Words to the songs are included. Kar-Ben Copies, Inc. (All ages)

Secret in Bubbe's Attic. The High Holy Days, Sukkot, and Chanukah come alive in this 43 minute video in which holiday symbols are the focus of songs and stories. Ergo Media Inc. (Grades PK-5)

Shofar: How and Why. Wall chart, also available in notebook size. Torah Umesorah Publications. (Grades 3 and up)

Fasting on Yom Kippur

יום צום

OVERVIEW

"And this shall be to you a law for all time. In the seventh month, on the tenth day of the month, you shall afflict your souls" (Leviticus 16:29).

In the Mishnah, the Rabbis interpreted the phrase "afflict your souls" to mean practicing various forms of self-denial. These included abstention from washing, anointing oneself with oil, wearing shoes, sexual intercourse, and food or drink (*Yoma* 8:1). At least from Rabbinic times on, fasting became central to the observance of Yom Kippur.

In the Bible fasting is a common practice with a variety of purposes. Fasts were proclaimed when calamity threatened or struck a community, upon the death of a national leader, in preparation for communing with God, as an act of penance, an act of contrition, or as an expression of remorse. In the main, these fasts are spontaneous responses to particular circumstances.

There is no record of annual fast days prior to the destruction of the First Temple. Fasting on the Day of Atonement may have begun as an emergency rite and was not fixed until the sixth century B.C.E.

During the Second Temple period, fasting was increasingly common: daily or bi-weekly fasts were sometimes proclaimed, especially when much needed rains did not occur at their usual times. These fasts were proclaimed by a community's leaders. Some ascetic Jewish groups instituted fasts as part of their regular observance as a way of becoming closer to God.

Mainstream Judaism, however, rejected fasting as a ritual except on prescribed days. Besides Yom Kippur, these include:

9th of Av - commemorating the destruction of the First and Second Temples and other catastrophes throughout Jewish history.

17th of Tammuz - commemorating the breaching of the walls of Jerusalem prior to the destruction of the First Temple in 586 B.C.E.

10th of Tevet - commemorating the seige of Jerusalem by the Romans in 70 C.E.

13th of Adar - commemorating the fast of Esther and the Jews of Persia prior to her visit to King Ahasuerus on behalf of her people.

13th of Nisan - fast of the firstborn, commemorating the slaying of the firstborn of Egypt in the days of Moses.

3rd of Tishre - commemorating the slaying of Gedaliah and his associates in the sixth century B.C.E.

In addition, it is a tradition that brides and grooms fast on their wedding day prior to the ceremony as a symbol that this day is like a mini-Yom Kippur for them. On this day all of their past transgressions are forgiven and they begin married life afresh.

On Yom Kippur, fasting is incumbent upon males age 13 and older and females age 12 and older. A year or two before reaching these ages, children begin training by fasting for part of the day, or by eating and drinking small amounts only.

Besides young children, those exempt from fasting include the sick, pregnant and nursing women, and those obliged to preserve their strength by eating or taking medicine or both.

Fasting on Yom Kippur means complete abstinence from food and drink from sundown until the end of the next day. A fast, therefore, is about 25 hours long. Even when Yom Kippur falls on Shabbat, fasting is required. All other fasts are moved back a day (or, in the case of the Fast of Esther and the Fast of the firstborn, moved up two days) if they would have fallen on Shabbat.

The medieval poet, Judah Halevi, saw fasting as a way to eliminate our animal instincts. Regarding the fast of a pious person, Halevi wrote: "All his physical faculties are denied their natural requirements, being entirely abandoned to religious service" (*The Kuzari* 3:5).

Louis Jacobs cites the following reasons for fasting on Yom Kippur: To show our penance and contrition as a means for self-discipline to focus our mind on the spiritual, to awaken God's compassion for us, and to awaken our own compassion for others (*A Guide to Yom Kippur*, pp. 17-20).

ACTIVITIES

Primary

1. Invite adults who have fasted for Yom Kippur, other holidays, or for other reasons to your class.

Each should briefly describe his or her fast. Point out the differences between fasting to lose weight and fasting for a holiday.

2. Ask the students to interview their family members about Yom Kippur and fasting. Work up a list of questions beforehand, such as the following: How old were you when you first fasted? Is it difficult for you to fast? Was there ever a time you did not fast? Why?

3. Poll the students to find out at what age they plan to begin fasting. Ask what might influence their decision.

4. Ask the class the following questions?
   a. What does it feel like to be hungry?
   b. What do you do when you are hungry?
   c. How is the hunger experienced on Yom Kippur different from the hunger of people who cannot get enough to eat?
   d. How can you help those who are hungry because they cannot get enough to eat?

5. When we fast on Yom Kippur, we feel hunger because our sense of taste is deprived. Other senses are also involved as we participate in this observance. Ask the students for additional examples of how our five senses are involved (e.g., the feel of holiday clothes, the aroma of Erev Yom Kippur meal, the smell of old prayer books, the touch of greeting friends and family, the sound of the Shofar, etc.).

6. Young students know, or should know, that they are too young to fast. Yet, the basic theme of Yom Kippur is afflicting the soul, or practicing self-denial. Ask students to suggest other things they can do in place of fasting which will remind them of the significance of the day (e.g., no bike riding, no watching television, etc.).

Intermediate

1. The Overview section above contains a list of fast days which commemorate events in Jewish history. Briefly describe these to your class. Create a list of additional days when it might be appropriate to fast. Some suggestions are: the anniversary of the massacre of Israeli athletes at the Munich Olympics; *Yom Hashoah*, Night of the Murdered Poets. Assign an event to each student to research and have each explain why we should or should not observe a fast.

2. Describe a magic box that is very special. It can be large or small and can contain anything the students want to put into it. Ask the class: If you could place one item in the magic box that would help make your Yom Kippur fast meaningful, what would you put in the box?

3. As a class create a list of five positive outcomes for the observance of fasting on Yom Kippur.

4. Ask each student to write a diary excerpt in which they describe their first Yom Kippur fast.

5. Do a "Proud Whip." Each student, in turn, fills in the blank: I am proud of my Yom Kippur observance, because this year _____.

6. Read and discuss the book *First Fast* by Barbara Cohen. Consider the following questions: Why doesn't Harry's mother want him to fast? How is Harry's synagogue similar to yours? How is it different? What does Harry do in order not to think about food? What does Bernie do to try to get Harry to break his fast? Who do you think sent Harry the marbles? For additional activities, see *A Teacher's Guide to First Fast* by Robert E. Tornberg.

Secondary

1. On Yom Kippur we give up food and liquid for one day. Some Christian churches observe Lent for a forty day period in the spring. Both observances require individuals to give up something. Invite a religion class from a church which observes Lent. Hold a group discussion which includes the differences and similarities between Lent and Yom Kippur, and the rationale behind these observances.

2. Read and discuss Isaiah 58, the *Haftarah* for Yom Kippur morning. What type of fast does Isaiah think God wants?

3. With students taking the various parts, read "Three Who Ate" by David Frishman. An adaptation can be found in *A Teachers Guide to Jewish Holidays* by Robert Goodman, pp. 57-60. Discuss the question which follows the text.

4. Read the following selections from the *Mishnah* (*Ta'anit* 1:4-7), which deal with fasting. Make a chart to show the period of time without rainfall and the corresponding length of the fast. Discuss

the importance of rainfall (for that time and place) and the connection between fasting and rainfall.

5. Distribute a list of unfinished sentences. Students may answer them individually followed by a group discussion.
   a. On Yom Kippur I feel _____.
   b. I choose to fast/not to fast on Yom Kippur because _____.
   c. The best part of Yom Kippur is _____.
   d. When I fast, I _____.

6. Louis Jacobs offers several reasons for fasting (see Overview section above). One reason is to awaken our own compassion for others. Elicit from the students concrete examples of compassionate acts they can carry out, and select one or two to do as a class.

ALL-SCHOOL PROGRAMS

1. Form a council of one or two students from each class. Have them design and carry out a publicity campaign urging members of the congregation to donate the equivalent of the cost of the meals they abstained from eating on Yom Kippur to a group which feeds the hungry, such as Mazon, or to a local soup kitchen.

2. While many people observe the Mitzvah of Fasting, they may not fully understand its significance. Prior to the High Holy Days, hold a study session with the older students about fasting. Suggested topics: Why fast? How fasting promotes introspection and repentance.

   References: "Fasting" in *Encyclopaedia Judaica*; *The Yom Kippur Anthology* by Philip Goodman.

3. The obligation to fast on Yom Kippur is a very personal Mitzvah, yet a very public statement of one's beliefs. Hold a forum during which "fasters" and "non-fasters" can have an open discussion.

4. Hold a school-wide mini-fast. At a time when a snack or treat would normally be served, gather the students together and explain that their snack is cancelled and that a mini-fast will be observed. (The reason for the fast might be the commemoration of a particular historical event.) The Rabbi or Director of Education can talk briefly about the tradition of fasting in Judaism. After-

ward, discuss with students how they felt about having to give up their usual snack.

RESOURCES

For the Teacher

Danby, Herbert, trans. *The Mishnah*. London: Oxford University Press, 1974.

"Fasting." In *Encyclopaedia Judaica*. Jerusalem: Keter Publishing House Jerusalem Ltd., 1972, vol. 6, cols. 1189-1196.

Goodman, Philip. *The Yom Kippur Anthology*. Philadelphia: The Jewish Publication Society of America, 1971.

Goodman, Robert. *A Teachers Guide to Jewish Holidays*. Denver: A.R.E. Publishing, Inc., 1983.

Halevi, Judah. *The Kuzari: An Argument for the Faith of Israel*. New York: Schocken Books, 1964.

For the Students

Abrams, Judith Z. *Yom Kippur: A Family Service*. Rockville, MD: Kar-Ben Copies, Inc., 1990. (Grades PK-2)

Bayar, Steven. *Did Darth Vader Repent?* Instant Lesson. Los Angeles: Torah Aura Productions. (Grades 7-adult)

Cohen, Barbara. *First Fast*. New York: UAHC Press, 1987. (Grades 4-6)

———. *Yussel's Prayer: A Yom Kippur Story*. New York; Lothrop, Lee & Shepard Books, 1981. (Grades K-2)

Frishman, David. "Three Who Ate." In *A Teachers Guide to Jewish Holidays* by Robert Goodman. Denver: A.R.E. Publishing, Inc., 1983, pp. 57-60. (Grades 7 and up)

Oppenheim, Peter, and Diane E. Berg. *The Yom Kippur Crisis*. Instant Lesson. Los Angeles: Torah Aura Productions. (Grades 6-Adult)

Saypol, Judyth Robbins, and Madeline Wikler. *My Very Own Yom Kippur*. Rockville, MD: Kar-Ben Copies, 1978. (Grades PK-6)

Wise, Ira J. *A Long, Penitent Season*. Instant Lesson. Los Angeles, Torah Aura Productions, 1990. (Grades 3-5)

———. *Missing the Mark*. Instant Lesson. Los Angeles: Torah Aura Productions, 1990. (Grades 6-7)

———. *T'shuvah She Wrote*. Instant Lesson. Los Angeles: Torah Aura Productions, 1990. (Grades 6-7)

Audiovisual

Beryl the Tailor. This 8 minute video of a tale by I.L. Peretz shows the connection between prayer and action. Torah Aura Productions. (All ages)

The Fast I Have Chosen. This film explores the paradox of poverty in the midst of plenty in America within the framework of the Yom Kippur liturgy. Alden Films (Grades 7 and up)

Guilt and Repentance. A 60 minute discussion by theologians on the major themes of Yom Kippur. Video includes the chanting, translation, and interpretation of the prayers. Jewish Theological Seminary. (Grades 9 to adult)

Kol Shofar — The Sound of the Shofar. Audio-cassette. The filmstrip explains how a shofar is made and the laws regarding the sounding of the shofar. Torah Umesorah. (Grades 4-6)

OVERVIEW

The primary Mitzvah of Sukkot, the fall harvest festival, is to dwell in a *sukkah*, a booth. On the fifteenth day of the seventh month, when you have gathered in the yield of your land, you shall observe the festival of the Lord seven days . . . . You shall live in booths seven days; all citizens of Israel shall live in booths, in order that future generations may know that I made the Israelite people live in booths when I brought them out of the land of Egypt, I the Eternal am your God" (Leviticus 23:39-43).

One is supposed to sleep each night and to eat all meals in the *sukkah* during the holiday. However, rainfall exempts one from these obligations. Women are exempt because eating or sleeping in the *sukkah* is a positive time-bound commandment.

Upon entering a *sukkah*, one recites the following blessing:

בָּרוּךְ אַתָּה, יְיָ אֱלֹהֵינוּ, מֶלֶךְ הָעוֹלָם, אֲשֶׁר קִדְּשָׁנוּ בְּמִצְוֹתָיו
וְצִוָּנוּ לֵשֵׁב בַּסֻּכָּה.

Blessed are you, O Eternal our God, Ruler of the universe, Who has made us holy with Mitzvot and commanded us to dwell in the *sukkah*.

This Mitzvah is one of the few in the Torah which includes the reason for its observance: as a reminder that the Israelites lived in booths during their wanderings in the wilderness. The Rabbis disagreed as to whether the booths literally or symbolically represent the clouds of glory which sheltered the Israelites during the Exodus (*Sukkot* 11b).

Historians point out that in ancient days farmers would often erect temporary booths in their fields at the end of the harvest and live in them. Because of this and because of its association with the harvest, *Sukkot* is called *Chag Ha-Asif*, the holiday of the ingathering.

It is traditional to erect a *sukkah* outside one's home. In Israel many Jews erect a *sukkah* on their balconies. Some Jews begin building a *sukkah* immediately after the conclusion of Yom Kippur. A *sukkah* must have 2½, 3, or 4 sides, corresponding to the sides of the Hebrew letters of the word *sukkah* (סכה). One of the walls may be shared with a house or other permanent structure. The roof is covered with branches (called *s'chach*) so that there is more shade than sunlight in the booth, but not so densely that one is unable to see through it to the stars.

A *sukkah* may be decorated with gourds, fruit, vegetables, tapestries, paper chains, furniture, etc. It is traditional to invite guests to share a meal in the *sukkah*. It is also a custom to "welcome" *ushpizin*, seven different biblical persons, as symbolic *sukkah* guests each night.

A second important Mitzvah pertaining to Sukkot is to wave the *lulav*. The Torah instructs: "On the first day you shall take the product of *hadar* trees, branches of palm trees, boughs of leafy trees (which has come to mean myrtle), and willows of the brook, and you shall rejoice before the Lord your God seven days" (Leviticus 23:40). The fruit of the *hadar* tree has come to mean the *etrog*. The *etrog*, in order to be fit for use, must have a short stem called a *pitom*.

The word *lulav* means palm branch, but has come to refer to all four species together. The palm branch is combined with two willow branches and three myrtle branches in a special holder woven of palm. This cluster is held in the right hand, while the *etrog* is held in the left hand. The following blessing is recited:

בָּרוּךְ אַתָּה, יְיָ אֱלֹהֵינוּ, מֶלֶךְ הָעוֹלָם, אֲשֶׁר קִדְּשָׁנוּ בְּמִצְוֹתָיו
וְצִוָּנוּ עַל נְטִילַת לוּלָב.

Blessed are you, O Eternal our God, Ruler of the universe, Who has made us holy with Mitzvot and commanded us concerning the waving of the *lulav*.

On the first day, the *Shehecheyanu* is also recited.

The four species are waved in six directions, three times in each direction in the following order: east, south, west, north, up and down. While waving the four species, it is customary to say:

אָנָּא יְיָ, הוֹשִׁיעָה נָּא!

We implore you, Eternal One, save us.

The *lulav* is waved either before or during the morning service on the seven days of Sukkot. It is not waved on Shabbat because of a concern that one might carry it outside of the *eruv* thus transgressing Sabbath law.

According to *Sefer Hachinuch* each of the four species (based on its shape) represents a part of the body through which one serves God. The *etrog* resembles the heart, the place of wisdom and understanding. The *lulav* resembles the backbone, which reminds us of uprightness. The myrtle resembles the *eyes*, which bring us enlightenment. And the willow resembles the lips through which we serve God with prayer.

Women are exempt also from waving the *lulav* because it is a positive time-bound commandment.

It is also a Mitzvah to rest on the first day of Sukkot, and on the eighth day, which is called Shemini Atzeret (Leviticus 23:35-36).

ACTIVITIES

Primary

1. Take your class on a walk through the neighborhood adjoining the synagogue. Ask students what changes in nature are taking place (e.g., temperature is getting colder, leaves are turning color, the birds are flying south, etc.). Ask if they know what is happening on farms and in orchards during the fall season. Introduce Sukkot as the Jewish celebration of the fall harvest. Share stories and pictures of harvest time.

   References: *How Do You Know It's Fall* by Allan Fowler; *Exploring Autumn* by Sandra Markle; *Why Do Leaves Change Color?* by Chris Arvetis and Carole Palmer.

2. Follow up activity #1 by taking a field trip to an orchard or farm and participate in the harvest. Choose appropriate fall crops, such as apples or pumpkins. Use the produce to decorate the synagogue's *sukkah* or to create a treat such as muffins, applesauce, or cake (obtain recipes from any good cookbook). Point out to the students that produce which is placed in the *sukkah* as a decoration is not to be consumed until the end of the holiday (*Sukkah* 10a-b).

3. On the chalkboard write out the verses from Leviticus quoted in the Overview (23:39-43). Read them to the class and discuss how the *sukkah* is derived from this biblical commandment.

4. There are many beautiful ways that the *sukkah* may be decorated. Birds made from eggshells are a unique decoration. The basis for this decoration is found in Isaiah 31:5: "As birds hovering, so will the Lord of hosts protect Jerusalem."

   Materials needed: Eggs, tempera or acrylic paint, feathers, sequins, construction paper, tape, string.

   Procedure: Outdoors, gently tap a small hole into both ends of a raw egg and blow out the contents. It may be helpful to hold on to the egg and swing it around before you blow it out. Use tempera or acrylic paints to decorate the eggshells. Also glue on feathers, sequins, beaks cut out of construction paper. When the eggs are dry, tape a string on each and hang in the *sukkah*.

5. At this age children enjoy using all their senses to experience new and unusual things. Display a *lulav* and an *etrog* for them to see, smell, and examine. Teach the children the pattern for shaking the *lulav* and *etrog* (see Overview above). Have each student in turn hold the *lulav* and *etrog* and shake them.

6. Once the holiday of Sukkot is over, the *etrog* and *lulav* still have many uses. The *lulav* may be stored away and used at Passover to sweep up the bread crumbs during the search for *chametz* (leavened products). Try this with your class.

   The *etrog* may be used in a number of ways. It may be made into compote or jelly (though it is very bitter and needs a lot of sugar), the peel may be grated and used in a cake for flavoring, or the *etrog* may be "embalmed" and used as *besamim* (spices) for the ceremony of Havdalah. This latter project requires the help of an adult to poke shallow perforations in the *etrog* with a sharp object, such as an ice pick. Have children place cloves into the holes (use pliers if necessary). Let the *etrog* dry in a warm sunny location for a few days; then it is ready to use.

Intermediate

1. Have students write an illustrated how-to

pamphlet entitled, "Building and Decorating a Sukkah." Photocopy the pamphlet and send it home to parents.

2. It is traditional to invite *ushpizin*, biblical characters, into the *sukkah* as guests. Traditionally, these *ushpizin* were Abraham, Isaac, Jacob, Joseph, Moses, Aaron, and David. Other biblical guests might include Rebekah, Rachel, Leah, Miriam, Deborah, and Hannah. Create a batik greeting containing the names of these biblical figures.

Materials needed: A large sheet or cotton fabric; fabric pen (disappearing ink good for 12-48 hours, available in sewing and craft stores, or use something more permanent); 1 jar cold textile wax; newspapers; assorted colors of textile or acrylic paint; various sizes of brushes.

Procedure: Pre-wash and dry the fabric. Draw design onto the fabric. Layer newspapers on a flat surface and place the fabric on top. Paint the design. Outline each part of the design with a think black line. When the batik is dry, iron the design to make it permanent. Paint the wax on the paint areas and those areas you want to leave plain white. When dry, roll up the fabric into a ball cracking the wax. Open fabric and paint all over with a dark color paint. Wash out in cold water to remove wax and excess paint. Dry, then iron out the rest of the wax. To iron, place fabric between layers of newspaper to absorb the wax.

3. Paper cuts date from the eighteenth century as a decoration for European *sukkot*. Following are directions for creating paper cuts:

Materials needed: Tracing paper; sharp medium pencils; black pens with a fine point; masking tape; ruler; sharp pointed curving scissors (e.g., cuticle or embroidery scissors); fine quality white paper, such as linen-finish stationery; white glue; dark or bright colored construction paper; plain white paper.

Procedure: On sheets of plain white paper, students create a design reflecting the themes of Sukkot or Judaism in general. Using the tracing paper, trace over the design with the fine-pointed black pen. Tape each tracing to a window. Place a piece of white paper over the tracing and tape in place. Using the pencil, lightly trace pattern. Remove paper from window and place a second sheet of paper under the white paper and tape

edges to hold. It is easier to cut through two sheets rather than one. Using the sharp curved scissors, the students cut out their designs. Punch the scissors through making a tiny hole, then insert the scissor blade and cut out the space. Instruct students to keep the scissors moving in a steady rhythm with small cuts. When finished mount the paper cut on a piece of construction paper of contrasting color. Hang in the *sukkah* at the synagogue or at home.

References: See the papercuts in the books *Jewish History — Moments and Methods* by Sorel Goldberg Loeb and Barbara Binder Kadden and *Seasons of Our Joy* by Arthur Waskow.

4. Learn to read the blessings and practice with the *lulav* and *etrog*. See *Hebrew Blessings Ditto Pak* by Frances Borovetz, pp. 24 and 25, or use a prayerbook.

5. With your students create a "You Are There" television or radio show based on Sukkot observances in other countries and historical periods. Make the production live or, if you have video equipment available, tape it. Use the references below to help students write scripts and create scenery.

References: *The Sukkot and Simchat Torah Anthology* by Phillip Goodman; *The Jewish Holiday Kitchen* by Joan Nathan; *The Book of Jewish Holidays* by Ruth Kozodoy; *The Family Treasury of Jewish Holidays* by Malka Drucker.

6. Stage the play "Sukkot — Why Is This House Different?" from *Class Acts: Plays & Skits for Jewish Settings* by Stan J. Beiner.

7. Have students design an application form for a "*sukkah* builder."

Secondary

1. A *midrash* compares the *lulav* and *etrog* to four types of Jews. Have your students match the symbol with the type of Jew:

   I. The fruit of goodly trees is the *etrog* which has a sweet smell (fragrance) and is good to eat (taste).

   II. The palm branches which have good fruit to eat (taste), but no sweet smell (fragrance).

III. The myrtle branches which have a sweet smell (fragrance), but not good fruit (taste).

IV. The willows which have no fragrance and no fruit (taste).

a. An individual who knows Torah and does good deeds.

b. An individual with no knowledge and no good deeds.

c. An individual with no knowledge, but who does good deeds.

d. An individual with knowledge but no good deeds.

(Answers: I — a; II — c; III — d; IV — b).

Discuss with your class if it is preferable to be a Jew who lacks knowledge, but performs good deeds, or a Jew who has knowledge, but does no good deeds.

2. As discussed in the Overview, *ushpizin* are traditional guests invited to dwell in the *sukkah*. These guests are Abraham, Isaac, Jacob, Joseph, Moses, Aaron and David. With your students create a new list of *ushpizin* to invite. Utilize historical and contemporary figures. Paint the names on a mural to be placed in the *sukkah*.

3. It has been traditional to use micrography as decoration for the *sukkah*. Micrography is a unique Jewish decorative art form consisting of miniature Hebrew writing used to outline geometric and flora designs and to create the human form and animals. Have students create their own micrography using fine-point marking pens on drawing paper. Following are some verses to include:

a. "You shall live in booths seven days" (Leviticus 23:42).

b. "You shall rejoice in your festival" (Deuteronomy 16:14).

c. "A land of wheat and barley, of vines, figs, pomegranates, a land of olive oil and honey" (Deuteronomy 8:8).

The students may also wish to use poetry about nature or thanksgiving for this project.

Reference: An example of micrography can be found in the article "Art" in the *Encyclopaedia Judaica*, vol. 3, across from cols. 523-524.

4. Read the following story adapted from one in *The Sukkot and Simhat Torah Anthology* by Philip Goodman, p. 97:

The Sukkah That Love Built

Rabbi Nachman of Bratzlav was invited by a humble Jew to visit his *sukkah*, on which he had spent more than he could afford. Rabbi Nachman accepted the invitation and paid a visit during the festival, accompanied by a disciple. When they entered the booth, the disciple whispered to Rabbi Nachman that the *sukkah* was not constructed according to all the laws, but the latter remained silent.

After they left the *sukkah*, Rabbi Nachman observed to his disciple, "This Jew went to so much trouble and spent so much money for the booth, and you raise questions as to its validity because of legal stringencies?"

Discuss: Which is more important to you: doing the Mitzvah correctly or the act of trying to fulfill it? If the Mitzvah is done incorrectly and others "learn" the Mitzvah this way, isn't this a threat to the integrity of the Mitzvah? Or is the simple attempt to try and to do the Mitzvah adequate in terms of preserving some form of its observance?

5. The commandment for the observance of Sukkot tells us we are to dwell in the *sukkah*. Hold an overnight with the upper grades and sleep in the *sukkah*. Utilize activities from this section for programming. (If it is not feasible to sleep in the *sukkah*, have a *shul*-in and sleep in the synagogue.)

6. Share the following information with the class: Sukkot is one of three harvest festivals, the other two being Shavuot and Passover. It is thought that originally these were ancient observances that became associated with Jewish historical events. Passover commemorates the spring harvest and the liberation from Egyptian slavery. Shavuot celebrates the harvesting of first fruits in early summer and the giving of Torah at Sinai. Finally, Sukkot recalls the fall harvest and the dwelling in temporary huts while the Israelites wandered in the desert.

Discuss the following: If these three holidays had not become attached to events of Jewish history, would they still be celebrated in a non-agricultural society? Is it important to recreate the experiences of our ancestors? Why or why not?

ALL-SCHOOL PROGRAMS

1. Hold an all-school quiz on the holiday of Sukkot. Mix age and grade levels on the teams. The number and size of teams will depend on your school. Team size should not be so large as to preclude discussion of quiz questions. Score 10 points for each correct answer. Use the following questions as a starting place. Add or delete questions based on your own preference and on what students have studied. Suggested questions:
   a. What is the Hebrew name for the temporary dwellings?
   b. What is the roof covering on a *sukkah* called?
   c. How many sides must a *sukkah* have?
   d. Recite by heart the blessing for dwelling in a *sukkah*.
   e. In how many directions are the *lulav* and *etrog* waved?
   f. In which directions are the *lulav* and *etrog* waved?
   g. What three branches compose a *lulav*?
   h. What is a *pitom*?
   i. Sukkot is one of three holidays called what in Hebrew?
   j. Can one eat the foods put up in the *sukkah* as decorations?
   k. Why do we build *sukkot* for this holiday?
   l. What is the Hebrew word for the guests who are traditionally invited to the *sukkah*?
   m. Identify the seven traditional guests invited to the *sukkah*.
   n. Recite the blessing for waving the *lulav*.
   o. The holiday of Sukkot is observed for how many days?

2. Each class selects or is assigned one of the *ushpizin*, either a biblical figure or another important figure from Jewish history. The class is to create a short presentation which will give the other classes a clue to his or her identity. Bring all the classes together. Each in turn makes its presentation, after which students can guess aloud. If you wish to add competition, each class can write down its guess. At the end of the presentations, the class with the most correct answers is declared the winner.

3. Sukkot commemorates the wanderings of the Jews in the wilderness for forty years. Organize four stations for students to visit. Each station represents either a place where an event happened, or a specific incident that occurred during the Israelites' forty year trek. To emphasize the tie-in of this activity to Sukkot, have each station take place under a *sukkah*. Divide the students into four equal groups. After they complete the activity at each station, the group will receive a representation of one of the four species (myrtle, willow, palm, *etrog*).

Station I: Mount Sinai (Exodus 19-20)
   Student have to identify and place in order the Ten Commandments. Provide them with a list containing the Ten Commandments and five additional Mitzvot in mixed sequence. Students decide together which are the real commandments and put them in order.

Station II: The Waters of Meribah (Numbers 20:2-13)
   Have three teachers or aides reenact Numbers 20:2-13. The students then debate whether or not Moses deserved the punishment given him.

Station III: Rebellion of Korach (Numbers 16:1-35)
   Two teachers or aides take the roles of Korach and Moses. Each presents a short, impassioned speech attempting to gain the students' allegiance. After the speeches the students vote on whom they want to follow. Discuss the students' reasons for their choices and the outcome of the biblical episode.

Station IV: At the Jordan River at the End of the Forty Years (Deuteronomy 31-34)
   Have the Rabbi or a teacher lead a brief memorial service in memory of Moses. Include a Psalm, eulogy, *El Malay Rachamim* and the mourner's *Kaddish*. Give students the opportunity to add their own thoughts about Moses.

RESOURCES
For the Teacher

Beiner, Stan J. *Class Acts: Plays & Skits for Jewish Settings.* Denver: A.R.E. Publishing, Inc., 1992.

Goodman, Philip. *The Sukkot and Simhat Torah Anthology.* Philadelphia: The Jewish Publication Society of America, 1973.

Goodman, Robert. *A Teachers Guide to Jewish Holidays.* Denver: A.R.E. Publishing, Inc., 1983.

Kozodoy, Ruth. *The Book of Jewish Holidays.* West Orange, NJ: Behrman House, 1981.

Loeb, Sorel Goldberg, and Barbara Binder Kadden. *Jewish History — Moments and Methods: An Activity Source Book for Teachers.* Denver: A.R.E. Publishing, Inc., 1982.

Nathan, Joan. *The Jewish Holiday Kitchen.* rev. ed. New York: Schocken Books, 1988.

Sher, Nina Streisand, and Margaret Feldman. *100+ Jewish Art Projects for Children.* Denver: A.R.E. Publishing, Inc., 1996.

Strassfeld, Sharon; Michael Strassfeld; and Richard Siegel, comps. and eds. *The First Jewish Catalog.* Philadelphia: The Jewish Publication Society of America, pp. 73-78, 126-130.

Waskow, Arthur. *Seasons of Our Joy: A Celebration of Modern Jewish Renewal.* New York: Beacon Press, 1991.

For the Students

Adler, David A. *A House on the Roof: A Sukkot Story.* New York: Bonim Books, 1976. (Grades K-4)

Arvetis, Chris, and Carole Palmer. *Why Do Leaves Change Color?* Middletown, CT: Field Publications, 1986. (Grades 4-6)

Beiner, Stan J. "Sukkot — Why Is This House Different?" In *Class Acts: Plays & Skits for Jewish Settings.* Denver: A.R.E. Publishing, Inc., 1992, pp. 33-42. (Grades 4-12)

Drucker, Malka. *The Family Treasury of Jewish Holidays.* New York: Little, Brown & Co., 1994. (All ages)

Fowler, Allan. *How Do You Know It's Fall?* Chicago: Children's Press, 1992. (Grades PK-2)

Gellman, Ellie. *Tamar's Sukkah.* Rockville, MD: Kar-Ben Copies, Inc., 1988. (Grades PK-2)

Gersh, Harry. *Midrash: Rabbinic Lore.* West Orange, NJ: Behrman House, 1985, pp. 27-28. (Grades 9 and up)

Grishaver, Joel Lurie. *Building Jewish Life: Sukkot and Simhat Torah.* Los Angeles: Torah Aura Productions, 1987. (Grades 2-5)

Gross, Judith. *Celebrate: A Book of Jewish Holidays.* New York: Platt and Munk, 1992. (Grades K-4)

Hall, Donald. *Ox Cart Man.* New York: Viking Press, 1979. (Grades 2-5)

Model of Nineteenth Century Decorated Sukkah. Palm Beach, FL: The Learning Plant. (Grades 4 and up)

Markle, Sandra. *Exploring Autumn.* New York: Atheneum, 1991. (Grades 3-6)

Saypol, Judyth Robbins, and Madeline Wikler. *My Very Own Sukkot.* Rockville, MD: Kar-Ben Copies, Inc., 1980. (Grades K-2)

Audiovisual

"Build a Sukkah." On the audiocassette *Aleph Bet Boogie* by Rabbi Joe Black and on his video of the same name. A rock and roll instruction on how to build a sukkah. Lanitunes Music. Available from A.R.E. Publishing, Inc. (All ages)

Miracle Days. In this 30 minute video, the Jewish calendar comes to life through Yoni, a magical minstrel, who sings and dances his way through the holidays. (Grades PK-5)

"Sukkot Song." On the audiocassette and songbook *Especially Wonderful Days* by Steve Reuben. A sing-along song about Sukkot. A.R.E. Publishing, Inc. (Grades K-6)

UNIT 5

OVERVIEW

Stories and their telling are integral to Judaism. But the telling of one particular story, the story of the Exodus from Egypt, is a Mitzvah when performed on Erev Passover at a *Seder*. Outside of Israel it is traditional to have a *Seder* on the first two evenings of Passover; some communities have a "*Seder*" on other nights as well, sometimes with a special theme.

Holding a *Seder* and telling the story of the Exodus fulfills the injunction, "And you shall explain to your son on that day, 'It is because of what the Eternal One did for me when I went free from Egypt'" (Exodus 13:8). This Mitzvah of retelling the story is incumbent on all Jews. As the Haggadah teaches, even if all of us were wise, all of us were people of understanding, all of us were elders, all of us were knowledgeable in the Torah, it would still be our obligation to tell of the Exodus from Egypt. And all who tell at length of the Exodus are praiseworthy. In keeping with this idea, the *Haggadah* records an anecdote of four Rabbis who gathered for *Seder* in B'nai B'rak at the time of the rebellion against Rome. They discussed the Exodus all night until their students came to them the next morning to tell them it was time to recite the *Sh'ma*.

The ritual for the *Seder* and the story of the Exodus are contained in the *Haggadah* (telling). Additionally, the *Haggadah* includes an account of the beginning of Jewish history from "My father was a wandering Aramean . . . ." and continues through the early Rabbinic period. Some *Haggadot* continue the history to contemporary times, using the Exodus as a paradigm of freedom for oppressed communities. Indeed, more editions of the *Haggadah* have been published than any other Jewish book.

Besides the *Seder*, the central ritual observance associated with Passover is the eating of unleavened bread, *matzah*. It is forbidden during Pesach to eat *chametz* (leavened food products especially those made from wheat, barley, spelt, oats, or rye). Ashkenazic Jews expand this prohibition to include corn, rice, peas, and most varieties of beans (those which are legumes). *Matzah*, which is made of wheat flour and water, is permitted because it is made under strict supervision which assures that no more than 18 minutes pass from the time the flour is mixed with water to the time the dough is put in the oven, thus precluding against the possibility of it rising.

The prohibition against eating *chametz* lasts throughout Passover: seven days in Israel and for liberal Jews outside of Israel, and eight days for those who observe the tradition of the diaspora. One should refrain from eating *chametz* or any product with *chametz* in it beginning the middle of the day prior to the *Seder*. It is forbidden not only to eat *chametz*, but to possess any during Passover. It is a tradition to search for *chametz* the evening before the holiday begins. After the home has been cleaned and all *chametz* disposed of, several crumbs of bread reserved for this purpose are "planted" in the home. Using a lighted candle, children are encouraged to search for them. When found, the crumbs are swept up with a feather into a wooden spoon. Spoon, feather, and crumbs are then burned the following morning.

Some Jews remove all *chametz* during Passover. Others put the *chametz* into a special cabinet which is locked during the holiday. In either case it is traditional to sell one's *chametz* to a non-Jew during the holiday. Afterwards, it is permissible to buy it back, although one is not allowed to sell it with this intention in mind.

While one must not eat *chametz* during Passover, one is required to eat *matzah* only on the first day of Passover (or the first two days for those observing the holiday for eight days). Even women and servants are obligated to eat *matzah*.

Two blessings are said before eating *matzah* on the first day:

בָּרוּךְ אַתָּה, יְיָ אֱלֹהֵינוּ, מֶלֶךְ הָעוֹלָם, אֲשֶׁר קִדְּשָׁנוּ בְּמִצְוֹתָיו וְצִוָּנוּ עַל אֲכִילַת מַצָּה.

Blessed are You, O Eternal our God, Ruler of the universe, Who has made us holy with Mitzvot and commanded us concerning the eating of *matzah*.

בָּרוּךְ אַתָּה, יְיָ אֱלֹהֵינוּ, מֶלֶךְ הָעוֹלָם, הַמּוֹצִיא לֶחֶם מִן הָאָרֶץ.

Blessed are You, O Eternal our God, Ruler of the universe, Who brings forth bread from the earth.

The Torah bases the eating of *matzah* on the tradition that when the Jews fled Egypt, "they baked unleavened cakes of the dough" because they left in such a hurry (Exodus 12:39). Some historians, however, claim that a holiday of unleavened bread was originally a celebration of the spring wheat harvest and only later was the Exodus appended to the observance.

The first and last days of the holiday are, much as Sabbath, days of rest on which no work is done. Because this is one of the three major festivals of the year, a *Yizkor* Service is held on the last day of Pesach at the synagogue.

ACTIVITIES

Primary

1. Read or tell the story of the Exodus to your class, beginning with Moses in the basket.
   a. Create small felt cut-outs which illustrate the story. Mount these on a flannel board as you speak.
   b. Draw, paint, or use paper cut-outs to illustrate the story. Glue these onto poster boards and, for durability, laminate.
   Whether following steps A or B, have these materials available for your students to manipulate and retell the story themselves.

2. Have the following items available for your students to use: a table, tablecloth, candles and holders, *Seder* plate, *matzah* cover, *Haggadot*, cup of Elijah, pillows for the chairs, plates, utensils, wine cups. Have them practice setting a *Seder* table.

3. Passover provides us with a richness of symbolism that lends itself to discussion and learning. Bring in a *Seder* plate and its symbols. With the students taste them and discuss the meaning of the symbols. Utilize any standard *Haggadah* for a list of these items and an explanation of their symbolism.

4. Prepare *charoset* from several different Jewish cultures (see recipes below). Bring a globe to class and point out the countries of origin of these recipes. For additional recipes see the two recommended cookbooks.

Reference: *The Jewish Holiday Kitchen* by Joan Nathan; *The Complete Passover Cookbook* by Frances R. AvRutick.

Yemenite *Charoset*
(serves 20)
30 dates, chopped
30 figs, chopped
4 tablespoons sesame seeds
2 teaspoons ginger powder
Dash of coriander
Matzah meal, as desired
Dry, red wine
1 chili pepper (optional)

Mix to form a paste.

Ashkenazic *Charoset* (Eastern Europe)
(serves 20)
1 pound grated or chopped apples
1/3 pound chopped nuts
2 teaspoons cinnamon
Dry wine or sweet wine to mix

Blend to form a paste.

Israeli *Charoset*
(serves 20)
3 apples, peeled
6 bananas
Juice and rind of 1 lemon
Juice and rind of 1 orange
30 dates
2 teaspoons cinnamon
1/2 pound ground peanuts
1 cup dry, red wine
Matzah meal, as desired
1 can dried fruit peel, if desired
Sugar to taste

Grate, mash or grind fruits. Mix with seasonings and wine.

5. Make pillow cases for pillows to be used for reclining at the *Seder*.
   Materials needed: One standard size white pillow case for each child; fabric crayons for each child (available at craft stores and sewing shops).
   Procedure: Each child creates his/her own design on paper, then draws it on a pillowcase.

6. There are many songs associated with the *Seder*. "*Dayenu*" and "*Chad Gadya*" are two which have special appeal to children. Teach these to the students, or listen to some recordings to learn the tunes. References: *One Little Goat: A Passover Song*; *Seder Melodies*; "Pesach Is Here Today" on the cassette tape *Especially Wonderful Days* by Steve Reuben; *A Singing Seder* by Cindy Paley.

Intermediate

1. Determine what students know by giving them a pretest, or organize a competition between two or three teams. Some suggested questions: Why did the Israelites settle in Egypt? (Invited by Joseph during a famine.) What is the best known Hebrew name for Passover? (Pesach.) In what season of the year does Passover occur? (Spring.) On what Hebrew date does Passover begin? (15th of Nisan.) What replaces leavened foods at Passover? (*Matzah*.) How many days do we observe Passover? (Eight for traditional Jews outside of Israel and seven for Jews in Israel and liberal Jews.) From what two ingredients is *matzah* made? (Flour and water.) Name four items on the *Seder* plate. (Egg, *maror* or horseradish, shank bone, *charoset*, parsley.) How many cups of wine are drunk at the *Seder*? (Four.) Which sea did the Jews cross after leaving Egypt? (Red Sea or Sea of Reeds.) When is the *Haggadah* used? (At the *Seder*.) In what book of the Bible is the story of Passover? (Exodus.) What does the *charoset* represent? (Mortar used with the bricks.) What does the parsley represent? (Springtime, season of Passover.) What does the salt water represent? (Tears shed by the Israelites because of slavery.) What does the horseradish represent? (Bitter life of slavery.)

   Follow up this activity by giving each student an opportunity to finish this statement: "I learned (or re-learned) that _____."

2. Have your students learn to read or chant the four questions in Hebrew. Ask the music specialist or one of the Hebrew teachers for help if needed.

3. Do a Values Whip with the class. Go around the room giving each student the chance to finish this statement: "The observance of Passover teaches me _____" or "Passover reminds me that _____."

4. In the United States, many holidays are commemorated by the issuing of special postage stamps. Have each student design a Passover commemorative stamp. Make it full size (8½" by 11"), as the tiny detail work may be impossible to accomplish. These can be laminated and used for display or as placemats.

5. After reading the story of the Exodus to your class, ask students to imagine that Pharaoh did not harden his heart against the Hebrews. Have them each rewrite the Exodus experience with this in mind.

6. Create a *Haggadah* display in an area of your classroom. Have each student read and examine the *Haggadot* you have collected. Next, determine with students what goes into a *Haggadah*, what "must" be there, and what is optional or the personal choice of the editor. Create lists of these items.

Secondary

1. Take this opportunity to conduct a traditional study session with your students. Provide each student with a copy of the book of Exodus. Also provide various commentaries, such as Rashi, Plaut, *Midrash* on Exodus, and any additional material suggested by the principal and/or Rabbi. Do a line-by-line reading of the text and utilize the commentary material.

2. Pose the following dilemma to the class: Can Pharaoh's actions be justified? Discuss.

3. Create a show using a format similar to the television show called "Sunday Morning," hosted by Charles Kuralt. Use the story of the Exodus as your theme. "Sunday Morning" reviews and comments on events of the previous week. You can arbitrarily choose from which point you want to work back. You might consider working back from the start of the 40 year period of wandering, or earlier. Obtain a segment of "Sunday Morning" to show your students how it is organized. If that is not possible, here are some other suggestions: First person interviews of Egyptians and Israelites, interviews of key characters from the Exodus, a food or cooking segment (featuring unleavened bread or manna), a piece on water in the desert, fashion in ancient Egypt, etc.

4. "Face the Nation" is another T.V. show with a format that would be very interesting for the students to script and tape. The invited guest might be Pharaoh, who could be questioned by a group of three Egyptian journalists. Moses might be the guest during another segment, and he could be questioned by a group of three Hebrew/Israelite journalists.

5. Have students create primary school activities for Passover, then become teachers for a younger grade. Some examples are: A maze which leads to the *Afikoman*, a Passover word search, word jumbles, riddles, simple board games using material from the *Haggadah*, running or action games.

6. Many non-Jewish groups enjoy experiencing a Passover *Seder*. Consider inviting a Christian group of students to share a *Seder*. The Anti-Defamation League of B'nai B'rith, together with The Liturgy Training Program of the Archdiocese of Chicago, has issued a *Haggadah* which is particularly appropriate for interfaith and Christian groups. Included is a packet with the music and Hebrew pronunciations.

   Reference: *The Passover Celebration: A Haggadah for the Seder*, edited by Leon Klenicki.

7. *Ma'ot Chittim* is a community fund which provides Passover staples to Jewish needy individuals and families. As a class decide on a fund-raising project to raise money for *Ma'ot Chittim*. Turn the funds over to a community group which distributes these foodstuffs.

ALL-SCHOOL PROGRAMS

1. Conduct an all-school search for *chametz*. Split the classes into several evenly divided teams. Provide each team with a teacher, adult volunteer, or synagogue staff person. There will be 10 locations where *chametz* needs to be found. Each location will be found by means of a clue. The adult leader should have a complete list of clues and locations so that he/she can give further hints. The *chametz* is represented by squares of paper with the location number on it. These are collected as the game proceeds. Each location also provides the clue for the next stop. The first clue is handed out to each team.

   a. Genesis 41:35 - "Let all the food of these good years that are coming be gathered, and let the grain be collected under Pharaoh's authority as food to be in the cities." (refrigerator or a store room)

   b. Genesis 49:20 - "Asher's bread shall be rich, and he shall yield royal dainties." (oven or *Oneg* table)

   c. Exodus 4:12 - "Now go, and I will be with you as you speak and will instruct you what to say" (telephone, or public address system).

   d. Exodus 15:1 - "Then Moses and the Israelites sang this song to the Lord." (choir area, musical instrument, piano, Cantor's study, music specialist, area where music books are kept)

   e. Exodus 16:27 - " . . . there were twelve springs of water . . ." (water fountain, faucet, or sink)

   f. Exodus 25:8 - "And let them make Me a sanctuary that I may dwell among them." (sanctuary, chapel)

   g. Exodus 25:16 - "And deposit in the Ark the tablets of the pact which I will give you." (Ark)

   h. Numbers 11:2 - "The people cried out to Moses. Moses prayed to the Lord, and fire died down." (fire extinguisher or fire alarm or a smoke alarm)

   i. Deuteronomy 6:9 - "Inscribe them on the doorposts of your house and on your gates." (*Mezuzah* mounted on front door or elsewhere in the building)

   j. Deuteronomy 15:4 - "There shall be no needy among you. . . ." (food cart for the hungry or a *Tzedakah* box)

2. Hold an all-school model *Seder* with a twist. Each class is responsible for a creative interpretation of one section of the *Haggadah*. They may use art; drama; dance; creative readings; audiovisual aids, such as slides; short student-made films; etc.

3. If you are lucky enough to have a *matzah* factory in your area, arrange for your school to take a tour. If not, organize your own *matzah* factory in your school.

4. Play the *Seder Board Game*. This game teaches the order and liturgy of the *Seder*, and reinforces the idea of a *Seder* as a "telling" and "sharing."

5. To experience Passover as Soviet Jews experience it, do "Passover in Soviet Union." (For a description this activity, see Unit 23 "*Pidyon Shevuyim,*" All-school Program #4.)

RESOURCES

For the Teacher

Ashkenazi-Hankin, Gail. *Passover Lite Kosher Cookbook.* Gretna, LA: Pelican Publishing Co., Inc., 1996.

Goodman, Philip. *The Passover Anthology.* Philadelphia: The Jewish Publication Society of America, 1961.

Goodman, Robert. *A Teachers Guide to Jewish Holidays.* Denver: A.R.E. Publishing, Inc., 1983.

Klenicki, Leon, ed. *The Passover Celebration: A Haggadah for the Seder.* Chicago: The Anti-Defamation League of B'nai B'rith and the Liturgy Training Program of the Archdiocese of Chicago, 1980. (Liturgy Training Publications, 155 East Superior Street, Chicago, IL 60611)

Maimonides, Moses. *The Commandments.* New York: The Soncino Press, 1967, vol. 1, pp. 166-171, vol. 2, pp. 194-199.

Nathan, Joan. *The Jewish Holiday Kitchen.* rev. ed. New York: Schocken Books, 1988.

Siegel, Richard; Michael Strassfeld; and Sharon Strassfeld, comps. and eds.*The First Jewish Catalog.* Philadelphia: The Jewish Publication Society of America, 1973, pp. 139-145.

Waskow, Arthur. *Seasons of Our Joy: A Handbook of Jewish Festivals.* New York: Beacon Press, 1991.

For the Students

Gold-Vukson, Marji. *Torah Tales Copy Pak™: Exodus and Leviticus.* Denver: A.R.E. Publishing, Inc., 1995. (Grades 2-5)

Grishaver, Joel Lurie. *Building Jewish Life/Passover.* Los Angeles: Torah Aura Productions, 1988. (Grades K-2)

Hirsch, Marilyn. *One Little Goat: A Passover Song.* Northvale, NJ: Jason Aronson, 1990. (Grades K-3)

Marcus, Audrey Friedman, and Raymond A. Zwerin. *But This Night Is Different: A Seder Experience.* New York: UAHC Press, 1980. (Grades PK-3)

Oren, Rony. *The Animated Haggadah.* New York: Sure Sellers, 1990. (Grades K-3)

Saypol, Judyth, and Madeline Wikler. *My Very Own Haggadah.* Rockville, MD: Kar-Ben Copies, Inc., 1983. (Grades 2-5)

Seder Board Game. Los Angeles: Torah Aura Productions. (Grades 3 and up)

The Seder Game. In *Holiday Game Pak.* Denver: A.R.E. Publishing, Inc., 1977. (Grades K-3)

Audiovisual

The Animated Haggadah. A half-hour videotape about one family's *Seder.* Board of Jewish Education of Greater New York. (Grades K-6)

Celebrate with Us: Passover. Audiocassette with engaging stories and joyful songs told and sung by professional actors. Jewish Family Productions. Available from A.R.E. Publishing, Inc. (Grades PK-3)

Complete Haggadah. A Windows or Macintosh program for creating one's own family Haggadah. Includes English translation. Davka Corporation. (Grade 7 and up)

The Joy of Passover: How To Create Your Own Passover Seder. 35 minute video which presents highlights of an actual *Seder,* along with descriptions and historical origins of symbolic foods and ritual objects, preparation for the *Seder,* and songs. Institute for Creative Jewish Media. (Grades 4-adult)

Mostly Matzah. This audiocassette by Fran Avni tells the ancient tale of the Exodus in story and song. Lemonstone Records. Available from A.R.E. Publishing, Inc. (Grades PK-3)

My Exodus. A half-hour videotape of six children telling their version of the Exodus. Torah Aura Productions. (Grades 3-6)

Passover Adventure. A 28 minute video which features a native born Israeli who tries to follow the route of the Exodus in order to celebrate Passover in a special way. Ergo Media Inc. (Grades 3 and up)

Passover at Bubbe's. Pan-Imago, Inc. In this 42 minute video, muppet characters help Bubbe prepare for and celebrate Passover. (Grades PK-3)

Passover: Traditions of Freedom. A 57 minute musical exploration on video of the festival of Passover. Features traditions from around the world. National Center for Jewish Film. (All ages)

"Pharaoh, Pharaoh." On the audiocassette *Jewish Rock and Roll Singer* by Mah Tovu. A rock and roll retelling of the Exodus story that kids will love. BeeZee Productions. Available from A.R.E. Publishing, Inc. (All ages)

"A Song of Freedom." On the audiocassette *Bible People Songs: Sing Along Songs for Primary Grades* by Jeff Klepper and Jeff Salkin. Denver: A.R.E. Publishing, Inc., 1981. (See also "The Ten Plagues" and "The Righteous Midwives" on the same recording.) (Grades PK-6)

Sounds of Freedom: Exodus in Song. A contemporary anthology featuring a song for every Torah portion in the Book of Exodus. Sounds Write Productions, Inc. Available from A.R.E. Publishing, Inc.

"Story of Nachshon" and "Nachshon." On the audiocassette *Everybody's Got a Little Music* by Rabbi Joe Black. LaniTunes Music. Available from A.R.E. Publishing, Inc. (Grades 3 and up)

Sanctifying the New Moon
ראש חֹדֶשׁ

OVERVIEW

"This month shall mark for you the beginning of the months; it shall be the first of the months of the year for you" (Exodus 12:2). Not only is the preceding verse the basis for the Mitzvah pertaining to the observance of Rosh Chodesh (New Moon), it is also the basis for the establishment of the Jewish calendar.

Long ago the beginning of a new month was declared when two independent witnesses reported to the Sanhedrin in Jerusalem that the crescent of a new moon had appeared. This declaration was relayed from Jerusalem to other cities by signal fires set on hill tops. However, the Samaritans, who objected to the Rabbis setting the calendar, set their own fires a day early in order to confuse the people. To counter this, messengers on horseback were sent by the Rabbis to proclaim the new month. This was a slower process, of course, causing a delay in announcing the new month. To make certain that all holidays were still celebrated on their proper day, an extra day was added to the biblically prescribed number. The custom of adding an extra day to the festivals and to Rosh Hashanah continues to be observed by many Jews living in the diaspora.

Since twelve lunar months of 29½ days each equals 354 days, a year of 12 lunar months is 11 days shorter than a solar year. To synchronize the lunar year with the solar, a thirteenth month is added seven times in every 19 year period. This leap month is added at the end of the calendar year and called V'Adar — Adar II.

The first month of the year, referred to in the verse from Exodus cited above, is Nisan, which occurs in the spring. Therefore, Passover is actually the first holiday of the Jewish year. Rosh Hashanah, the Jewish New Year, occurs on the first day of the seventh month — the time which the Torah tells us is a "memorial proclaimed with the blast of horns" (Leviticus 23:24). How then a new year in a seventh month? In Rabbinic times there were three new years besides Rosh Hashanah each year: Tu B'shevat, the new year for trees; Nisan 1, new year for the reign of kings; Elul 15, the new year for tithes. Thus, a new year for agriculture, a fiscal year, a royal calendar, and a new year for the spirit. The latter became the time of the turning of a new leaf, of the spirit, and of the calendar.

It takes approximately 29½ days for the moon to circumscribe the earth. Since half days are not possible, some months are 29 days and some months are 30. The months Iyar, Tammuz, Elul, Tevet, and Adar II are always 29 days; the months Nisan, Sivan, Av, Tishri, and Shevat are always 30 days. Cheshvan and Kislev are sometimes 29 days and sometimes 30 days. Adar is 30 days in a leap year and 29 days in a non-leap year.

Rosh Chodesh, a minor holiday marking the new moon, is celebrated for one or two days each month. If a month contains 30 days, then the last day of that month and the first day of the next month comprise Rosh Chodesh. If a month contains 29 days, then only the first day of the following month is Rosh Chodesh. Because of Rosh Hashanah, there is no Rosh Chodesh celebration in Tishri.

It is customary to announce and to bless the new moon after the reading of the Haftarah at the Shabbat service prior to Rosh Chodesh. Rosh Chodesh itself is observed as a half-holiday. In the Bible it included festive meals, abstention from business, and visiting prophets. While it is permitted to work on Rosh Chodesh, it is traditional that women not work. This was as a reward for not donating their jewelry toward the making of the golden calf. In some circles Rosh Chodesh has become a women's holiday with special services and celebrations. This is especially appropriate because of the similarity in timing of a woman's monthly cycle with the lunar cycle.

The worship service on Rosh Chodesh includes a special Musaf service, the addition of prayers in the Amidah, part of the Hallel, and the reading of Numbers 28:1-15.

ACTIVITIES

Primary

1. Create a permanent bulletin board on which you display a large Hebrew calendar. Gather the students around the calendar at the beginning of

each month to review the month, day, and Hebrew year.

2. At the beginning of each new Hebrew month, each student will make a personal calendar. It should include the following in Hebrew: name of the month, the days of the week, the numerical dates, and any holidays or special events occurring in that month. The students can decorate their calendars with original pictures reflecting the month's special occasions.

3. Teach your students the names of the seasons in Hebrew:

Winter - *Choref*
Summer - *Kayitz*
Spring - *Aviv*
Fall - *Stav*

Cut a large circle from white construction paper. Divide it into fourths. Decorate each quadrant for one of the seasons. Print the Hebrew name of the season on wooden clothespins. The students can quiz themselves by clipping the correct Hebrew name to the corresponding English translation. Self-check by looking at the answer on the reverse side of each quadrant.

4. The start of the new month is called Rosh Chodesh. Teach this term to your students. It is considered a minor holiday and is traditionally celebrated by announcing and blessing the new moon. A festive meal is included.
Plan a monthly celebration for the new moon (new month). Announce the new month's name and ask each of the children what they hope for in the new month. Mention the holidays and special events that fall during the month, and include a special treat for the students. For an unusual treat, make cookies in the shapes of the stages of the moon. Use a simple sugar cookie recipe and let the students shape the dough.

5. Create decorations for Rosh Chodesh. (Choose a month that has several special occasions or holidays.) The students can write appropriate biblical verses on streamers and decorate their room, door, or hallway. They can make simple paper cuts of the various stages of the moon. Have the students use black or blue paper as the background and cut representations of the stages

of the moon from a sheet of white construction paper. Add glitter stars on the paper cut to create the illusion of a night sky.

6. In the Overview section above, Rosh Chodesh is described as a half-holiday on which women did not work. Perhaps this was the prototype for Mother's Day. Rosh Chodesh then provides a monthly occasion when students can do something special with or for their mothers. Help students to choose one of the following activities, or brainstorm for additional ideas:
   a. Choose a chore to do for your mother.
   b. Take your mother out for a special walk.
   c. Plan some special time together.
   d. Make a small gift, write a poem, or just say, "Thanks, Mom, for all you do."

Intermediate

1. Distribute a current Jewish calendar to each student. Ask each to determine the Hebrew and civil dates of the following: Rosh Hashanah, Yom Kippur, Sukkot, Chanukah, Purim, Passover, Shavuot, and their birthdays. Then distribute a Hebrew calendar for the prior year and have the students do the same thing. Compare the two calendars and explain why the dates change.

2. There are various rhymes and songs used to learn the names and order of the civil months and the corresponding number of days in each month. With your students create a rhyme or song for learning the Hebrew months. Use a tune of a popular song or write it as a rap (a spoken song done to a loud, recurring beat). See the Overview above for the names of the months and their lengths.

3. Some traditional Jews consider Rosh Chodesh to be a minor Yom Kippur. They fast and repent of their misdeeds. Have your students write resolutions for an upcoming month.

4. Design a Hebrew calendar. For each Hebrew month create a human tableau which illustrates an event or events in that month. Take snapshots of each tableau. Reproduce the calendar to distribute to all class members and possibly to the entire school. Include the following information on the calendar pages: Torah portions for each Shabbat, important dates, holidays, days of the week in Hebrew and English. Ask students to suggest other information to include.

5. In addition to learning the names of the seasons (see Primary Activity #3 above), teach the class Hebrew vocabulary which describes each season.

winter - *Choref*
snow - *sheleg*
cold - *kar*
spring - *aviv*
rain - *geshem*
wind - *ruach*
lightning - *barak*
thunder - *raam*
summer - *kayitz*
hot - *cham*
sun - *shemesh*
fall - *stav*
leaves - *aleem*
chilly - *kareer*

6. Read the following selection from the *Mishnah* (*Rosh Hashanah* 2:5-7) which describes how witnesses reported the new moon to the Sanhedrin in the early Rabbinic period. Ask students to identify some other questions that the Sanhedrin might have asked the witnesses to determine if they were telling the truth.

There was a large courtyard in Jerusalem called *Beit Yaazek*, where all the witnesses assembled, and there the Court examined them . . . How do they examine witnesses? The pair which comes first, they examine first. They bring in the elder of the two and say to him, "Tell us how you saw the moon: Facing the sun or turned away from it? To the north or to the south? How high was it? To which side was it leaning? And how broad was it? . . ." Afterward, they bring in the second witness and examine him. If their words are found to agree, their evidence is accepted . . . The chief of the court says, "It is hallowed." And all the people respond: "It is hallowed, it is hallowed."

Secondary

1. Hebrew months have long been associated with the signs of the zodiac. Have your students create a series of applique banners or one large quilt which displays the name of each Hebrew month and the corresponding sign of the zodiac. Tishri - scales; Cheshvan - scorpion; Kislev - archer/bow; Tevet - goat; Shevat - bucket/water carrier; Adar - fish; Nisan - ram;

Iyar - bull; Sivan - twins; Tammuz - crab; Av - lion; Elul - virgin/young girl.

2. Rosh Chodesh celebrates the appearance of the new moon. Read the following Talmudic explanation for the size of the moon, which has been adapted from *Chullin* 60b:

According to Jewish tradition, the sun and the moon were originally the same size. The moon asked God, "How can the sun and I be of equal importance?" God answered: "Make yourself smaller." The moon complained, "Just because I asked the question, why must I be smaller?" God replied, "You will shine both during the day and during the night." The moon responded, "What good will I be in the daylight?" God said, "All right, the Jews will determine the calendar by you." The moon replied, "For that the sun is needed as well." God said, "Some of the most important Jews will be called small like you are: Jacob will be called 'small,' and Samuel will be called 'small,' and even King David will be called 'small.' Being small will be an honor for you.

Discuss the following with the class: When two are competing for the same honor, position, or award, must one always be the winner and the other the loser? Give examples of individuals or groups who have had to make themselves smaller and to accept less because "two could not wear one crown" (e.g., women, minorities, the disabled). What was the moon attempting to say? (That we each have our own unique "crown" or qualities.)

3. Share some original Rosh Chodesh services with the class. Assign students to write their own creative Rosh Chodesh service. Utilize the service in your synagogue prayerbook as a basis. Encourage the students to add material of their own choosing or creation which reflects the themes of Rosh Chodesh (e.g., moon, changing seasons, passage of time, renewal and hope).

References: "This Month Is for You: Observing Rosh Hodesh As a Women's Holiday" by Arlene Agus in *The Jewish Woman: New Perspectives* edited by Elizabeth Koltun; *Miriam's Well: Rituals for Jewish Women Around the Year* by Penina V. Adelman.

4. The ceremony of *Kiddush Levana*, hallowing the moon, is always done outdoors and only if the moon is visible. One evening, a few days after Rosh Chodesh, have a *Kiddush Levana* with your students. You might include a potluck or dessert party with the ceremony.

Reference: *Seasons of Our Joy* by Arthur Waskow, pp. 299-230.

5. Ask students to create a series of public service announcements encouraging the congregation to celebrate Rosh Chodesh. If possible, print these in the synagogue bulletin on a monthly basis. Students can also create readings for welcoming the new month and share them at worship services and/or assembly programs.

6. Rosh Chodesh is considered a special time for women. Celebrate the contributions women have made to Jewish life throughout the ages. Create a time line from a length of cord strung like a clothesline in the classroom. Students write thumbnail sketches of notable Jewish women and put them in sequential order on the time line.

References: *Written Out of History: Our Jewish Foremothers* by Sondra Henry and Emily Katz; *Encyclopaedia Judaica* (see names of individual women).

ALL-SCHOOL ACTIVITIES

1. Throughout the school year, announce each Hebrew month at an assembly. Assign a each class the responsibility of presenting a skit or song, etc., to announce a particular month and to describe the special events and holidays that fall during it.

2. Rosh Chodesh is considered a time of renewal and hope. It provides an opportunity for a fresh start each month. Make an all-school "Wish Tree" in time for the beginning of a new month.

    Materials needed: Tree branch, plaster of paris, construction paper, pens, pencils, hole punch.

    Procedure: Pre-cut construction paper tree leaves. In class, imbed a branch from a tree in plaster of paris. When the plaster dries, the branch will be held firmly in place. On the pre-cut leaves, students write personal wishes and hopes for the new month. Punch holes into the leaves, thread with yarn, and hang on the tree

branch. Display the wish tree in the synagogue. Attach a sign describing what it is and the name of the new Hebrew month.

3. Have a Rosh Chodesh service and *Oneg* for the Religious/Hebrew school. Include the blessing for the new month, recitation of the *Hallel*, and the Torah reading for Rosh Chodesh, Numbers 28:1-15. Include a special festive snack. Ask the Rabbi, Cantor, and Director of Education to help create a meaningful observance for all ages. Repeat monthly as feasible.

RESOURCES

For the Teacher

Adelman, Penina. *Miriam's Well: Rituals for Jewish Women Around the World.* New York: Biblio Press, 1990, pp. 8-10, 28-31.

Agus, Arlene. "This Month Is for You: Observing Rosh Hodesh As a Women's Holiday." In *The Jewish Woman: New Perspectives.* Elizabeth Koltun, ed. New York: Schocken Books, 1976, pp. 84-93.

Berrin, Susan. *Celebrating the New Moon: A Rosh Chodesh Anthology.* Northvale, NJ: Jason Aronson, 1995.

Henry, Sondra, and Emily Taitz. *Written Out of History: Our Jewish Foremothers.* Fresh Meadow, NY: Biblio Press, 1983.

Maimonides, Moses. *The Commandments.* New York: The Soncino Press, vol. 1, pp. 159-163.

Siegel, Richard; Michael Strassfeld; and Sharon Strassfeld, comps. and eds. *The First Jewish Catalog.* Philadelphia: The Jewish Publication Society of America, 1973, pp. 96-102.

Waskow, Arthur. "Feminist Judaism: Restoration of the Moon." In *On Being a Jewish Feminist: A Reader.* Susannah Heschel, ed. New York: Schocken Books, 1983, pp. 261-272.

———. *Seasons of Our Joy: A Handbook of Jewish Festivals.* New York: Beacon Press, 1991.

For the Students

Gersh, Harry. *When a Jew Celebrates.* West Orange, NJ: Behrman House, 1971, pp. 105-115. (Grades 4-6)

My Very Own Jewish Calendar. Rockville, MD: Kar-Ben Copies, Inc. Annual. (Grades K-4)

Shekel. Michal. *The Jewish Life Cycle Book.* Hoboken, NJ: KTAV Publishing House, Inc., 1996, pp. 58-62. (Grades 6-8, Teacher Guide available)

Weilerstein, Sadie Rose. *What the Moon Brought.* Philadelphia: The Jewish Publication Society of America, 1942. (Grades K-3)

Zwerin, Raymond A. *The Jewish Calendar.* Denver: A.R.E. Publishing, Inc., 1975. (Grades 8 and up)

Audiovisual

Back to Tishri. In this 23 minute video, a girl gets lost in a magical Jewish calendar. She reunites with her mother after she has gone through all the months of the year. Bureau of Jewish Education of Greater Boston. (Grades K-2)

"Rosh Chodesh Moon." On the audiocassette *MIRAJ: A Moon Note.* A contemporary song of blessing on Rosh Chodesh. New Legends. (Grades 9-adult)

Circumsizing Sons

בְּרִית מִילָה

OVERVIEW

Brit Milah (Covenant of Circumcision) is one of the oldest and most enduring rites in Judaism. "This is the covenant that you shall keep, between Me and you and your offspring to follow: every male among you shall be circumcised. You shall circumcise the flesh of your foreskin, and that shall be the sign of the covenant between Me and you" (Genesis 17:10-11).

Circumcision predates Judaism, and was practiced by some ancient peoples as a rite of puberty. The procedure involves removing part or all of the foreskin which covers the glans of the penis. The Jewish people adopted this practice, transforming it into a religious ceremony in which an eight-day-old boy becomes a member of the Jewish community. In addition to the above citation, circumcision is mentioned a number of other times in the Bible.

After receiving the above command, Abraham, at age 99, circumcised himself, his son Ishmael, and all males of his household, including his servants. When Isaac is born, he is circumcised on the eighth day.

When the Hivites want to intermarry with the Hebrews, Jacob's sons insist that they be circumcised (Genesis 34:14). Three days after the males are circumcised, two of Jacob's sons kill all the males of Shechem in revenge for raping their sister Dinah.

When Moses is returning from Midian to Egypt, God seeks to kill him, apparently for failing to circumcise his son. Moses is spared when his wife Zipporah circumcises him (Exodus 4:24-26).

While all of the Jews who left Egypt were circumcised, the Jews born in the wilderness were not circumcised until Joshua circumcised them prior to entering Canaan (Joshua 5:2-8).

Circumcision was abandoned in the kingdom of Israel for a time (I Kings 19:14). Elijah is credited with helping reinstate the practice. Throughout the Bible those who are uncircumcised, such as the Philistines, are spoken of with contempt.

Under the influence of Hellenism, many Jews abandoned the practice in keeping with Greek tradition. Some who had been circumcised underwent operations to disguise the fact in order to participate nude in Greek games. Antiochus IV, of Chanukah infamy, prohibited circumcision. Some women who nonetheless circumcised their sons were killed.

Circumcision was also prohibited by Hadrian in the first century, leading, in part, to the Bar Kochba revolt. However, the practice of circumcision by Jews endured throughout the periods of Rabbinic Judaism and the Middle Ages.

In the nineteenth century some Reform leaders sought to abolish the practice of circumcision as barbaric. However, other Reform leaders defended the practice, and it remains today widely observed among all Jews.

Traditionally, a father is responsible for circumcising his son. Because most fathers are unable to perform the medical procedure, it is common practice to designate a *mohel* to act for him. A *mohel* is a ritual circumcisor who is trained in both the medical procedure and in the details of Jewish law and ritual relating to circumcision. If a *mohel* is not available, a Jewish physician may perform the circumcision, usually in conjunction with a Rabbi. While a woman is legally eligible to be a *mohel*, within the Orthodox community the tradition is that only men become *mohalim*.

The training of *mohalim* is now being done under the auspices of the Reform movement. Men and women are learning to perform the rites and rituals of this ancient life cycle event.

Circumcision, since biblical times, has been performed on the eighth day of a child's life, usually in the morning. Even if the eighth day is Shabbat or Yom Kippur, the circumcision takes precedence. However, if the child is not strong enough to undergo the circumcision on the eighth day, the *Brit Milah* is postponed. If the circumcision is not done on the eighth day, then, when it is finally performed, it may not be done on Shabbat or a holiday.

The *Brit Milah* is usually performed at the home or at the synagogue. Prior to the ceremony, the parents select three friends or relatives to honor: the *kvatterin* (godmother) brings the child into the room where the circumcision is to occur and hands him to the *kvatter* (godfather). The *kvatter* hands the baby to the *mohel*, who recites the introductory prayers, and then places the child on the lap of the *sandak,* traditionally a grandfather, who holds the child during the ceremony. Some synagogues have a special chair called the chair of Elijah, on which the *sandak* sits. According to Jewish tradition, Elijah is the guardian of the child during circumcision, and is spiritually present at all such ceremonies.

The *mohel* recites the following blessing and performs the circumcision:

בָּרוּךְ אַתָּה, יְיָ אֱלֹהֵינוּ, מֶלֶךְ הָעוֹלָם, אֲשֶׁר קִדְּשָׁנוּ בְּמִצְוֹתָיו וְצִוָּנוּ עַל הַמִּילָה.

Blessed are you, Lord our God, ruler of the universe, Who has made us holy with Mitzvot and commanded us concerning circumcision.

The father then recites this blessing:

בָּרוּךְ אַתָּה, יְיָ אֱלֹהֵינוּ, מֶלֶךְ הָעוֹלָם, אֲשֶׁר קִדְּשָׁנוּ בְּמִצְוֹתָיו וְצִוָּנוּ לְהַכְנִיסוֹ בִּבְרִיתוֹ שֶׁל אַבְרָהָם אָבִינוּ.

Blessed are you, Lord our God, ruler of the Universe, Who has made us holy with Mitzvot and commanded us to enter him into the covenant of Abraham our father.

All those present say:

כְּשֵׁם שֶׁנִּכְנַס לַבְּרִית כֵּן יִכָּנֵס לְתוֹרָה וּלְחֻפָּה וּלְמַעֲשִׂים טוֹבִים.

As he has entered the covenant, so may he be brought to the study of Torah, to the marriage canopy, and to a life of good deeds.

After the wine is blessed and shared by the parents and the child, a prayer for the well-being of the child and his family is read and the child is given his Hebrew name.

While the traditional ceremony is usually followed, some parents do compile or write their own ceremony, incorporating the traditional prayers. Often in these ceremonies, the role of the mother is made more prominent.

The *Brit Milah* ceremony is customarily followed by a *Seudat Mitzvah,* a meal in celebration of the child's birth and his entering into the covenant. It is considered praiseworthy to make this as grand a celebration as possible.

Circumcision not performed in infancy may be done later. It is traditional for a male who converts to Judaism to be circumcised. If the convert was already circumcised, then a symbolic circumcision is performed — a drop of blood is taken from the penis (*hatafat dam brit*) right after the person emerges from the *Mikvah.*

ACTIVITIES

Primary

1. At the *Brit Milah,* a child receives his Hebrew name. Take a photo of each child in the class and mount each on a piece of construction paper. Next to the photo write the child's Hebrew name, its meaning, and possibly a picture illustrating the meaning. Make a bulletin board display of these name posters, or laminate them with clear contact paper and use as placemats.

2. A traditional treat eaten at a *Brit Milah* is honey cake. Bake this cake with your students using this recipe:

    Honey Cake
    (From the kitchen of Julia Soroken)
    Combine and beat well: 2 eggs, 1 cup sugar, 1 cup honey, 1 cup water or black coffee, 2 tablespoons cooking oil. Sift together: 3 cups flour, 1 teaspoon baking powder, 1 teaspoon baking soda, 1 heaping teaspoon cinnamon, 1/2 teaspoon allspice, 1/2 teaspoon cloves. Alternately add flour mixture to honey mixture. Mix well. Stir in 1 cup floured nuts. Bake at 350 degrees in a 9" x 13" greased and floured pan for one hour.

3. Ask students if they had a *Brit Milah* or naming ceremony. Have them share photos, certificates, and mementos of this occasion. (Send home a note prior to this lesson asking for parents' help in providing these items.)

4. *Brit Milah* is one outward sign of being Jewish. There are many others. Make life-sized poster cut-outs of each child in your class.
    Materials needed: White or brown shelf paper unrolled, felt marking pens.
    Procedure: Each child should lie down on the paper and the teacher or another student should trace that child's body shape. The student can then cut out his/her form and decorate it with other outward symbols of Judaism, such as a *kipah,* a *Tallit,* a necklace with Jewish objects on it, a hand holding a Jewish ritual object, etc.

5. Discuss the following: Parents provide a *Brit Milah* or naming ceremony as a sign of the promise to raise their child as a Jew. What does a child have to do to help fulfill that promise?

6. *Brit Milah* is a physical sign that a baby boy has become a part of the Jewish community. The baby's family is participating in an age-old ceremony which reinforces its commitment to Judaism. Jewish tradition is passed from generation to generation, and the Jewish family is the link which holds it all together. Have each student create a family tree which documents how Judaism has evolved in his or her particular family. Depending on the age group, the dates of Jewish life cycle events may be included and special family traditions and observances may be described. (Be especially sensitive to children with a non-Jewish parent or grandparent.)

Intermediate

1. At a *Brit Milah*, the infant is given his Hebrew name. Have students do some research on their own names. Find out after whom they were named and the meaning of the name. Students who do not have a Hebrew name should take this opportunity to choose one. Have students design a wall pennant to illustrate the meaning of their Hebrew names.

    Materials needed: Large piece of felt, smaller pieces of felt in various colors, scissors.

    Procedure: Students cut out the smaller pieces of felt into the letters of their Hebrew name and symbols, flowers, etc., to decorate their pennant. Glue the cut-outs in a variety of colors on the large piece of felt for an applique effect. After displaying the pennants in the hallway of the religious school, each student may take his/her pennant home to hang.

    References: *The Name Dictionary* or *The Complete Dictionary of English and Hebrew First Names*, both by Alfred J. Kolatch.

2. The Torah speaks of three covenants between God and human beings. Divide the class into three groups. Assign each group one of the following passages: Genesis 9:9-17, Genesis 17:1-14, and Exodus 24 and 31:18. Each group should read their assigned verses and then create a three dimensional depiction of it.

3. A Torah binder, or *wimpel*, is made from fabric which swaddles an infant during the *Brit Milah*. The *wimpel* is composed of three sections three feet long, sewn together and decorated with the infant's name, birth date, and the threefold blessing of Torah, *chupah* and *ma'asim tovim* (good deeds). This *wimpel* is then used on important Jewish occasions in the infant's life, e.g., the first time he goes to synagogue, at his Bar Mitzvah, on his wedding day. Have each student design and make a Torah binder. Directions can be found in *The Second Jewish Catalog* by Sharon Strassfeld and Michael Strassfeld, pp. 42-43.

    References: *The New Work of Our Hands: Contemporary Jewish Needlework and Quilts* by Neil R. Tupa. *Torah Binders of the Judah L. Magnes Museum* by Ruth Eis.

4. The birth of a new baby is cause for much celebration. Brainstorm several ways in which the Jewish community can honor the arrival of a new baby.

5. In *The Eternal Light*, Harry M. Epstein wrote, "The child stands between the generations, inheriting from the one and transmitting to the other" (p.33). Discuss how the observance of *Brit Milah* exemplifies this saying.

6. Stage a mock *Brit Milah*. Assign each of the traditional parts to your students and have a *Seudah Mitzvah* afterwards. For help with the ceremony and for suggestions for a meal for a *Brit Milah*, see the references listed immediately below.

    References: *The Second Jewish Catalog* by Sharon Strassfeld and Michael Strassfeld; *The Jewish Holiday Kitchen* by Joan Nathan.

7. Spend two class sessions studying the mini-course *Circumcision* by Raymond A. Zwerin, Audrey Friedman Marcus, and Leonard Kramish.

Secondary

1. Invite a *mohel* to your class for a brief lecture followed by a question and answer period.

2. While there is a standard service for *Brit Milah*, there is no traditional equivalent for baby girls.

Some suggested naming ceremonies have been called *Brit Kedushah* (Covenant of Holiness), *Brit Haneirot* (Covenant of the Candles), or *Brit HaBat* (Covenant of the Daughter). Share the titles of these ceremonies with your students. In small groups develop a ceremony for one of the titles listed above.

References: *The Second Jewish Catalog* edited by Sharon Strassfeld and Michael Strassfeld, pp. 32-34; *Jewish and Female: A Guide and Sourcebook for Today's Jewish Woman* by Susan Weidman Schneider, pp. 121-131.

3. Hold a public debate on the following: "Resolved: Jews should continue to practice *Brit Milah*." Divide the class in half and have one group take the pro position and other group defend the con position.

4. The Union of American Hebrew Congregations has developed guidelines for Reform *mohelim*. Write to them at 838 Fifth Avenue, New York, NY 10021 for "Program Perspective on Training Physicians as *Mohalim* for the Reform Movement." Share this with your class and discuss the need for *mohalim* who are familiar with the specific requirements of a particular denomination.

5. All religions celebrate in some formalized way the birth of a new baby. Invite clergy of other faiths to explain the ceremonies and traditions associated with their respective faiths. The format for the presentations could be a panel discussion or a less formal open forum. Allow time for questions and answers.

6. View and discuss the film *Judaism*. Ask students to identify the significance of the *Brit Milah* ceremony according to the film.

ALL-SCHOOL PROGRAMS

1. In addition to *Brit Milah*, Jews participate in many special life cycle ceremonies. Assign a different observance to each class from among the following: *Brit Milah*, *Pidyon Haben*, consecration, Bar/Bat Mitzvah, Confirmation, wedding. The presentation may take the form of a banner, a skit, slide presentation, or any other form a class decides to utilize.

2. *Brit Milah* is a symbol of the covenant between God and the Jewish people. According to tradition, the covenant relationship was established when the Jewish people received the Torah at Mt. Sinai. At an assembly program, students will assume the identity of one of the people in the *midrash* below. (Don't read the *midrash* until after the exercise.) The Rabbi or Director of Education enters the room with a Torah and says, "God has just offered us the Torah, which contains many important teachings. We have to decide whether or not to accept it." Students are divided into several groups, each with a pre-selected leader. Each group will assume the identify of one of the groups.

Group 1: The leader explains that they are the children of Esau. Their father Esau was a hunter and, therefore, a killer by nature. He lived by the sword, and it is their practice to do so as well. The group must decide whether to change its practice or reject the Torah.

Group 2: The leader explains that they are the children of Ammon and Moab. It is their custom to be able to be married to whomever they wish, even taking more than one wife or more than one husband. The Torah, however, forbids this practice. The group must decide whether to change its practice or reject the Torah.

Group 3: The leader explains that they are the children of Ishmael. Their father, Ishmael, was a thief by nature and, in their community, it is permitted to steal. The Torah, however, forbids stealing. The group must decide whether to change its practice or reject the Torah.

Group 4: The leader explains that they are the Israelites and that they have to decide whether or not to accept the Torah. If the students ask what is in the Torah, the leader should try to convince them to accept or reject it without knowing what is in it. If the students do not ask this question, steer the conversation in that direction.

Each group must come to a decision, but the decision does not necessarily have to agree with the *midrash*. Group leaders should be sure that all sides of the issue are considered.

Reconvene the group as a whole. One student from each group reports on its decision. The Rabbi or Director of Education should wrap up the assembly by telling the following *midrash* from *Sifre* to Deuteronomy 33:2:

The Nations Refuse the Torah

When God was ready to give the Torah to Israel, God first offered it to other nations. First, God went to the descendants of Esau.

"Will you accept the Torah?" asked God.

They replied, "What is written in it?"

God answered, "You shall not kill."

They said, "Master of the universe, our father Esau was a killer by nature and lived by the sword."

So God went to the children of Ammon and Moab.

"Will you accept the Torah?" asked God.

They said, "What is written in it?"

God answered, "You shall not commit adultery."

They replied, "Master of the universe, it is our custom to behave that way."

Then God approached the children of Ishmael and said, "Will you accept the Torah?"

They asked, "What is in it?"

And God answered, "You shall not steal."

They replied, "Master of the universe, our father was a thief by nature and we have inherited his practices."

After offering the Torah to all other nations, God approached Israel and said, "Will you accept the Torah?"

The people replied, "We will observe it and we will hear it" (Exodus 24:7).

3. The following assembly program will help each student feel personally connected to the covenant. Prepare on a bulletin board the outline of an open Torah scroll. Distribute to each student a 3" x 5" card and a pencil. Explain the concept of covenant as a contract between God and the Jewish people. Each student is to select one aspect of Judaism which is most meaningful and to write it on the card (e.g., lighting Shabbat candles, Jewish summer camp, Holocaust, *Kashrut*, *Tzedakah*, etc.). Students gather in groups and share their responses. Collect the cards and mount them on the bulletin board.

RESOURCES

For the Teacher

Barth, Lewis M., ed. *Berit Mila in the Reform Context.* New York: UAHC Press, 1990.

"Circumcision." In *Encyclopaedia Judaica.* Jerusalem: Keter Publishing House Jerusalem Ltd., 1971, vol. 4, cols. 567-576.

Cohen, Eugene J. *Guide to Ritual Circumcision and Redemption of the First-Born Son.* Hoboken, NJ: KTAV Publishing House, Inc., 1984.

Diamant, Anita. *The New Jewish Baby Book.* Woodstock, VT: Jewish Lights Publishing, 1993.

Donin, Hayim Halevy. *To Be a Jew: A Guide to Jewish Observance in Contemporary Life.* New York: Basic Books, Inc., 1991, pp. 273-276.

Klein, Isaac. *A Guide to Jewish Religious Practice.* New York: The Jewish Theological Seminary of America, 1979, pp. 419-432.

Kolatch, Alfred J. *The Complete Dictionary of English and Hebrew First Names.* New York: Jonathan David Publishers, Inc., 1984.

Nathan, Joan. *The Jewish Holiday Kitchen.* rev. ed. New York: Schocken Books, 1988.

Orenstein, Debra, ed. *Life Cycles: Jewish Women on Life Passages & Personal Milestones. Vol. 1.* Woodstock, VT: Jewish Lights Publishing, 1994, pp. 57-82.

Strassfeld, Sharon, and Michael Strassfeld, comps. and eds. *The Second Jewish Catalog.* Philadelphia: The Jewish Publication Society of America, 1976, pp. 11-45.

Tupa, Neal R. *The New Work of Our Hands: Contemporary Jewish Needlework and Quilts.* Radnor, PA: Chilton Books, 1994.

Weber, Douglas, and Jessica B. Weber. *The Jewish Baby Handbook: A Guide for Expectant Parents.* West Orange, NJ: Behrman House, 1990.

For the Students

Gersh, Harry. *When a Jew Celebrates.* West Orange, NJ: Behrman Hosue, Inc., 1971, pp. 17-34. (Grades 4-6)

Grishaver, Joel Lurie. *The Life Cycle Workbook.* Denver: A.R.E. Publishing, Inc., 1983, pp. 14-25. (Grades 4-6)

Pasachoff, Naomi. *Basic Judaism for Young People: God.* West Orange, NJ: Behrman House, Inc., 1987, pp. 35-42. (Grades 4-7)

Zwerin, Raymond A.; Audrey Friedman Marcus; and Leonard Kramish. *Circumcision.* Denver: A.R.E. Publishing, Inc., 1983. (Grades 5 and up)

Audiovisual

Judaism. A 15 minute film about the basic practices of Judaism, including circumcision. Alden Films. (Grades 4 and up)

The Eighth Day: Circumcision/Hanukah. A 25 minute video that highlights the conflict between traditional and assimilating Jews in the time of the Maccabees. A mother and father must decide whether to circumcise their son in defiance of the Greek edict. Ergo Media Inc. (Grades 5 and up)

It's a Boy! A controversial 52 minute video in which a circumcision goes wrong. Disturbing and powerful film on the realities of the procedure and its possible after effects. Filmakers Library. (Adult)

Ritual: Three Portraits of Jewish Life. Jewish Theological Seminary. A 60 minute video that looks at three rituals as they pertain to Jewish life: prayer, building a *sukkah*, and *Brit Milah*. (Grades 9-adult)

UNIT 8

Redeeming the Firstborn Son
פִּדְיוֹן הַבֵּן

OVERVIEW

The Mitzvah of *Pidyon HaBen*, redemption of the (firstborn) son, is best understood in relation to the privileged status granted to firstborn males in the biblical tradition. They are the favored of the Lord, as can be inferred from the following verses: "You shall give Me the firstborn among your sons" (Exodus 22:28). (Firstborn sons were not given for the purpose of being sacrificed as occurred in some other ancient societies, but in order that they might be priests who served God.) And, ". . . he [a father] must accept the firstborn, [even if he is] the son of the unloved one [wife], and allot to him a double portion of all he possesses . . ." (Deuteronomy 21:17).

According to the Torah, every firstborn belongs to God because "at the time that I smote every firstborn in the land of Egypt, I consecrated every firstborn in Israel, man and beast, to Myself" (Numbers 3:13). the God of Israel had a claim on the first offspring of human beings and animals, as well as on the first fruits of the earth. Firstborn male cattle were to be offered as sacrifices to God, but firstborn asses were to be redeemed through the offering of a sheep (Exodus 13:12-13). Since the days after the destruction of the Temple, cattle are given to a *Kohen*. He keeps them until they die a natural death or suffer a blemish which would make them unfit for sacrifice and, therefore, usable by the community for work or food.

There is some confusion as to whether or not firstborn males could qualify for the priesthood. One tradition teaches that they lost their special position during the incident of the golden calf. When Moses returns to the camp to see what the people have done, his anger rises within him. He calls out: "Whoever is for the Lord, come here," and the tribe of Levi steps forward (Exodus 32:26). Therefore, the Levites were chosen to serve God in place of the firstborn.

Yet, later in the Torah we read: "The first issue of the womb of every being, man or beast, that is offered to the Lord shall be [the priest's]; but, you shall have the firstborn of man redeemed" (Numbers 18:15). The ceremony at which this redemption takes place is called *Pidyon HaBen*.

The ceremony of *Pidyon HaBen* takes place when the child is 31 days old. This is because a child is only considered a viable life after 30 days; an infant who dies before the 31st day has no burial ceremony, for instance. However, the ceremony of *Pidyon HaBen* is delayed until the next day if the 31st day is Shabbat or a festival. The ceremony may take place in the home or in the synagogue.

The father presents his son, sometimes on a special tray, to a *Kohen*, a descendant of the priests. The *Kohen* asks in Aramaic if the father wants to redeem his son or leave him with the *Kohen*. The father says that he wants to keep him, and redeems him from the *Kohen* with the payment of silver coins. The traditional payment was five shekels (Numbers 18:16). Now the custom is to use five silver coins of the monetary unit of the country in which the ceremony takes place.

The father then recites the following blessings:

בָּרוּךְ אַתָּה, יְיָ אֱלֹהֵינוּ, מֶלֶךְ הָעוֹלָם, אֲשֶׁר קִדְּשָׁנוּ בְּמִצְוֹתָיו וְצִוָּנוּ עַל פִּדְיוֹן הַבֵּן.

Blessed are you, O Eternal our God, Ruler of the universe, Who has made us holy with Mitzvot and commanded us concerning the redemption of the firstborn.

בָּרוּךְ אַתָּה, יְיָ אֱלֹהֵינוּ, מֶלֶךְ הָעוֹלָם, שֶׁהֶחֱיָנוּ וְקִיְּמָנוּ וְהִגִּיעָנוּ לַזְּמַן הַזֶּה.

Blessed are you, O Eternal our God, Ruler of the universe, Who has given us life, has sustained us, and has enabled us to reach this time.

The *Kohen* then acknowledges that the child has been redeemed and returns him to his father. The ceremony concludes with the blessing over the wine, the priestly benediction, and a joyous feast. After the ceremony the *Kohen* may return the money to the father, although the Mitzvah is obviated if this was the intention before the ceremony began. Often the father will make a contribution to the synagogue or other charity in honor of his firstborn son.

If, for some reason, a person should have been

redeemed by his father but was not, he must redeem himself after he becomes a Bar Mitzvah. Often, in place of the father, another adult male relative will perform the redemption ceremony at the appropriate time.

Pidyon HaBen is not performed if the father or the maternal grandfather is a *Kohen* or *Levi*. Also, because the firstborn must be the first to open the womb, the redemption is foregone if the firstborn son was delivered by Cesarean section, or if the mother had previously had an abortion or miscarried a fetus after 40 days.

The Karaites, a Jewish sect which began in the eighth century, abolished *Pidyon HaBen*, asserting that it was irrelevant following the destruction of the Temple. For similar reasons, some Rabbis of the Middle Ages also attempted to let the ritual die out, but it has remained a widely observed ceremony among Orthodox and Conservative Jews. The Reform Movement does not recognize priestly status, therefore, has abandoned this ritual, although individual Reform families may choose to observe it. In modern times some Jews have celebrated a *Pidyon HaBat* (redemption of the daughter) if the firstborn is female.

ACTIVITIES

Primary

1. Read the story of "Puss-in-Boots" to your class (readily available at your local public library). While this is not a Jewish story, it illustrates how first, second, and third born children were treated differently. Discuss with your class whether such treatment is fair or unfair.

2. Have each student state where they stand in birth order in their families (oldest, middle, youngest). Discuss with them what special responsibilities and privileges they have. Ask if birth order makes a difference. Do parents treat you equally? If you are the oldest, how do you view the youngest? If you are the youngest, how do you view the oldest?

3. Have each student create a scrapbook of personal firsts. These might include first words spoken, first steps, first day of school, first Chanukah, first two-wheel bicycle, etc. Students will need help from their families in order to get this information. They may add photos or draw-

ings to the scrapbook. Discuss what makes "firsts" so special.

4. Based on the Overview section above, outline the *Pidyon HaBen* ceremony in brief. Part of this ceremony is the recitation of *Shehecheyanu*. Have the children learn to recite or to sing this blessing.

5. The ceremony of *Pidyon HaBen* is followed by a joyous feast called a *Seudah Mitzvah*. Prepare a festive Jewish dish that might be used on such an occasion. Many Jewish cookbooks give menu suggestions for life cycle events.

   Reference: *The Jewish Holiday Kitchen* by Joan Nathan.

6. To help the students understand what it means to redeem something, prepare a booklet of coupons that the students redeem for certain items or privileges. For example: a trip to the synagogue's library, a sticker, being first in line, leading *HaMotzi* before snack, etc.

Intermediate

1. Announce to the class that each student will have a chance to go to the library (or to other desirable place or activity, such as the playground, or music). Then ask the class who wants to go first. Discuss with the group members why or why not they desired to go first. Broaden the discussion to include how they feel when they are chosen for an activity first, last, or somewhere in the middle. Explain the special status of the firstborn in Judaism and the ritual of *Pidyon HaBen*.

2. Read and discuss the story of Hannah in I Samuel 1:1-2:11. Explain that the ceremony of *Pidyon HaBen* is held to release the firstborn son from the obligation of serving in the Temple. Although the Temple is no longer standing, this ceremony is observed in remembrance of that time.

3. Extend activity #2 by having the students investigate the dress of the *Kohanim*. Bring in fabric, trim, plastic "jewels," etc., to recreate the dress of the *Kohanim*.

Reference: "Priestly Vestments" in *Encyclopaedia Judaica*, vol. 13, cols. 1063-1069.

4. Have the students learn about the additional responsibility of being a firstborn son, the fast of the firstborn.

   References: "Firstborn" in *Encyclopaedia Judaica*, vol. 6, col. 1310; *A Guide to Jewish Religious Practice* by Isaac Klein, pp. 109-110.

5. *Pidyon HaBen* emphasizes the special status of the firstborn in Judaism. Direct the students to create a book of Jewish firsts. Things to include: first Jew, first king, first Prime Minister of Israel, first Jew to set foot in America. Students should generate additional "firsts" to research and include.

6. So that students will better grasp the concept of redeeming, present situations in which a person has fallen short of the mark, such as doing poorly on a test, shoplifting, fighting with one's parents, failing to help someone in need, etc. Ask students for suggestions of how the person could redeem himself or herself in each of these situations. Explain how and why a child is redeemed in the *Pidyon HaBen* ceremony.

Secondary

1. Have the students research the following:
   a. What determines firstborn status?
   b. Which of the following were firstborn: Abraham, Isaac, Jacob, Joseph, Moses, David?
   c. Based on the students' research, is birth order important in Jewish tradition? In determining qualifications for leadership?

2. Discuss with the class why the destruction of the Temple might encourage the abandonment of the *Pidyon HaBen* ceremony.

3. One of the privileges of being firstborn was a double inheritance, at the time of one's father's death. A daughter, however, originally could not inherit. Read and discuss the story of the daughters of Zelophehad (Numbers 27:1-11). See also Deuteronomy 21:15-17.

4. The ceremony of *Pidyon HaBen* can be found in *The Second Jewish Catalog* by Sharon

Strassfeld and Michael Strassfeld, pp. 38-39. Share this with the students. Together, write a ceremony of *Pidyon HaBat* (redemption of the firstborn daughter).

5. Direct the students to research the duties and responsibilities of the *Kohanim* and the *Levites*.

   References: Numbers 3:11-13; "Priests and Priesthood" in *Encyclopaedia Judaica*, vol. 13, cols. 1069-1091.

6. Share with the class the following verses from II Kings 3:1-27. Sacrificing firstborn children seems repugnant to our modern sensibilities, yet in the ancient world it was practiced by some peoples. Also read Micah 6:7-8. How does Micah's approach differ from that of II Kings?

ALL-SCHOOL ACTIVITIES

1. Stage a *Pidyon HaBen* or *Pidyon HaBat* ceremony. Include a *Seudah Mitzvah* as part of the festivities.

2. Have a group of students or the teacher write a dramatization of the daughters of Zelophehad (Numbers 27:1-11). Perform this for the rest of the student body.

3. Divide the students into groups of 6-10, mixing the grade levels. Each group is assigned a birth order (first, second, third). Discuss the advantages and disadvantages of being in that position in the family. Each group reports to the whole and a list of guidelines for the treatment of children can then be developed.

RESOURCES

For the Teacher

Donin, Hayim Halevy. *To Be a Jew: A Guide to Jewish Observance in Contemporary Life*. New York: Basic Books, Inc., 1991, pp. 273-276.

Cohen, Eugene J. *Guide to Ritual Circumcision and Redemption of the First-Born Son*. Hoboken, NJ: KTAV Publishing House, Inc., 1984.

Encyclopaedia Judaica. Jerusalem: Keter Publishing House Jerusalem Ltd., 1972, vol. 6, col. 1310; vol. 13, cols. 1669-1091; vol. 14, cols. 1442-1447.

Klein, Isaac. *A Guide to Jewish Religious Practice.*

New York: The Jewish Theological Seminary of America, 1979, pp. 430-432.

Maimonides, Moses. *The Commandments*. New York: The Soncino Press, 1967, vol. 1, pp. 179-180.

Nathan, Joan. *The Jewish Holiday Kitchen*. rev. ed. New York: Schocken Books, 1988.

Strassfeld, Sharon, and Michael Strassfeld, comps. and eds. *The Second Jewish Catalog*. Philadelphia: Jewish Publication Society of America, 1976, pp. 34-40.

For the Students

Borovetz, Frances. *Hebrew Blessings Ditto Pak*. Denver: A.R.E. Publishing, Inc., 1980, p. 23. (Grades 3 and up)

Gersh, Harry. *When a Jew Celebrates*. West Orange, NJ: Behrman House, Inc. 1971, pp. 23-24. (Grades 4-6)

Grishaver, Joel Lurie. *The Life Cycle Workbook*. Denver: A.R.E. Publishing, Inc., 1983, pp. 14-17. (Grades 4-6)

UNIT 9

Caring for the Dead
חֶסֶד שֶׁל אֱמֶת

OVERVIEW

Caring for the dead is among the most altruistic of acts. The Mitzvah is performed with the sure knowledge that it cannot be paid back. The importance of this Mitzvah is illustrated by the fact that during wartime or outbreaks of plague or other diseases, it was the responsibility of every Jew to see that bodies were given proper burial. Such treatment for a corpse was known as a *mayt mitzvah*, literally, a "corpse of the commandment." Even a High Priest who, in all other cases was forbidden to touch a corpse (which would render him ritually impure), must see to the burial of a *mayt mitzvah*.

The Torah, with reference to a person who has been put to death for committing a capital offense states: "You must not let the corpse remain on the stake overnight, but must bury it the same day" (Deuteronomy 21:23). From this verse we learn that burial is to be on the day of death; if death occurs in the evening, burial is to be the next day. In ancient times this practice was especially important to prevent decay of the body. In our day this tradition is followed as much as possible. There is latitude taken, however, since relatives often need to travel great distances to attend the funeral. Thus, Jewish burial occurs as soon after death as practical, and can take place even on the second day of holidays in order to avoid undue delays.

With these principles as a basis, the Rabbis greatly expanded the responsibility of the Jewish community in caring for its dead. The following are among the traditions relating to care for the deceased.

Shemirah (watching the body): A body is not to be left alone from the moment of death until burial. In fact, one is not supposed to leave the room of a dying person, lest the person die alone. The person watching the body will often recite Psalms during the vigil. The responsibility for *shemirah* is usually shared among a number of individuals, each taking a shift of a few hours.

Taharah (ritual purification): Water is poured over the body in a prescribed manner as a means of ritual purification.

Tachrichim (shrouds): A shroud is the traditional garment in which the body is dressed for burial. It is a simple outfit, made of white linen or cotton, without pockets. Men are traditionally buried with their *Tallit*, the *tzitzit* of which have been removed since the deceased can no longer observe the 613 commandments.

To carry out these practices, the *Chevra Kadishah* (Sacred Fellowship) was created. It is considered a privilege to serve on a *Chevra Kadishah*. Many Orthodox and some non-Orthodox congregations utilize a *Chevra Kadishah* to arrange for preparation and burial of the deceased. Most commonly, Jewish funeral homes will arrange for the traditional practices to be followed upon request.

It is traditional to allow the body to decompose naturally. Therefore, both embalming and cremation are prohibited by Jewish law. In addition, in order to disturb the body as little as possible, autopsies are generally not allowed. Only in situations where information is required for criminal cases, or if the information might contribute to the saving of lives is an autopsy permitted.

Donations of organs are, by and large, permitted by Jewish law. Some authorities insist that the organ be directly transplanted to another person, while others support donating to such institutions as eye banks. The general principle here is that the prohibitions of deriving benefit from the dead, or of desecrating the dead, or of delaying the burial of the dead are all set aside because of the consideration of saving a life. Even donating an eye to restore the sight of an individual is considered saving a life.

If a person had a limb amputated during his or her lifetime, it is traditional for the limb to be buried in the person's future gravesite.

Burial in a simple, all wood coffin, sometimes referred to as a "plain pine box" symbolizes the idea that all are equal in death. Placing the casket in a cement vault is only allowed if required by law. The use of an above-ground crypt is not in keeping with Jewish custom, although in some swampy areas it is mandated by practicality.

It is a Mitzvah to accompany the body to the cemetery. At the beginning of the service, it is customary for the close relatives of the deceased (parents, children, siblings, and spouse) to tear one of their garments (a tie, scarf, or vest). Often a small black ribbon is used instead. This ritual, called *kriah* (tearing) is a symbol of mourning and is a substitute for any inclination to tear or cut one's self as a sign of abject grief.

The funeral service usually consists of the reciting of Psalms, a eulogy *(hesped)*, *El Malay Rachamim*, and the Mourner's *Kaddish*. Those present participate in the burial by shoveling dirt into the grave. Following the funeral, it is a Mitzvah to comfort the mourners. The first meal, called *Seudat Havra'ah* (the meal of condolence), is to be provided by family friends. Visiting during the seven-day mourning period *(shiva)* and participating in a *minyan* so that the mourners may say *Kaddish* are additional Mitzvot.

ACTIVITIES

Primary

1. Often a child's first experience with death comes when a pet dies. As a discussion starter, read one of the books listed below, all of which deal with the death of a pet. Open the discussion by asking if any of the students have had a pet that died. Be prepared for a variety of responses and questions, including such issues as life after death and burial practices.

    References: *Badger's Parting Gift* by Susan Varley; *I'll Always Love You!* By Hans Wilhelm; *Sounds of Summer* by David Updike.

2. Share with your students the following Talmudic tale:

    #### Honi

    Honi the Circle Maker was out taking a walk one day when he happened by an elderly man planting carob trees. Honi told the man that he would never live long enough to see the carob trees bear fruit. The man replied that this was fine, for just as the ancestors had planted for him, he would plant for his children and grandchildren.

    Ask the students: Why was the old man planting for his children and grandchildren? What lessons had he learned from his ancestors? Were his descendants going to inherit more than fruit trees? Ask the students to list at least five things which

they have inherited from their ancestors. Now have them list at least five things which they want to leave to their children and grandchildren.

3. Our tradition tells us that an individual lives on in the memories of those who loved them and by the good deeds they have accomplished. Instruct students to choose an individual they love. Have them describe that person's special qualities and list those things they especially cherish. (You may wish to allow the students to choose a pet.)

4. Read *Bubby, Me, and Memories* by Barbara Pomerantz, a moving book about memories of a Jewish grandmother. Ask students if they have someone special in their lives like the *Bubby* in this story. Talk with them about how they might feel if that person could no longer be a part of their lives.

5. Invite the Rabbi to visit your class and discuss with the students any questions they have about death.

    Reference: *Talk to God . . . I'll Get the Message* by Norman Geller.

6. It is traditional for Jews in mourning to eat round-shaped foods after the funeral at a meal known as *Seudat Havra'ah*. This meal of consolation is usually prepared by friends. Most often the meal would include hard cooked eggs, lentils, and bagels. These round foods remind us of the cycle of life. Let the students make additional suggestions for other round-shaped food they could help prepare for the meal of consolation.

Intermediate

1. This activity will enable students to describe the *Kaddish* and also to gain a deeper understanding of this prayer which is recited by mourners. Using a variety of Jewish prayerbooks representing various traditions (i.e., traditional, liberal, egalitarian), have students compare the English translations of the Mourner's *Kaddish*.

2. Prepare a tape of the *Kaddish* and place it at a listening station (a quiet area with a tape player). Assign the students to learn at least the congregational responses.

3. There is a *midrashic* commentary on the book of Ecclesiastes which states: "None can say to the Angel of Death, 'Wait until I make up my accounts.'" Share this with your students and ask them what it means.

4. Introduce students to the beauty of the biblical book of Ecclesiastes by reading with them chapter 3:1-8.
   a. Have students create a series of felt banners which illustrate these biblical verses.
   b. Create a slide-tape show based on these verses.
   c. Play the rock song, "Turn, Turn, Turn" by the Birds or Pete Seeger.

5. Have students research the history of the local *Chevra Kadishah*. Some sources to investigate are old synagogue records, interviews with older members of the congregation, and possibly a trip to your community's original Jewish cemetery.

6. View and discuss the film *The Day Grandpa Died*. Use the film to trigger a discussion about students' experiences with death. (Be especially sensitive to any students who have experienced recent deaths of relatives.) Ask the following questions: Has anyone close to you ever died? How did you find out? How did you react? What were some of the things done to care for the deceased?

7. Contact a *Chevra Kadishah* or a Jewish funeral home to borrow a burial shroud (*tachrichim*). Pass it around to the students. Ask what is unusual about it (i.e., what doesn't it have that most garments have?) Hopefully, the students will guess that it has no pockets. Discuss why a shroud is so made (because "you can't take it with you"). Talk about the Jewish concept of being equal in death, which is demonstrated by the tradition of burying in a shroud (as opposed to being buried in one's clothes) and also by the practice of using a simple wood casket.

Secondary

1. We are most often fearful of those things which we understand the least. Invite a funeral director (Jewish if available), a Rabbi, and a member of the *Chevra Kadishah* (if one exists in your community) to present a panel discussion on Jewish ritual practices and beliefs concerning death and dying. If possible display *tachrichim* (burial shrouds) and the black ribbons used by mourners in some traditions to symbolize *kriah*, the tearing of one's garment. Be sure to include a discussion about indigent Jews who are not able to leave provisions for their own burial.

2. Many individuals have written living wills, documents detailing what kinds of treatment they want in case they are incapacitated to the point of not being able to communicate their wishes. Write to: Concern for Dying, 250 West 57th Street, New York, NY 10107 to request information and brochures to share with your students. Based on these materials, have your students write their own versions of a living will.

   Reference: *Bioethics: A Jewish View* by James L. Simon, Raymond A. Zwerin, and Audrey Friedman Marcus.

3. Invite a Rabbi to discuss traditional Jewish beliefs concerning death, burial, afterlife, and resurrection.

4. Assign each student (or pair of students) to investigate the beliefs and practices of a different religion regarding death and dying. They may interview clergy or lay leaders and share their findings with each other. During a summary discussion, students determine which issues and practices are common to all religions.

5. The passage in Deuteronomy containing Moses' plea to God to be able to cross the Jordan River into the Promised Land is very brief. The *midrash* on this event, however, contains a lot of material. Together with your students, read *Deuteronomy Rabbah* 11:10 or "Moses' Prayer for Suspension of Judgment" in *Legends of the Jews* by Louis Ginzberg, pp. 419-428. These accounts show that Moses fought death. Have your students list possible reasons for this (e.g., he did not want to give up his position of power and authority, his wish to see the Promised Land, fear of the unknown, a desire to cling to life). Relate the students' perceptions of Moses at this time in his life to modern day fears and anxieties concerning death and dying. If possible, invite an expert in this field to your class to facilitate this discussion.

6. Ask students if any of them have ever made a condolence call. Have them share the experience. Read Chapter 207 of *The Code of Jewish*

Law: *Kitzur Shulhan Arukh* by Solomon Ganzfried, which describes appropriate behavior for comforting mourners. As a group, brainstorm a list of guidelines students can incorporate into their own Jewish behaviors. As a follow-up, compare what the Talmud says with *Living a Jewish Life: Jewish Traditions, Customs and Values for Today's Families* by Anita Diamant and Howard Cooper.

ALL-SCHOOL PROGRAMS

1. View the film *Echoes of a Summer* which deals with the death of a teen-ager. Break up into small groups for discussion and sharing time. Have a teacher or other adult with each group. Note: This film is rated PG and would be suitable only for intermediate grade students and older. If possible have the staff preview the film first with a mental health professional in attendance to provide added insights.

2. The following is a suggested format for participation in a memorial service. Each class within your school should decide how it would like to memorialize the children who perished during the Holocaust. An all-school assembly can be held during which each class makes a presentation. The structure of the assembly could be a worship service with students' participation, and/or poetry readings, short dramatic skits, art displays, and the establishment of a permanent memorial. You may choose to hold this on Yom Hashoah or on one of the holidays when a *Yizkor* service is traditionally held: Passover, Shavuot, Yom Kippur, or Sukkot.

3. Locate and visit an old Jewish cemetery in your community or nearby. A local Jewish historical society will most likely be able to help you. Sometimes there are specific tasks which students can do to help preserve or beautify the cemetery. At the cemetery discuss the responsibility of caring for the dead in Jewish tradition. Hold a brief memorial service which might include a Psalm, readings, or the recital of *Kaddish*.

RESOURCES

For the Teacher

Brener, Anne. *Mourning & Mitzvah: A Guided Journal for Walking the Mourner's Path through Grief to Healing.* Woodstock, VT: Jewish Lights Publishing, 1993.

Diamant, Anita, and Howard Cooper. *Living a Jewish Life: A Guide for Starting, Learning, Celebrating, and Parenting.* New York: HarperCollins, 1991, pp. 289-301.

Freedman, Rabbi Dr. H., and Maurice Simon. *The Midrash Rabbah: Deuteronomy.* New York: The Soncino Press, 1977, pp. 180-188.

Ganzfried, Solomon. *Code of Jewish Law: Kitzur Shulhan Arukh.* rev. ed. Hyman E. Goldin, trans. Rockaway Beach, NY: Hebrew Publishing Co., 1991, vol. 4, ch. 197-221, pp. 98-137.

Goodman, Arnold. *A Plain Pine Box: A Return to Simple Jewish Funerals and Eternal Traditions.* Hoboken, NJ: KTAV Publishing House, Inc., 1981.

Isaacs, Ronald H., and Kerry M. Olitzky. *The Jewish Mourners' Handbook.* Hoboken, NJ: KTAV Publishing House, Inc., 1991. (Grades 6 and up)

Isaacs, Ronald H., and Richard Wagner. *The Chain of Life: A Curricular Guide for Teaching about Death, Bereavement and the Jewish Way of Honoring the Dead.* New York: Coalition for the Advancement of Jewish Education, 1993.

Lamm, Maurice. *The Jewish Way in Death and Mourning.* New York: Jonathan David Publishers, 1969.

Marcus, Audrey Friedman. "Teaching about Death and Dying." In *The New Jewish Teachers Handbook.* Audrey Friedman Marcus and Raymond A. Zwerin, eds. Denver: A.R.E. Publishing, Inc., 1994, pp. 437-445.

Mellonie, Bryan, and Robert Ingpen. *Lifetimes: The Beautiful Way To Explain Death to Children.* New York: Bantam Books, 1983.

Siegel, Richard; Michael Strassfeld; and Sharon Strassfeld, comps. and eds. *The First Jewish Catalog.* Philadelphia: The Jewish Publication Society of America, 1973, pp. 172-181.

Wolfson, Ron. *A Time to Mourn — A Time to Comfort.* New York: Federation of Jewish Men's Clubs, 1993.

For the Students

Adler, C.S. *Daddy's Climbing Tree.* Boston: Clarion Books, 1993. (Grades 4-7)

Geller, Norman. *Talk to God . . . I'll Get the Message.* (Jewish Version.) Lewiston, ME: Norman Geller, Publisher, 1983. (Grades 1-4)

Howard, Ellen. *The Tower Room.* New York:

Atheneum Books for Young Readers, 1993. (Grades 3-7)

Isaacs, Ronald H., and Kerry M. Olitzky. *Doing Mitzvot: Mitzvah Projects for Bar/Bat Mitzvah.* Hoboken, NJ: KTAV Publishing House, Inc., 1994, pp. 87-101. (Grades 6 and up)

Kay, Alan. *Pebbles on a Stone.* Instant Lesson. Los Angeles: Torah Aura Productions, 1992. (Grades 4-6)

————. *The Red in My Father's Beard.* Instant Lesson. Los Angeles: Torah Aura Productions, 1992. (Grades 4-6)

Ish-Kishor, Sulamith. *Our Eddie.* New York: Alfred A. Knopf, 1992. (Grades 7 and up)

Kroll, Virginia. *Helen the Fish.* Morton Grove, IL: Alfred Whitman Concept Books, 1992. (Grades K-3)

Lanton, Sandy. *Daddy's Chair.* Rockville, MD: Kar-Ben Copies, Inc. 1991. (Grades 1-3)

Marcus, Audrey Friedman; Sherry Bissell; and Karen S. Lipschutz. *Death, Burial & Mourning in the Jewish Tradition.* Denver: A.R.E. Publishing, Inc., 1976. (Grades 5 and up)

Pomerantz, Barbara. *Bubby, Me and Memories.* New York: UAHC Press, 1983. (Grades K-3)

Rosman, Steven. *Deena and the Damselfly.* New York: UAHC Press, 1992. (Grades 2-4)

Simon, James L.; Raymond A. Zwerin; and Audrey Friedman Marcus. *Bioethics: A Jewish View.* Denver: A.R.E. Publishing, Inc., 1984. (Grades 8 and up)

Techner, David, and Judith Hirt-Manheimer. *A Candle for Grandpa: A Guide to the Jewish Funeral for Children and Parents.* New York: UAHC Press, 1993. (Grades K-3)

Updike, David. *Sounds of Summer.* New York: Pippin Press, 1993. (Grades 2-5)

Varley, Susan. *Badger's Parting Gifts.* New York: Lothrop, Lee, and Shepard Books, 1984. (PK-2)

Viorst, Judith. *The Tenth Good Thing about Barney.* New York: Atheneum Publishers, 1971. (Grades K-2)

Warburg, Sandol. *Growing Time.* New York: Houghton Mifflin Co., 1969. (Grades K-3)

Wilhelm, Hans. *I'll Always Love You!* New York: Crown Books for Young Readers, 1988. (Grades K-2)

Audiovisual

The Corridor: Death. In this 25 minute video, a car accident involving two young Americans visiting Israel becomes a trigger for a debate about the meaning of death, afterlife, and the Jewish perspective. Ergo Media Inc. (Grade 9 and up)

The Day Grandpa Died. An 11 minute film about a young Jewish boy whose grandfather dies. BFA Educational Media. (Grades 4 and up)

"Hamakom." On the audiocassette *Where Heaven and Earth Touch* by Craig Taubman. A song containing the traditional prayer recited at the house of mourning. Sweet Louise Productions. Available from A.R.E. Publishing, Inc.

A Plain Pine Box. A 30 minute film about the *Chevra Kadishah* at Adath Jeshurun Congregation in Minneapolis. Committee on Congregational Standards of the United Synagogue of America. (Grades 7 and up)

Saying Kaddish. A 58 minute video about a family facing a death. The underlying theme is the importance of community in a time of personal crisis. The Jewish Theological Seminary of America. (Adult)

UNIT 10

Blessing After Eating
בִּרְכַּת הַמָּזוֹן

OVERVIEW

"You shall eat and be satisfied and bless the Lord your God for the good land which God has given you" (Deuteronomy 8:10). This biblical verse is the basis for the Mitzvah of reciting the blessing after meals. *Birkat HaMazon* is Hebrew which means literally "the blessing of the food." The Yiddish term for grace after meals is to *Bensch*, a word thought to derive from Latin and Old French for "blessing."

On Shabbat and festivals *Birkat HaMazon* is preceded by the singing of Psalm 126 (*Shir HaMa'alot*) which speaks as if out of the Babylonian Exile of the restoration of Zion. The Sephardic tradition is to include Psalm 23 in the *Birkat HaMazon*. The Talmudic tradition of reciting Psalm 137 (which refers to the destruction of the Temple) prior to the *Birkat HaMazon* is no longer followed.

Traditionally, when three or more males age 13 or older eat together, the *Birkat* is recited by the group. *Bensching* is introduced by a responsive formula known as *zimmun*. It takes the form of the leader asking ascent of the group to bless God. The group praises God for the food of which all have partaken, and the leader proceeds to the body of the *Birkat*.

The *Birkat HaMazon* itself consists of four blessings. The first praises God for providing food for all creatures. The second expresses gratitude for the good land God has given us, for the redemption from Egypt, for the covenant of circumcision, and for the revelation of Torah. The third asks God to have mercy on Israel and to restore the Temple and the Davidic kingdom. The fourth expresses thanks to God and includes petitions for God to fulfill specific desires, such as blessing the house in which one has eaten and sending Elijah the Prophet.

Certain additions are made to *Birkat HaMazon* on Shabbat and festivals. On Chanukah and Purim a section beginning *Al Hanisim* (on account of the miracles) is included. At a wedding feast, the *Sheva Brachot* (seven blessings) are recited right after the *Bensching* is concluded. At a house of mourning, passages are added which refer to the Mitzvah of Comforting Mourners.

A shortened version of *Birkat HaMazon* may be recited if one is working. In an extreme emergency

the line "Blessed be the Merciful One, the King, the Master of the land" is sufficient to fulfill the Mitzvah of having recited the *Birkat*.

The first three blessings are among the oldest in Jewish tradition. The Talmud attributes the first to Moses upon receiving manna from heaven, the second to Joshua when he conquered the land of Canaan, and the third to David and Solomon [because of David's role in making Jerusalem the capital and Solomon's role in building the Temple] (*Berachot* 48b).

The Bible, however, does not corroborate any of this even though certain lines of the blessing are taken from the biblical text.

The fourth blessing was added after the Bar Kochba rebellion (second century C.E.). The Rabbis of Yavneh added it in gratitude for the fact that the corpses of Betar did not decay and spread disease and that permission to bury them was finally granted to the Jews by the Romans. Certain parts of the fourth blessing have been added in more recent times, including, in some versions, lines reflecting Jewish life today.

Birkat HaMazon may be recited in any language (*Sota* 7:1). It is often sung, using any of a variety of melodies. It must be said at the table at which one has eaten. It is said only after a meal at which bread is consumed. If no bread is eaten, a shorter form is used.

It is customary to leave some bread on the table during *Birkat HaMazon* as a symbol of hope that there should never be a lack of food. A custom peculiar to Passover, is to conclude the *Bensching* with the blessing over wine, which is considered to be a cup of blessing, and is shared by all.

Some people remove utensils, especially knives, from the table before reciting *Birkat HaMazon*. The reason for this is that the table is considered to be an altar, and the altar of the Temple was constructed of stones not hewn with tools. Tools can become weapons and the table should be a place associated with peace.

ACTIVITIES

Primary

1. Bring a loaf of bread to class. Ask the students

49

where it comes from. (Remember to go beyond the grocery store!) Record all the steps in bread production that the students suggest. Then read *From Grain to Bread* by Ali Mitgutsch or another children's book about making bread. Compare the steps in the story with the steps the students listed. What steps, if any, did the students leave out?

2. Discuss: When a parent, relative, or friend does something nice, how do you show your appreciation? Continue the discussion by telling the students that the Jewish people have a special prayer which shows our appreciation to God for the food we eat. Read selected parts of the *Birkat HaMazon* to the students.

3. The song "*Oseh Shalom*" is part of *Birkat HaMazon*. Learn one or more melodies for this song.

    References: *Songs NFTY Sings #1*; *Traditional Sabbath Songs for the Home*.

4. In *Birkat HaMazon* we express our thanks to God for many things, especially the food we eat. Help the students create mobiles which will display the things for which they are thankful.

    Materials needed: Coat hangers, 4″ x 6″ cards, light colored construction paper.

    Procedure: On a card, write the title: "Things for Which I Am Thankful." Tape the card in the center of a coat hanger. Cut the construction paper into pieces of various sizes. On the pieces students write or draw pictures of things for which they are thankful (parents, peace, etc.). Hang these from the bottom of the coat hanger using string.

5. If a snack is a regular part of your program, teach the students the last line of the first paragraph of *Birkat HaMazon*: "*Baruch Atah Adonai, Hazan et Hakol*" (Blessed are You, God, who provides everything). Recite this blessing each week after the snack.

Intermediate

1. Use the ditto in *Hebrew Blessings Ditto Pak* by Fran Borovetz, p. 14, to help students review the first blessing of *Birkat HaMazon*.

2. Create an illustrated version of *Birkat HaMazon*. After a careful reading of the prayer, identify the main ideas.

Materials needed: Scraps of fabric in various colors, larger pieces of fabric for the backing.

Procedure: Using the technique of applique, create a design depicting the blessing. Either by machine or by hand, applique the design made out of various colors and textures of fabric onto the backing.

3. Discuss: What is the importance of blessing God after eating a meal?

4. As discussed in the Overview above, *Birkat HaMazon* was not fully composed at one time. Rather, as Jewish history evolved, additions were made. After thoroughly reading *Birkat HaMazon*, ask the students to compose their own contemporary additions to this prayer.

5. There are two very interesting Rabbinic selections dealing with the concept of blessing and eating:

    "A person is forbidden to enjoy anything of this world without saying a blessing. Whoever does so, commits an act of theft against God" (*Berachot 35a*).

    "A person should not taste without first saying a blessing, because it teaches in the Psalms (24:1), 'The Earth is the Lord's and the fullness thereof.' Someone who gets enjoyment out of this world without a blessing has defrauded the Lord."

    Consider the following: How is eating and not blessing like a theft? Try to think as the Rabbis did. How do you show your appreciation for the food you eat? Whom do you thank? Is it important to you to express your appreciation beyond the person who has cooked the meal?

6. Read Psalm 126, which is sung at the beginning of the *Birkat HaMazon* on Shabbat and holidays. Discuss the meaning of this Psalm. Write the verses on the chalkboard which present visual images. Choose one of the following techniques to create a poster series illustrating the Psalm.
    a. Students clip pictures from magazines and newspapers.
    b. Students use pastel chalk sticks to create their own images.

Secondary

1. Refer to the sections of the Book of Psalms mentioned in the Overview section above. Read them

through and discuss why they were chosen to be part of *Birkat HaMazon.*

2. The Rabbis felt that it wasn't adequate simply to say a blessing prior to eating. They added a much longer series of blessings after the finish of a meal. Discuss what might have been their reasoning. Is it easier to be thankful after you eat than before? Why?

3. It is a custom on Shabbat to sing *zemirot* (songs) after the meal. Two popular *zemirot* are *"Yah Ribon Olam"* and *"Tzur Mishelo Ochalnu."*
   a. Find recordings of these *zemirot* and listen to them.
   b. Learn to sing these songs.
   c. Read them in English translation.
   Discuss what the themes, ideas, and moods of these songs are. Extend the activity by locating and learning additional songs from Jewish tradition which would reflect similar ideas.

References: *Authorized Daily Prayerbook* by Joseph H. Hertz; *A Shabbat Haggadah* by Michael Strassfeld; *The Art of Jewish Living: The Shabbat Seder* by Dr. Ron Wolfson; *Traditional Shabbat Songs for the Home* sung by Velvel Pasternak.

4. Read through the blessing after meals with the commentary by Joseph H. Hertz found in *The Authorized Daily Prayer Book,* pp. 964-983. Ask the following questions: Does this prayer include things which do not deal with food or its consumption? Identify those elements. Why do you think these things were dealt with in this blessing?

5. It says in *Birkat HaMazon:* "I have been young and now I am old, yet have I not seen the righteous forsaken, nor his children begging for bread." In his commentary Joseph H. Hertz asserts that the Psalmist who inspired these lines is discussing Jewish social conditions and that no Jew ever went without food. A helping hand always aided him or her. In addition, Jewish children would never have to beg for bread. Ask: Is this true today? Was it ever true? Do Jews who have always share with those who have not? Should our responsibility extend to others besides Jews? Would you feed your enemy if he or she was hungry?

6. During the holidays of Chanukah and Purim, special blessings are added to *Birkat HaMazon* known as *Al Hanasim* (On account of the miracles). These blessings set up an interesting paradox: the intent of *Birkat HaMazon* is to thank God for the beneficence of this world. Included within the blessing is mention of two key moments in Jewish history: when the Israelites enter the Promised Land after wandering 40 years in the wilderness and the occasion of the Babylonian Exile. Research the origins of both Chanukah and Purim. Ask students: Why, out of all other Jewish historical experiences, were these two chosen for special attention during this blessing? Bear in mind that both holidays have no mention of God playing a direct role in the initial occurrences which led to these holidays being observed.

ALL-SCHOOL PROGRAMS

1. Include *Birkat HaMazon* at all congregational dinners and teach the words and melodies. Versions of *Birkat HaMazon* can be found in many prayerbooks and in the references listed immediately below.

References: *The Art of Jewish Living: The Shabbat Seder* by Dr. Ron Wolfson; *A Shabbat Haggadah* by Michael Strassfeld; "Jewish Prayers for the Home Table: Birkat HaMazon."

2. Plan ways to implement an anti-hunger drive within your community (refer to Secondary activity #5 above). Possible avenues to explore: community food banks, synagogue food collection efforts, soup kitchens, etc. Organizations that fight hunger on a national and international level are: Mazon, 2940 Westwood Blvd., Suite 7, Los Angeles, CA 90064; Oxfam America, P.O. Box 2176, Boston, MA 02106. Contact your local American Red Cross and Salvation Army.

3. Write for information about Mazon (see activity #2 immediately above for the address). Mazon is a Jewish organization that donates to causes which alleviate hunger on the national and local levels. Institute a campaign to encourage congregants to donate to Mazon 3% of the cost of their joyous celebrations at which food is served.

RESOURCES

For the Teacher

Birkat HaMazon: *Grace after Meals.* Miami: Central Agency for Jewish Education, 1984.

Glosser, Joanne; Beth Huppin; and Bill Kunin. *Feed the World: Hazan Et Hakol.* New York: Coalition for the Advancement of Jewish Education, 1986.

Hertz, Joseph H. *Authorized Daily Prayer Book.* New York: Block Publishing Co., 1948.

"Jewish Prayers for the Home Table: Birkat HaMazon." New York: Central Conference of American Rabbis, 1987.

Kelman, Vicki. *Family Room: Linking Families into a Jewish Living Community.* Los Angeles: Shirley and Arthur Whizin Institute for Jewish Family Life, 1995, pp. 31-41.

Strassfeld, Michael, comp. *A Shabbat Haggadah for Celebration and Study.* New York: Institute of Human Relations Press, 1981.

Wolfson, Ron. *The Art of Jewish Living: The Shabbat Seder.* New York: The Federation of Jewish Men's Clubs and the University of Judaism, 1985.

For the Student

Borovetz, Fran. *Hebrew Blessings Ditto Pak.* Denver: A.R.E. Publishing, Inc., 1980. (Grades 3-7)

Grishaver, Joel Lurie, and Beth Huppin. *Tzedakah, Gemilut Chasadim and Ahavah.* Denver: A.R.E. Publishing, Inc., 1983, pp. 54-57.

Mitgutsch, Ali. *From Grain to Bread.* Minneapolis: Carolrhoda Books, Inc., 1981. (Grades K-3)

Audiovisual

The Bridge. An audiocassette by Kol B'Seder featuring a variety of contemporary songs, including *"Oseh Shalom."* Jeffrey Klepper and Daniel Freelander. Available from A.R.E. Publishing, Inc. (All grades)

Songs NFTY Sings #1. Sound recording which includes a rendering of *"Oseh Shalom."* NFTY Resources. (All grades)

"Birkat Hamazon." On the audio recording *Whispers in the Wind* by Doug Cotler. Wail and Blubber Music. Available from A.R.E. Publishing, Inc. (Grades 4 and up)

UNIT 11

Affixing the Mezuzah

לִקְבּוֹעַ מְזוּזָה

OVERVIEW

"Hear, O Israel, the Lord is our God, the Lord is One. You shall love the Lord your God with all your heart, with all your soul and with all your might. And these words which I command you this day shall be upon your heart. . . . You shall write them upon the doorposts of your house and upon your gates . . ." (Deuteronomy 6:4-9).

The literal meaning of the word *Mezuzah* is "doorpost," but it has come to refer to the biblical passages and encasement which are affixed to the doorposts of Jewish houses. Some sources trace the origin of the *Mezuzah* to the time of the enslavement in Egypt, basing that practice on an Egyptian custom of placing a sacred document at the entrance to their houses.

It is thought that, originally, biblical verses were actually carved into the doorpost. Later, they were written on parchment which was then fastened to the doorpost. Eventually, the parchment was placed for protection in a hollow reed or other casing, as is the current custom.

The earliest evidence of a *Mezuzah* is from the Second Temple period. A *Mezuzah* parchment containing Deuteronomy 10:12-11:21 was found among the Dead Sea Scrolls at Qumran.

The *Mezuzah* has been considered by some to be an amulet which protects the house. This view may be based upon the final verse of the *Mezuzah*: "So that your days and the days of your children will be multiplied upon the earth" (Deuteronomy 11:21). The Jewish mystics even added symbols and inscriptions to enhance its protective function.

Yet, Maimonides, among others, strongly objected to considering the *Mezuzah* an amulet. Rather, he explained that by the commandment of the *Mezuzah*, we are reminded, when entering or departing, of God's unity, and are stirred into love for God. We are "awakened from slumber and from worldly thoughts to the knowledge that nothing endures in eternity like knowledge of the 'Rock of the World.'" This contemplation, Maimonides goes on, brings us back to ourselves and leads us on to the right path. (*Yad Hazakah, Mezuzah,* 6:13)

Other explanations of the significance of the *Mezuzah* are: It identifies a home as the residence of Jews, it reminds us to make our home a place worthy of God's blessing, and it reminds us each time we leave the house of our responsibility to follow ethical practices in business and professional life.

The *Mezuzah* is a piece of parchment (made from the skin of a kosher animal) on which are written the first two paragraphs of the *Sh'ma,* Deuteronomy 6:4-9 and 11:13-21. These passages are written in 22 lines by hand by a scribe called a *Sofer STaM* (one who qualifies to write a *Sefer Torah, Tefillin,* and *Mezuzah*). On the back of the parchment the letters *shin, daled,* and *yod* are written. As a word, they are pronounced *Shaddai,* one of the biblical names of God, usually translated "God Almighty." As an acronym, they stand for the phrase *Shomer Daltot Yisrael* (Guardian of the doors of Israel); some say *Shomer Dat Yisrael* (Guardian of the faith of Israel). Also on the reverse side of the parchment is an encoded phrase: "כוזו במוכסז כוזו." Each letter represents the previous letter in the Hebrew alphabet (for example, the *kaf* represents *yod,* the *vav* represents *hey,* etc.), forming the words "*Adonai Elohaynu Adonai,*" meaning "The Eternal our God is Eternal."

The parchment is rolled with the text on the inside so that *Shaddai* can be seen through an opening in the case. If there is no opening, the word or its first letter *Shin* appears on the case itself.

One is required to affix a *Mezuzah* not only to the doorpost at one's entrance, but also to the doorpost of every room except a bathroom, storeroom, or kitchen. Although there is no requirement to affix a *Mezuzah* to the entrance of public buildings (unless used for residential purposes), it has become a common practice for synagogues and Jewish community buildings to put up a *Mezuzah.* The Mitzvah of affixing a *Mezuzah* applies only to permanent structures and not to temporary or casual places. Thus, no *Mezuzah* is affixed to a *sukkah* or to a camping tent.

The *Mezuzah* is affixed on the right-hand side of the doorpost as one enters, within the upper one-third of the doorpost, but at least one handbreadth from the top. The *Mezuzah* is placed diagonally, with the top toward the inside; it may be placed vertically if the doorpost is too narrow. In either case, both the top and bottom must be fastened to the doorpost with nails. The tradition of affixing the *Mezuzah* at an angle may have been the result of a compromise in the Middle Ages between those who believed it should be vertical and those who believed it should be horizontal. As such, it symbolizes the spirit of compromise that should prevail in the home.

Before affixing a *Mezuzah*, one says these blessings:

בָּרוּךְ אַתָּה, יְיָ אֱלֹהֵינוּ, מֶלֶךְ הָעוֹלָם, אֲשֶׁר קִדְּשָׁנוּ בְּמִצְוֹתָיו וְצִוָּנוּ לִקְבּוֹעַ מְזוּזָה.

Blessed are You, O Eternal our God, Ruler of the Universe, Who has made us holy with Mitzvot and commanded us to affix a *Mezuzah*.

בָּרוּךְ אַתָּה, יְיָ אֱלֹהֵינוּ, מֶלֶךְ הָעוֹלָם, שֶׁהֶחֱיָנוּ וְקִיְּמָנוּ וְהִגִּיעָנוּ לַזְּמַן הַזֶּה.

Blessed are You, O Eternal our God, Ruler of the Universe, Who has given us life, sustained us, and brought us to this time.

The *Mezuzah* is sometimes put up as part of a *Chanukat HaBayit* (dedication of the house) ceremony. Twice every seven years, the *Mezuzah* should be inspected by a scribe to be sure that the writing is still legible.

ACTIVITIES

Primary

1. Hold a *"Mezuzah* Hunt." Search the synagogue, school, and/or homes to see where *Mezuzot* have been placed. Also, identify those doorways which do not have *Mezuzot*. Ask students to draw conclusions about where *Mezuzot* should and should not be located,

2. Open the Torah scroll and find the *Sh'ma*. Ask the Rabbi or other resource person for help if necessary. Have the students memorize the first line of the *Sh'ma* in Hebrew. Explain that the first two paragraphs of the *Sh'ma* are written on the parchment in the *Mezuzah*.

3. Discuss the following: If you pass by a house and see a *Mezuzah* on the doorpost, what does it tell you about the family that lives there?

4. Using an ordinary doll house, create a Jewish home in miniature. Make *mezuzot* on a small scale and affix them to the appropriate doorposts of the doll house. This might be an ongoing class project, using different Jewish symbols.

5. Read and discuss the book *Hear O Israel: First I Say the Shema* by Molly Cone. Ask the following questions: When do you say the *Sh'ma*? Where can you find the *Sh'ma*? Who says the *Sh'ma*? Why do you think the *Sh'ma* was chosen to be written on the *Mezuzah* parchment?

6. Create a *Mezuzah* finger puppet. You might name it *"Mezuzah* Man" or "Miriam *Mezuzah."* Begin by introducing students to your new friend. Let the character describe what it does. Allow students to ask questions. Directions for making a *Mezuzah* finger puppet:

   Materials: felt, needle, thread, glue, real scroll or small felt or paper facsimile.

   Procedure: Use a rectangle of felt (any color) measuring about 5″ x 2″ (long and wide enough to fit on your finger). Fold the felt lengthwise. Using a running stitch, sew up the long side. Glue felt eyes, nose, and mouth to form the character's face. Cut a small hole at the back of the *Mezuzah*. Use either a real scroll or a small felt or paper facsimile and glue it to the inside of the finger puppet.

Intermediate

1. Imagine that the *Mezuzah* on your doorpost could speak. Have each student conduct an interview with his/her *Mezuzah*. What would the *Mezuzah* have to say about Judaism and Jewish practice? About the family that affixed the *Mezuzah*? Remember, the *Mezuzah* contains the first two paragraphs of the *Sh'ma* (Deuteronomy 6:4-9 and 11:13-21). Read these verses in preparation for the interviews.

2. View and discuss the video *The Perfect Gift: Jewish Religious Articles,* with particular attention to the references to the *Mezuzah*. Consider these questions: What biblical passages does the *Mezuzah* contain? How is the *Mezuzah* scroll made? What is the correct procedure for affixing a *Mezuzah*?

3. Discuss the following: Why is it important to you to place a *Mezuzah* on your doorpost?

4. The *Mezuzah* contains the *Sh'ma* and the

V'ahavtah. Listen to a variety of recordings of the *Sh'ma* and *V'ahavta* in Hebrew and English. How do the different melodies make you feel? Is the music fast or slow? Are there low notes or high notes?

References (sound recordings): "*Sh'ma*" and "*V'ahavta*" on *Sing Unto God* by Debbie Friedman; "*V'ahavta*" on *Walk with Me* by Julie Silver; "*Sh'ma/You Shall Love*" on *And the Youth Shall See Visions* by Debbie Friedman.

5. Read the first two paragraphs of the *Sh'ma* in English (Deuteronomy 6:4-9 and 11:13-21). Have the students design and draw their own slides illustrating the Mitzvot mentioned therein. Obtain supplies for making slides from a camera supply store.

6. Have the students role play and discuss the following situation: A Jewish family moves into a new neighborhood and has put up a *Mezuzah*. As this family's eleven-year-old daughter brings home friends, each responds differently. Among the possible responses are: "What's that?" "You aren't Jewish, are you?" "My grandparents have one of those." Encourage students to generate additional responses.

7. Learn the blessing for affixing the *Mezuzah*. Utilize the ditto stencil on page 19 of *Hebrew Blessings Ditto Pak* by Frances Borovetz.

8. Have students make their own *Mezuzah* cases. There are many different ways to make the casing. They might also make their own scrolls.

References for making *Mezuzah* cases: *Arts and Crafts the Year Round* by Ruth Sharon, vol. 2, pp. 96-103; *The First Jewish Catalog* by Richard Siegel, Michael Strassfeld, and Sharon Strassfeld, p. 14.

Reference for making scrolls: *The First Jewish Catalog* by Richard Siegel, Michael Strassfeld, and Sharon Strassfeld, pp. 185-195, 206.

Secondary

1. Plan a *Chanukat Habayit* (dedication of the house) ceremony. Choose a location where the group will conduct the ceremony and affix a *Mezuzah*. Possible locations include: a Jewish home for the elderly, synagogue, religious school classrooms, home of one or more students, Jewish organizational office or building.

References: *Gates of the House*; *The First Jewish Catalog* by Richard Siegel, Michael Strassfeld, and Sharon Strassfeld, p. 15.

2. As noted in the Overview section above, the Israelites may have borrowed the idea of placing a sacred document on their doorposts from the Egyptians who would place a sacred document at the entrance to their homes. Imagine you are one of the following people: An American patriot in 1776, a cave dweller from prehistoric times, a volunteer for the underground railroad which spirited slaves to free states prior to the Emancipation Proclamation, an astronaut. What sacred document or object would you place at your door? Why? What gives those documents or objects significance to these figures? Why do you think Jews gave special significance to the *Sh'ma*?

3. Research the requirements for the Mitzvah of *Mezuzah*.

References: *Code of Jewish Law* by Solomon Ganzfried, vol. 1, pp. 34-39; *The Commandments* by Maimonides; *A Guide to Jewish Religious Practice* by Isaac Klein, pp. 49-51.

4. Explain to students that Jews in the Soviet Union are not free as we are to observe Jewish practices. Have each student imagine that he/she is a Jew living in the Soviet Union. Write a diary excerpt in which you describe your thoughts and feelings about your desire to affix a *Mezuzah* on your doorpost. Include the reaction(s) of other family members. Within the excerpt, state what you ultimately did.

5. Read the first two paragraphs of the *Sh'ma* in English (Deuteronomy 6:4-9 and 11:13-21). Have the students design and draw their own filmstrip illustrating these Mitzvot. To obtain supplies for making filmstrips, contact The Film Makers, P.O. Box 592, Arcadia, CA 91006.

6. A recent Confirmand receives a *Mezuzah* as a gift. He decides to place it on the front doorpost. His parents are uncomfortable with this public display of Judaism. Role play this conflict

between the Confirmand and his parents. Create three possible resolutions of this conflict.

ALL-SCHOOL PROGRAMS

1. Invite a *sofer* (Jewish scribe) to speak about his craft and to inspect *Mezuzot* brought in by the students. The *sofer* may make repairs on the *Mezuzot* and/or Torah scrolls.

2. After making *Mezuzot* (see Intermediate activity #8) or purchasing them, design a *Chanukat Habayit* ceremony and put a *Mezuzah* on each classroom doorpost.

   References: *Gates of the House*, pp. 103-107; *The First Jewish Catalog*, p. 15.

3. This assembly program can be held at the conclusion of a unit of study on the *Mezuzah* or as a one-shot program on the Mitzvah of *Mezuzah*.
   a. Opening remarks: Have a representative from each class report on one aspect of its study of *Mezuzah*. If this is to be a one-time only program, the Rabbi or Director of Education can present a brief five minute talk on *Mezuzah*.
   b. Torah reading: Have a post-Bar or Bat Mitzvah student read the *Sh'ma* and the *V'ahavta*, verses which are contained in the *Mezuzah*.
   c. Presentation: Each class receives a *Mezuzah* for the door of their classroom.
   d. Each class returns to its respective room and affixes the *Mezuzah*. All present recite the appropriate blessings. The Rabbi, Cantor, and/or Director of Education can go around to each room to help and to be a part of the ceremony.

RESOURCES

For the Teacher

Ganzfried, Rabbi Solomon. *Code of Jewish Law: Kitzur Shulhan Arukh.* rev. ed. Hyman E. Goldin, trans. Rockaway Beach, NY: Hebrew Publishing Co., 1991, vol. 1, ch. 11, pp. 34-39.

Klein, Isaac. *A Guide to Jewish Religious Practice.* New York: The Jewish Theological Seminary of America, 1979, pp. 49-51.

"Mezuzah." In *Encyclopaedia Judaica.* Jerusalem: Keter Publishing House Jerusalem Ltd., 1972, vol. 11, cols. 1474-1477.

Sher, Nina Streisand, and Margaret Feldman. *100+ Jewish Art Projects for Kids.* Denver: A.R.E. Publishing, Inc., 1996. (Grades PK-6)

Siegel, Richard; Michael Strassfeld; and Sharon Strassfeld, comps. and eds. *The First Jewish Catalog.* Philadelphia: The Jewish Publication Society of America, 1973, pp. 12-15, 185-195, 206.

Stern, Chaim, ed. *On the Doorposts of Your House.* New York: Central Conference of American Rabbis. 1994, pp. 138-142.

For the Students

Borovetz, Frances. *Hebrew Blessings Ditto Pak.* Denver: A.R.E. Publishing, Inc., 1980, p. 19. (Grades 3 and up)

Cone, Molly. *Hear O Israel: First I Say the Sh'ma.* New York: UAHC Press, 1971. (Grades K-3)

Ray, Eric. *Sofer: The Story of a Torah Scroll.* Los Angeles: Torah Aura Productions, 1986. (Grades K-6)

Weisser, Michael. *My Synagogue.* New York: Behrman House, Inc., 1984, pp. 2-3. (Grades K-3)

Zwerin, Raymond A., and Audrey Friedman. *Our Synagogue.* New York: Behrman House, Inc., 1974, Series C, Topic 6. (Grades K-2)

Audiovisual

"The Mezzuzah Song." On Kol B'Seder's audio-cassette *Growin' — New Songs for Jewish Families.* Jeffrey Klepper and Daniel Freelander. Available from A.R.E. Publishing, Inc. (Grades PK-3)

The Perfect Gift: Jewish Religious Articles. A 29 minute video introducing students to the ritual objects of *Mezuzah, Tallit, Tefillin,* and *Ketubah.* Ergo Media Inc. (Grades 3 and up)

UNIT 12

Wearing Tallit and Tefillin
טַלִּית וּתְפִלִּין

OVERVIEW

Two of the most important symbols used during prayer are the *Tallit* and *Tefillin*. The wearing of a *Tallit* derives from the Mitzvah of putting fringes on the corners of one's garments. "The Lord said to Moses: Speak to the Israelite people and instruct them to make for themselves fringes (*tzitzit*) on the corners of their garments throughout the ages. Let them attach a cord of blue to the fringe at each corner. That shall be your fringe. Look at it and recall all the commandments of the Lord and observe them, so that you do not follow your heart and eyes in your lustful urge. Thus you shall be reminded to observe all My commandments and to be holy to your God" (Numbers 15:37-40).

Putting *tzitzit* at the corners transforms any garment into a *Tallit*. Traditionally, a *Tallit* is worn by males, 13 years and older, during *Shacharit* (morning) and *Musaf* (additional) services every day. In some synagogues it is the custom that only married men wear a *Tallit*. It is also customary in some congregations for the leader of the *Minchah* (afternoon) service and the *Ma'ariv* (evening) service for Shabbat and festivals to wear a *Tallit*. It is also worn during the evening service on Yom Kippur.

While women are not required to wear a *Tallit* (because it is a positive, time-bound Mitzvah), neither are they prohibited from wearing one. In synagogues where women are called to the Torah, it is usual that they wear a *Tallit*. Some women wear a *Tallit* whenever the tradition prescribes its usage for men.

The *Tallit* is not worn in the evening, because in the passage from Numbers quoted above, one is supposed to "look at" the *tzitzit*. This has been interpreted to mean by the light of day.

During the reading of that passage, which is part of the third paragraph of the *Sh'ma*, it is traditional to gather the four *tzitzit* together and kiss them when the word *tzitzit* is read. Likewise, when called to the Torah, it is customary to touch the first word of the passage to be read with one *tzitzit*, which one then kisses before reciting the blessing.

Kohanim (descendants of the ancient priesthood) cover their heads with the *Tallit* during the *duchan* ritual — the priestly benediction recited over the congregation during the Shabbat morning *Amidah*.

A *Tallit* may be made of linen, wool, or silk. However, it may not contain both linen and wool. This is because of the prohibition against wearing a garment made of this mixture of materials (*sha'atnez*). The *tzitzit* must be of the same material as the *Tallit*. While a *Tallit* is usually of white material with black or blue stripes, it may be of any color, or combination of colors. The Torah commands that a thread of *techelet*, royal blue, be attached to each fringe. *Techelet* was an expensive blue dye extracted from the *hilazon* — a sea molusc found off the coast of Phoenicia. The use of this dye ceased during the Rabbinic period, either because of its scarcity and expense, or because the formula for obtaining the exact shade of blue was lost.

In addition to the *Tallit* being worn during prayer, it is a traditional practice for men to wear a *Tallit Katan*, a small *Tallit*, under their clothes at all times.

When putting on a *Tallit*, it is customary to recite Psalm 104:1-2: "Bless the Lord, O my soul; O Lord, my God, You are very great; You are clothed in glory and majesty, wrapped in a robe of light; You spread the heavens like a tent cloth." The following blessing is then recited:

בָּרוּךְ אַתָּה, יְיָ אֱלֹהֵינוּ, מֶלֶךְ הָעוֹלָם, אֲשֶׁר קִדְּשָׁנוּ בְּמִצְוֹתָיו וְצִוָּנוּ לְהִתְעַטֵּף בַּצִּיצִית.

Blessed are You, O Eternal our God, Ruler of the universe, Who has made us holy with Mitzvot and commanded us to wrap ourselves with fringes.

The *Tallit* is then touched to the eyes, kissed, and put on.

The purpose of the *tzitzit* is to remind us of the 613 commandments of Torah. The reminder is arrived at through *gematria*, numerology, in which each Hebrew letter has a numerical value. The letters in the word *tzitzit* add up to 600, plus the eight strands and five knots on each fringe, equal 613. Moreover, the pattern of wrapping the *tzitzit* at each corner is: double knot, seven coils, double knot, eight coils, double knot, eleven coils, double knot, 13 coils. Seven plus eight plus eleven equals 26, the value of the letters in the tetragrammaton —

God's name. Thirteen is the value of the word *echad*, which means "one." So the *tzitzit* also remind us of the last two words of the first line of the Sh'ma: "*Adonai* is One."

The tradition of wearing *Tefillin* is derived from four different verses in the Torah, each of which speaks of a "sign upon your hand and a symbol between your eyes" (Exodus 13:9, 13:16; Deuteronomy 6:8, 11:18). The word *Tefillin* is usually translated by the Greek term phylacteries, which means amulets, but they are not amulets. Rather, they are small leather boxes containing the above cited verses and wrapped around one's arm and forehead before prayer.

Tefillin are worn during the *Shacharit* (morning) service on weekdays. They are not worn on Shabbat or the festivals lest one carry them, thus transgressing the sanctity of the day. Another interpretation: because they are referred to as being an *ot*, a sign, and since Shabbat is also a sign of the covenant between God and Israel, to wear *Tefillin* on that day would be superfluous. Traditionally, *Tefillin* are worn by males 13 and older. Before his thirteenth birthday, a boy begins to practice putting them on. Because it is a positive, time-bound Mitzvah women are exempt, but not forbidden, from wearing Tefillin.

The *Tefillin* — box (*bayit*/house) and strap (*retzuah*) — are made from the skin of a kosher animal. The *bayit shel yad*, which is worn on the arm, has one compartment. This contains a piece of parchment on which are written the four verses cited above. The *bayit shel rosh* worn on the forehead also contains the four verses, one in each of its four separate compartments. It also has the Hebrew letter *shin* inscribed on one side of the *bayit* and a four-branched *shin* on the opposite side.

The letter *shin* stands for *Shaddai*, one of the biblical names of God. When the *Tefillin* strap is wrapped around the arm and hand in the appropriate way, the letters in the word *Shaddai* are formed.

When both are worn, *Tefillin* are put on after the *Tallit*. The following blessing is recited:

בָּרוּךְ אַתָּה, יְיָ אֱלֹהֵינוּ, מֶלֶךְ הָעוֹלָם, אֲשֶׁר קִדְּשָׁנוּ בְּמִצְוֹתָיו וְצִוָּנוּ לְהָנִיחַ תְּפִלִּין.

Blessed are You, O Eternal our God, Ruler of the universe, Who has made us holy with Mitzvot and commanded us to put on *Tefillin*.

Some recite this blessing twice, once for the arm and then again for the forehead. The *Tefillin shel yad* is put on one's "weaker" arm (left if one is right-handed, right if one is left-handed); the sleeve is rolled up and watch and ring removed so that nothing is between the *Tefillin* and the arm. The *bayit* is placed over the muscle of the upper arm and the strap is wound seven times around the forearm. This is to signify that our covenant with God is a daily matter. The *retzuah* is then wound three times around the hand and middle finger while the words of the prophet are recited: "And I will betroth thee unto Me for ever; . . . in righteousness . . . in justice . . . in lovingkindness . . . in compassion . . . in faithfulness; And you shall know the Lord" (Hosea 2:21-22).

ACTIVITIES

Primary

1. To introduce students to the study of *Tallit* or *Tefillin*, place first one and then the other in a bag. Allow the students to place one hand in the bag and touch the ritual object. After everyone has had a chance to do this, ask students to describe what they felt. Ask them to guess what is in the bag. If no one can do so, ask them what they think the object looks like. Take the ritual object out of the bag, show it to the students and explain its significance.

2. Have someone put on *Tallit* and *Tefillin* before the class. This individual should then explain what they are wearing and why.

3. Extend activity #1 by having each student put on the *Tallit* and *Tefillin*. Take an instant photo of each child. The students can then write a poem reflecting how they felt wearing the *Tallit* and *Tefillin*.

4. Bring in a variety of *Tallitot* to show the students. You might also wish to ask students to bring in *Tallitot* belonging to parents or older siblings. Have them describe the similarities and differences they observe. They can then draw conclusions as to what is required and what is left up to the discretion of the creator of a *Tallit*.

5. Take a field trip to the studio of a weaver (preferably a person who weaves *Tallitot*). The

weaver should demonstrate how cloth is made or how a *Tallit* is woven.

6. Play "What Am I?" first with *Tallit*, then with *Tefillin*. Begin by saying to the students: "I am something Jewish." Students ask questions that are answered yes or no (as in "Twenty Questions") and then guess what the object is. Questions might include: Are you a person? Are you bigger than a car? Are you found in the synagogue? When students guess correctly, or if they are stumped, display the object and explain its use.

Intermediate

1. Give pairs of students a copy of the Torah in English and instruct them to find the following verses: Exodus 13:9 and 13:16. Have each pair compose a statement explaining how *Tefillin* fulfill literally the words in these passages. Have them include their thoughts on how these verses might have been interpreted differently.

2. Choose one or more of the following *Torah Umesorah* filmstrips to view and discuss with your students: *How Tefillin Are Made, How Tefillin Are Worn, Tzitzis — The Badge of Israel, The Story of Sha'atnez.*

3. Obtain several sets of *Tefillin* and, with the students, learn how to put them on. *The First Jewish Catalog* by Richard Siegel, Michael Strassfeld, and Sharon Strassfeld contains a diagram and explanation for putting on *Tefillin*.

4. Tell students to imagine that each of them is a *Tallit* given to an almost thirteen-year old. Have them write a story about what they see and experience.

5. As a class create an illustrated dictionary about *Tallit* and *Tefillin*. This will require some research by the students. They may utilize the material from the Overview section above and other references listed in the Resources section below.

6. Discuss the following with your students: How is wearing *Tefillin* and/or *Tallit* like tying a string around your finger?

Secondary

1. Take the class to the sanctuary. Give each a *Tallit*.

Direct them to follow the traditional custom of wrapping oneself with the *Tallit* for a quiet moment of meditation. Afterward, discuss whether this might enhance worship and help develop a deeper sense of *kavanah*.

2. As a follow-up discussion for activity #1, have students create original poems describing the feeling of isolation and meditation they experienced while beneath the *Tallit*.

3. Have your students learn the blessings recited when putting on the *Tallit* and *Tefillin*.

   References: *Hebrew Blessings Ditto Pak* by Frances Borovetz, pages 17-18.

4. As described in the Overview section above, numerical symbolism has been used to interpret the knots and coils of the *tzitzit*. Create a bulletin board display which illustrates this use of *gematria*.

   References: "A Closer Look at the *Tzitzis* We Wear," a spirit master stencil available from Torah Umesorah; *The First Jewish Catalog* by Richard Siegel, Michael Strassfeld, and Sharon Strassfeld.

5. Invite a *sofer* (scribe) to visit your class and demonstrate how the scrolls are written for inclusion in the *Tefillin*.

6. Stage a debate on the following issue: Women may wear a *Tallit* (or Women should wear a *Tallit*). Bear in mind that the Torah does not specify gender regarding who wears a *Tallit*. The Talmud exempts women from time-bound Mitzvot so that they would be free for other responsibilities (child rearing and taking care of the home). Therefore, they are exempt from public worship and from wearing a *Tallit*. In many synagogues, however, women do wear a *Tallit*.

ALL-SCHOOL PROGRAMS

1. Hold a *Tallit*-making workshop. Directions for tying the *tzitzit* (fringes) can be found in *The First Jewish Catalog* by Richard Siegel, Michael Strassfeld, and Sharon Strassfeld. Judaica stores can provide you with packets of thread to be used. Encourage participants to be creative with their choice of fabrics. Each student may also want to make a special *atarah* (neckband) for the *Tallit*.

2. Begin a *Tallit* and *Tefillin* group at your synagogue which can meet on Sunday mornings. Participants should be encouraged to learn to put on *Tallit* and *Tefillin* and take part in the morning service.

3. Gather all the classes in a large room or, weather permitting, outdoors. Each class will need a large piece of fabric or a sheet under which all students can fit. Seat the classes in groups, with the groups forming one large circle. Each class or class representative reads an original statement, poem, or meditation which they have prepared about the significance of the *Tallit*. When the first class reads, their piece of fabric is spread out in the center of the circle. Each subsequent class joins its fabric to the others. Use extra large safety pins to attach one to another. Once all the classes have added their fabric pieces, attach large *tzitzit* to each corner. Together recite the blessings for putting on a *Tallit*. Gently lift up the giant "*Tallit*," a symbol of "*sukkat shalom*," a shelter of peace, and have everyone gather under it. Together sing "*Ufros Aleynu Sukkot Shelomecha*" under the giant *Tallit*.

RESOURCES

For the Teacher

Donin, Hayim Halevy. *To Pray As a Jew: A Guide to the Prayer Book and the Synagogue Service.* New York: Basic Books, 1980, pp. 24-37.

Elder, Shim D. *Halochos of Tefillin.* Lakewood, NJ: Halacha Publications, n.d.

Elkins, Dov Peretz. *The Tallit.* New York: United Synagogue, n.d.

Glatzer, Shoshana; with Ellen Singer; Susan Shulman-Tesel; and Lisa Schachter. *Coming of Age as a Jew — Bar/Bat Mitzvah.* New York: Board of Jewish Education of Greater New York, 1989, pp. 39-55.

Jacobs, Louis. *The Book of Jewish Practice.* West Orange, NJ: Behrman House, Inc., 1987, pp. 31-40.

Siegel, Richard; Michael Strassfeld; and Sharon Strassfeld, comps. and eds. *The First Jewish Catalog.* Philadelphia: The Jewish Publication Society of America, 1973, pp. 51-63.

Stern, Jay B. *Syllabus for the Teaching of Mitzvah.* New York: United Synagogue Commission on Jewish Education, 1986, pp. 183-187.

For the Students

Borovetz, Frances. *Hebrew Blessings Ditto Pak.* Denver: A.R.E. Publishing, Inc., 1980. (Grades 3-7)

"A Closer Look at the Tzitzis We Wear." (Stencil explaining the numerical significance of the *tzitzit*.) New York: Torah Umesorah Publications. (Grades 4 and up)

"Do It Yourself Tzitzis Guide." (Stencil illustration on how to tie *tzitzit*.) New York: Torah Umesorah Publications. (Grades 4 and up)

Kaplan, Aryeh. *Tefillin.* New York: National Conference of Synagogue Youth, 1986. (Grades 6 and up)

Sandberg, Martin I. *Tefillin: "and you shall bind them."* New York: United Synagogue of America, 1992. (Grade 6 and up)

Tallit. Instant Lesson. Los Angeles: Torah Aura Productions, 1985. (Grades 5-adult)

Audiovisual

The Perfect Gift: Jewish Religious Articles. A 29 minute video introducing students to the ritual objects of *Mezuzah, Tallit, Tefillin,* and *Ketubah.* Ergo Media Inc. (Grades 3 and up)

Tefillin. A 30 minute video on how *tefillin* are made and a description of the components that are used in *tefillin.* Zersch Greenfield. (Grades 6 and up)

"Two Special Symbols (Tallit and Tefillin)." On the audiocasette *Especially Jewish Symbols* by Jeff Klepper and Susan Nanus. A.R.E. Publishing, Inc. (Grades 1-6)

UNIT 13

Observing Dietary Laws
כַּשְׁרוּת

OVERVIEW

Of the 613 Mitzvot, more than 15 pertain to *Kashrut*, Jewish dietary regulations. These can be divided into three categories: permitted and forbidden foods, proper slaughtering of meat and fowl, and separation of milk and meat

A number of special Hebrew and Yiddish terms are associated with the dietary laws. Kosher means fit or proper, and refers to food that can be eaten in accordance with Jewish dietary regulations. The verb *kasher* means to make something kosher and is used with regard to food itself or to dishes and utensils. Any food or utensil that is not kosher is regarded as *treif*. The term *treif* originally referred to meat that had been torn from an animal, but it has come to mean anything not kosher.

Food that contains milk or any milk product is called *milchik*. Food that contains meat, poultry, or any by-product of them is called *fleishik*. Food that is neither *milchik* nor *fleishik* is *pareve*.

With regard to land animals, any animal that has true hooves which are cloven and that chews the cud is permitted (Leviticus 11:3). Specifically prohibited are the camel, hare, and daman, because they have no true hooves, and the swine because it does not chew its cud (Deuteronomy 14:7-8).

Anything that lives in water which has both fins and scales is permitted (Leviticus 11:9). Shellfish or non-scaled fish such as shark and whale are not kosher.

With regard to fowl, the Torah says "You may eat any clean bird" (Deuteronomy 14:11), but does not specify any characteristics a bird must possess to be considered clean. Instead, the text lists more than 20 birds which are prohibited. The Talmud explains that "any bird that seizes its prey in its claws is unclean, and any that has an extra toe, a crop, and a gizzard that can be peeled is clean" (*Chullin* 59a). Most domestic birds may be eaten and most wild birds and birds of prey may not. In addition, eggs from non-kosher birds are not kosher, while eggs from kosher birds are kosher. However, if the egg contains a blood spot, it may not be eaten because of the prohibition against eating blood. In addition, one is forbidden to eat most insects.

Animals and fowl which are permitted to be eaten must be slaughtered in the proper manner in order to be kosher. Animals and fowl killed in any other way are not kosher. The Torah specifically prohibits eating the flesh of an animal that has died naturally (Deuteronomy 14:21) or flesh that has been torn from an animal (Exodus 22:30). Game taken through hunting, is therefore, prohibited. The term for proper slaughtering of animals is *shechitah*; the ritual slaughterer is known in Hebrew as a *shochet*.

The Torah does not specify how animals or fowl are to be slaughtered. However, the Rabbis interpret a biblical passage referring to the slaughtering of animals to mean that "just as the consecrated offerings must be killed in the prescribed manner, so animals killed for food must be killed in that manner" and insist that this manner was told to Moses (*Sifre* to Deuteronomy 12:21).

In a proper *shechitah*, the knife must be specially prepared and its blade examined to be certain that it does not contain nicks or other irregularities. "The method consists of cutting the throat with a single, swift, and uninterrupted horizontal sweep of the knife in such a way as to sever the trachea, esophagus, carotid arteries, and jugular vein." This process "is designed to cause the animal the least amount of pain, to bring about instant death, and to remove as much blood as possible" (*The Jewish Dietary Laws*, p. 66). After the animal has been killed, the *shochet* inspects certain of its internal organs to be sure that they are free of diseases or defects which would make the animal *treif*.

In order to remove as much of the blood as possible, the meat from the animal must be soaked and salted. This process is usually done by a kosher butcher.

The third aspect of the laws of *Kashrut* concerns the separation of milk and meat. This practice is based upon the verse: "You shall not boil a kid in its mother's milk" (Exodus 23:19, 24:26; Deuteronomy 14:21). Since this command is repeated three times, the Rabbis derived three prohibitions from it: not cooking the two together, not eating the two together, and not deriving benefit from cooking the two together. If meat (or fowl which is considered meat) is to be eaten at a meal, then nothing with milk or a milk product may be eaten. If milk or a milk product is to be eaten, then meat or a derivative may not be eaten. Food that is *pareve* may be eaten with either milk or meat. It is traditional to have separate dishes, utensils, and pots and pans for each, and to wait a certain length of time after eating meat to eat milk and vice versa.

The reasons for the dietary laws have been the source of ongoing debate. The Torah implies that the purpose of these laws is to make us holy (Leviticus 11:44-45 and 20:26). Being holy is usually interpreted to mean to be set apart, and to maintain a distinct identity from other peoples. By eating food which keep Jews out of the kitchens of other peoples, a certain distance is maintained. Maimonides posited that the food which is forbidden by the law is unwholesome (*The Guide for the Perplexed* 3:48). Others point out that these laws force us to demonstrate self-control over one of the basic activities of life, eating. Since animals also eat, these rules humanize the process. In addition, they demonstrate a reverence for life, particularly as they regulate the slaughter of animals.

While human beings continue to search for meaning to these practices, the traditionalist will insist that *Kashrut* is observed because it is God's commandment.

ACTIVITIES

Primary

1. Begin a discussion of *Kashrut* by showing the students photos of individuals from a variety of different cultures wearing their native dress. Ask the students how we can tell these people from different countries apart (i.e., by dress, language, housing, food). The key is to focus on differences concerning eating habits and food. Explain that historically Jews have had distinctive food and eating habits. Introduce in simple terms the separation of meat and dairy products, the neutral status of fruits, vegetables, and grains, and the prohibitions against pork and shellfish.

2. Extend activity #1 by showing your students a variety of pictures of food from magazines. In advance, prepare a poster board divided into four categories labeled *milchik*, *fleishik*, *pareve*, and *treif*. As you hold up each picture, students take turns categorizing them.

3. Take the class on a field trip to a kosher kitchen. Ask a knowledgeable person who relates well to young children to explain how the kitchen is organized.

4. Bring a variety of food product containers and boxes to class that are marked with a "K" or "Ⓤ" or with another symbol that identifies a product as kosher. Ask students to make an inventory of items in their home or at the supermarket which have these symbols.

5. Have students suggest a breakfast, lunch, and dinner menu for one day. Then go over with them the content of each meal and ask if it is kosher. If it is not, request that they make substitutions that will permit the meal to conform to the requirements of *Kashrut*.

6. Using pictures of food items, make a board game. Players decide which items are *milchik*, *fleishik*, *pareve*, or *treif*. Each in turn spins a spinner, moves his/her playing piece, then identifies the category of food on which the game marker lands. If a player guesses incorrectly, he/she returns the marker to the previous space.

Intermediate

1. View and discuss the filmstrip *An Introduction to Kashrut*. Consider the following questions: What are the special terms used in the filmstrip? What do they mean? What are the major practices associated with keeping kosher? Why has *Kashrut* been important to the Jews through the centuries? How would you have to change your eating habits to conform strictly to *Kashrut*?

2. In the Overview above, four reasons are given for the observance of *Kashrut*: (1) to keep us holy (separate), (2) to keep us away from unwholesome food, (3) to force us to exercise self-control over one of life's basic activities — eating, and (4) to encourage us to show reverence for all life. Poll students to see which reason(s) makes the most sense to them. Ask them to describe their Jewish lives in the future, making specific reference to the observance of *Kashrut*.

3. Brainstorm with students a list of positive values that one can learn from keeping kosher.

4. Assign students to conduct a multi-generational food survey. They need to ask at least three

generations about their eating habits regarding issues of *Kashrut*. It may be possible to include a fourth generation if grandparents can recall what their parents did. In a survey they design, have students find out where each respondent was born and their level of observance of *Kashrut*.

Compare the results of the survey and discuss how eating styles have changed. What are some reasons for these changes? (Note: Some students will have a parent or grandparents who are not Jewish. Sensitivity will be needed in these instances.)

5. As pointed out in the Overview above, there are a number of special Hebrew and Yiddish terms which are used in relationship to the dietary laws. Have your students research the meaning of these terms. Gather the information together and create a *Kashrut* dictionary. To expand this activity, utilize pictures (either drawn or from magazines) and create a *Kashrut* "pictionary."

6. Ask students to imagine that they have to explain the Jewish dietary laws to non-Jewish friends. Have each student prepare a pamphlet which describes the laws of *Kashrut*.

Secondary

1. Present the following statement by Y.L. Gordon to the class: "Be a Jew in your tent and a man in the street." Apply this statement to the observance of *Kashrut*. Ask: If you observed the dietary laws and found yourself in a social situation in which non-kosher food was served, how would you react? Ask students to describe additional ways people make their religious, ethnic, or cultural identity known. How do students let it be known that they are Jewish?

2. The Rabbi, Cantor, Director of Education, and other Jewish professionals are often considered role models for the community. Have students debate whether or not it is incumbent upon these individuals to observe *Kashrut*. Should they be expected to do things that many in the community do not?

3. In Genesis 32:25-50 Jacob struggles with a "man" and is wounded in the thigh muscle. In remembrance of this, no meat from the thigh muscle of any animal is kosher. After the struggle is over, Jacob, though injured, is the victor. He requests and receives a blessing. Jacob is also given a new name, Israel, meaning "one who struggles with God." Consider the following: How does this story reflect the Jewish experience regarding the dietary laws (struggling with food desires)?

4. Collect books from the public library on various groups that have a specific philosophy about food, such as vegetarians, Hindus, Moslems, Jews, etc. Give each student a different group to research. Then have them answer the following questions based on their reading: In what food prohibitions does the group believe? What is the basis for these prohibitions? Is the group promoting more than just eating styles? How so? Students should then present short oral reports. As a class compare and contrast the practices of the different groups to each other and to the Jewish observance of *Kashrut*.

5. Extend activity #4 by having each student prepare and share a dish typical of the group they studied.

6. Invite a *shochet* or a kosher butcher to discuss the requirements associated with these professions. Students can prepare questions in advance.

ALL-SCHOOL PROGRAMS

1. Prepare six different stations, all relating to *Kashrut*, for students to visit. Ask the following questions as a pretest and posttest to determine what students know prior to visiting the stations and what new knowledge they acquired through their visits.

Station I: A Pretest
   Students answer the following ten true-false questions:
   a. Pork products are prohibited. (True)
   b. Any kind of fish, including shellfish, is allowed. (False)
   c. Meat and milk must never be served together. (True)
   d. Fruits and vegetables are considered neutral and may be served any time. (True)
   e. To be permitted as food to eat, an animal must chew its cud and have a split hoof. (True)
   f. To be kosher fish must have fins and scales. (True)

g. A ritual slaughterer is called a *shochet*. (True)
h. A Ⓟ or J signifies that a product is kosher. (False)
i. Hunted game may be eaten according to the laws of *Kashrut*. (False)
j. One must keep separate dishes and utensils for meat and milk products. (True)

Station II: Filmstrips

View the filmstrips *An Introduction to Kashrut* and *The Koshering of Meat and Poultry*.

Station III: Kosher and *Treif*

Provide pictures of a variety of boxes and cans of food. The items pictured should be either obviously kosher or blatantly *treif*. The students will sort them into these two groups. In order for this activity to be self-correcting, place the answers on the reverse side of the pictures.

Station IV: The Meaning of *Kashrut*

Have students write on a graffiti board labeled: "Keeping Kosher Means _____" (Have plenty of different colored felt markers available.)

Station V: Menus

Present five menus to each group that comes to the station. Students must determine whether or not each meal is kosher and, if not, why not.

Menu #1
Spaghetti and meatballs
Salad
Garlic toast sprinkled with parmesan cheese

Menu #2
Fried chicken
Steamed carrots
Cole slaw
Sliced peaches

Menu #3
Hamburgers
Potato chips
Vegetable sticks
Milk and brownies

Menu #4
Broiled steak
Mushrooms sauteed in butter
Baked potato
Tomato slices

Iced tea
Fresh fruit

Menu #5
Filet of sole stuffed with crabmeat
Saffron rice
Steamed artichoke
Coffee

Station VI: Posttest

Students complete the posttest (see Station I above).

2. Invite one or more articulate individuals who observe *Kashrut* to speak at an assembly. Brief them to direct their remarks to an explanation of the details of the dietary laws, as well as to the reasons why they personally keep kosher. Leave adequate time for a question and answer period.

3. Show the film *How To Kosher a Kitchen and Why!* Break up into small discussion groups to review the steps required to *kasher* a kitchen, as well as the reasons for keeping kosher. Ask students to suggest other reasons why someone might keep kosher.

RESOURCES

For the Teacher

Donin, Hayim Halevy. *To Be a Jew: A Guide to Jewish Observance in Contemporary Life.* New York: Basic Books, Inc., 1991, pp. 97-120.

Dresner, Samuel H., Seymour Siegel, and David M. Pollock. *The Jewish Dietary Laws.* rev. ed. New York: The Rabbinical Assembly of America, 1982.

Greenberg, Blu. *How To Run a Traditional Jewish Household.* Northvale, NJ: Jason Aronson, 1993, pp. 95-119.

Klein, Isaac. *A Guide to Jewish Religious Practice.* New York: The Jewish Theological Seminary of America, 1979, pp. 301-378.

Lipschutz, Yacov. *Kashruth: A Comprehensive Reference to the Principles of Kosher.* Brooklyn, NY: Mesorah Publications, Ltd., 1988.

Siegel, Richard; Michael Strassfeld; and Sharon Strassfeld, comps. and eds. *The First Jewish Catalog.* Philadelphia: The Jewish Publication Society of America, 1973, pp. 18-36.

Welfeld, Irving. *Kosher: A Guide for the Perplexed.* Northvale, NJ: Jason Aronson Inc., 1996.

For the Students

Artson, Bradley Shavit. *It's a Mitzvah: Step-by-Step to Jewish Living.* West Orange, NJ: Behrman House and New York: The Rabbinical Assembly, 1995, pp. 84-95. (Grades 8-adult)

Jacobs, Louis. *The Book of Jewish Belief.* West Orange, NJ: Behrman House, 1984, pp. 132-139. (Grades 9 and up)

Miller, Deborah Uchill, and Karen Ostrove. *Fins and Scales: A Kosher Tale.* Rockville, MD: Kar-Ben Copies, Inc., 1992. (Grades 1-3)

Nathan, Joan. *The Jewish Holiday Kitchen.* rev. ed. New York: Schocken Books, 1988, pp. xv-xviii. (Grades 2-6)

Prager, Janice, and Arlene Lepoff. *Why Be Different? A Look into Judaism.* West Orange, NJ: Behrman House, 1986. (Grades 6-8)

Zakon, Miriam. *Kid's Kosher Cookbook.* Spring Valley, NY: Feldheim, 1991. (Grades 3 and up)

Audiovisual

Chicken Soup. A 14 minute humorous production (in 16mm only) about the making of kosher chicken soup. Alden Films. (Grades 3 and up)

God's Diet. A 6 minute video that briefly explains the laws of kashrut and emphasizes the spirituality of keeping kosher. Bureau of Jewish Education of Greater New York. (Grades 4 and up)

How To Kosher a Kitchen and Why! A 22 minute documentary film about all aspects of *Kashrut.* Alden Films. (Grades 5 and up)

"Kosher." On the audiocassette *Sparks of Torah* by Kol B'Seder. Jeffrey Klepper and Daniel Freelander. Song about *Kashrut.* Available from A.R.E. Publishing, Inc. (Grades 3 and up)

UNIT 14

Immersing in a Ritual Bath
מִקְוֶה

OVERVIEW

"And he shall bathe his flesh in running water and be clean" (Leviticus 15:13). From this verse we adduce the Mitzvah of immersion for purposes of ritual purity. The practice of this Mitzvah most likely goes back to the days of the Temples in Jerusalem and perhaps even to the days of the first priesthood after the Exodus. Since a river or sea may be used for ritual immersion, we have no evidence as to when the ritual first began.

Usage of a constructed *Mikvah* or ritual bath, however, can be dated. Because two such baths were unearthed at Masada, we know their history is at least some 2000 years old.

Rules pertaining to the *Mikvah* are quite specific. It must be large enough for an adult to immerse completely — some say at least 47" deep — and it must be filled from free flowing water or rain water, not tap water. However, once a *Mikvah* possesses the minimum quantity of valid water (40 *seahs*, which is approximately 60 gallons), tap water may be added to it.

A person immersing in a *Mikvah* must be completely naked. Jewelry, hair clips, bandages, and any other object that comes between one's skin and the water must be removed. Makeup and nail polish should also be removed. A person usually showers to remove dirt before entering a *Mikvah*, a clear indication that its purpose is not physical cleanliness. A person immerses completely, recites the following blessing, and then immerses again.

בָּרוּךְ אַתָּה, יְיָ אֱלֹהֵינוּ, מֶלֶךְ הָעוֹלָם, אֲשֶׁר קִדְּשָׁנוּ בְּמִצְוֹתָיו וְצִוָּנוּ עַל הַטְּבִילָה.

Blessed are You, O Eternal our God, Ruler of the universe, Who has made us holy with Mitzvot and commanded us concerning immersing.

The most common use of the *Mikvah* is by married women who, each month after their menstrual flow, immerse themselves in order to resume sexual relations with their husbands. This practice is based upon the verse: "You shall not come near a woman who is impure" (Leviticus 18:19). The laws pertaining to this practice come under the heading of *taharat hamishpachah*, the purity of the family. For this reason, the establishment of a *Mikvah* takes priority over the establishment of a synagogue. According to tradition, a married woman may not live in a community which has no provision for ritual immersion.

The regulations for going to the *Mikvah* are quite specific. A bride goes for the first time just prior to her wedding. Thereafter, she must abstain from sexual relations with her husband from the onset of each menstrual cycle until seven days after the cycle has ended. During these days she is considered *niddah*, removed or separated. Indeed, most couples who observe the laws of family purity sleep in separate beds and do not touch each other while the woman is *niddah*, and the husband will not take an object directly from his wife, but will pick it up only after she has set it down.

It has been said that this forced abstinence strengthens a couple's relationship. Rabbi Meir stated that because a woman is forbidden to her husband for about two weeks each month, it enhances and renews her charm in his eyes (*Niddah* 31b).

Observance of this Mitzvah may also increase the chances of a woman becoming pregnant, because her most fertile time would be when she can resume intimacy with her husband. There is no evidence, however, that this was the prime intention of the precept.

The primary purpose of *Mikvah*, according to one thinker, is "spiritual in character, involving a cleansing of the mind, heart, and emotions, enabling a wife to bring herself once again completely and without reservation to her husband and for her husband to receive her in a like spirit" (*To Be a Jew* by Rabbi Hayim Halevy Donin, p. 126). Other reasons for *taharat hamishpachah* are to extend self-discipline to drives and urges which often cause passions to overcome reason, and to enable a husband to see his wife as more than a sexual object.

While its detractors view *Mikvah* as a remnant of the antiquated attitude that a woman's menstrual flow is something impure, *Mikvah* is used today by many in the Orthodox and non-Orthodox community. There are many who choose to reinterpret this ritual as a celebration of womanhood.

From the Bible we learn that a woman must also immerse herself in a *Mikvah* seven days after the birth of a son and 14 days after the birth of a daughter (Leviticus 12:5). There is no explanation for this discrepancy. According to Nachmanides, the time is doubled for a girl because the aftereffects are prolonged due to the difference in the physical constitution of a female child as compared to a male (Nachmanides to Leviticus 12:5). It might also be that since a daughter will someday also bear children, the extra seven days is on behalf of her future situation. Some communities extend these periods to as many as 40 days for a son and 80 days for a daughter.

Although not required to do so, some men use the *Mikvah* as an aid to spirituality prior to Shabbat or a festival. A *sofer* (scribe) uses the *Mikvah* prior to writing God's name. Male and female converts to Judaism go to the *Mikvah* to symbolize their spiritual purification or rebirth. By performing a Mitzvah whose reason is not apparent, the convert demonstrates the depth of his or her commitment to Judaism.

A *Mikvah* may also be used to immerse new vessels such as pots, pans, dishes, and silverware.

ACTIVITIES

Primary

1. Read and discuss the story *Hurry, Friday's a Short Day: One Boy's Erev Shabbat in Jerusalem's Old City* by Yeshara Gold. This story is about a young boy immersing in the *Mikvah* as a pre-Shabbat activity. Discuss the following questions: Why is Friday a short day? What special things does Rafi do on Friday? Why does he go to the *Mikvah* with his father?

2. Ask students to list as many uses for water as they can. Discuss the use of water as a cleansing agent. Point out how using the *Mikvah* to purify oneself is different from taking a bath or using water to cleanse one's self.

3. Ask the students for examples of ceremonies which celebrate a change of status (e.g., birthday parties, graduation ceremonies, Bar/Bat Mitzvah observances). Explain to the students that *Mikvah*, in a sense, changes an individual (or an object). It helps a person prepare for Shabbat, it changes the status of dishes and utensils making

them ready for use in a *kosher* kitchen, and marks the change in religious affiliation for converts to Judaism.

4. Show the filmstrip *T'villas Keilim* which introduces children to the general idea of *Mikvah*. It explains the immersion of utensils and explains the origin of this Mitzvah.

5. Discuss with students how they feel when they are swimming or floating in the water. Relate this feeling to the Mitzvah of *Mikvah*.

6. With your class construct a model of a *Mikvah* out of a milk carton. Include a dressing room and a waiting room in the model. After it is completed, role play the *kashering* of toy pots and pans.

Intermediate

1. Prepare a list of questions for students to answer as they hear an explanation of *Mikvah*. Decide what you want to tell the students and derive the questions from your presentation.

2. The reasons for many of the Mitzvot remain unknown. These Mitzvot fall under the heading of *Chukim*. Create a bulletin board display of examples of *Chukim*, with some suggestions of how they enhance Jewish life. (Examples are *Mikvah, Kashrut, Sha'atnez*.)

3. Direct the students to learn to read the Hebrew blessing recited when using the *Mikvah* (see Overview above).

4. If there is a *Mikvah* in your community, invite a representative to come and give a presentation about it and its uses to your class.

5. Role play a congregational board meeting dealing with the following issue: The congregation is in the process of designing a new building. A few members want to include a *Mikvah*, since there is none within 100 miles. Although no women currently use the *Mikvah* on a regular basis, a few have said they would do so if it were close by. Furthermore, the Rabbi wants a *Mikvah* to make it easier for Jews-by-Choice, who immerse in a *Mikvah* as part of their conversion. The two major drawbacks are cost and space limitations.

6. During the rainy season, arrange to collect rain water. Bring it to class and compare it with tap water. Invite a chemistry teacher or a person from the local water district who is knowledgeable about the chemical content of the water to describe how rain water is different from tap water. Discuss the significance of using some rain water in a *Mikvah*, as opposed to using only tap water.

Secondary

1. The Christian ceremony of baptism has its roots in the observance of *Mikvah*. Invite a Christian clergyperson to explain baptism, how and where it is done, and its significance in the life of a Christian. Together discuss the similarities and differences between *Mikvah* and baptism.

2. The *Mikvah* has been referred to as a fountain of living waters, a place where an individual can experience a spiritual rebirth. For many individuals who choose Judaism, immersion in a *Mikvah* is part of the conversion process. Invite a Jew-by-Choice to share this experience with your class.

3. The study of ritual purity might be used as an opportunity to begin a unit on sex and sexuality. Two good references for teaching this topic are listed below. The second title is somewhat dated, but presents the material in a thoughtful, discussion provoking format. Be sure to point out that, traditionally, *taharat hamishpachah*, family purity, served to regulate sexual relations between husband and wife.

   References: *How to Run a Traditional Jewish Household* by Blu Greenberg, pp. 129ff; *Choosing a Sex Ethic: A Jewish Inquiry* by Eugene B. Borowitz.

4. Read and discuss the following translation from the Yiddish of a *techina*, a petitionary prayer or supplication:

   For a Woman going to the ritual bath . . . Great God! Through water You have shown great miracles many times: the righteous Noah was saved from the flood, our teacher Moses was pulled out of water, Miriam's well went with the Jews in the desert. Show Your miracle today, too, that I may be helped through water to bear a son who will be completely righteous, will study Torah day and night, and will light a path directly to paradise for me after I have lived a long life. May I, through his merit, deserve to sit together with the matriarchs in the world to come. Amen. (*Genesis 2: An Independent Voice for Jewish Renewal*, Autumn, 1978, vol. 18, no. 3)

5. Read and discuss "*Tumah* and *Taharah, Ends and Beginnings*" by Rachel Adler found in *The Jewish Woman: New Perspectives* edited by Elizabeth Koltun. Also read the editor's note following the article.

6. As a follow-up to activity #5, debate whether or not women should still use the *Mikvah*. Another helpful resource is the article "Take Back the Waters" by Rabbi Elyse M. Goldstein in *Lilith* Magazine.

ALL-SCHOOL PROGRAMS

1. If there is a *Mikvah* in or near your community, arrange a field trip there. A person from the *Mikvah* association can lead the tour and explain the significance of the Mitzvah of *Mikvah*.

2. At an assembly for older students, view *Mikvah, Marriage, and Mazel Tov*, a short film which explains the significance of the Mitzvah of *Mikvah* and its relationship to marriage. Follow up with a question and answer period.

3. Invite a panel of individuals who have experienced *Mikvah* to describe their experiences and answer questions about it. Or, have the Rabbi or Director of Education discuss the significance of *Mikvah* and field questions.

RESOURCES

For the Teacher

Adler, Rachel. "Tumah and Taharah, Ends and Beginnings." In *The Jewish Woman: New Perspectives*. Elizabeth Koltun, ed. New York: Schocken Books, 1976.

Borowitz, Eugene B. *Choosing a Sex Ethic: A Jewish Inquiry*. New York: Schocken Books, 1976.

Donin, Hayim Halevy. *To Be a Jew: A Guide to Jewish Observance in Contemporary Life.* New York: Basic Books, 1991, pp. 121-133, 136-139.

Goldstein, Elyse M. "Take Back the Waters." *Lilith,* no. 15, Summer 1986/5746.

Hirschman, Fran. *Mikvah and the Jewish Laws of Sex and Marriage.* Los Angeles: Torah Aura Productions, 1994.

Maimonides, Moses. *The Commandments.* New York: Soncino Press, 1967, vol. 1, pp. 111-112, 117-119.

"Mikveh." In *Encyclopaedia Judaica.* Jerusalem: Keter Publishing House Jerusalem Ltd., 1972, vol. 11, cols. 1534-1544.

Orenstein, Debra, ed. *Lifecycles: Jewish Women on Life Passages & Personal Milestones. Vol. 1.* Woodstock, VT: Jewish Lights Publishing, 1994, pp. 24-25.

Probe, Marilyn, and Susan Talve. "A Healing Ritual: Mikveh as Celebration." In *Jewish Education News,* Summer, 1988.

Stern, Jay B. *Syllabus for the Teaching of Mitzvah.* New York: United Synagogue Commission on Jewish Education, 1986, pp. 168-173.

For the Students

Gold, Yeshara. *Hurry, Friday's a Short Day: One Boy's Erev Shabbat in Jerusalem's Old City.* New York: Mesorah Publications, Ltd., 1986. (Grades K-4)

Audiovisual

Mikva, Marriage, and Mazel Tov. A 10 minute video or film which explains the significance of the Mitzvah of *Mikvah* and its relationship to marriage. Alden Films. (Grades 6 and up)

Still Waters Run Deep. A 30 minute video that presents information regarding mikvah and explains some of the misconceptions pertaining to the cermony. Higher Authority Productions. (Grades 8-adult)

Overview

The last of the Ten Commandments is a prohibition against covetousness. "You shall not desire *(Lo Tachmod)* your neighbor's house. You shall not desire your neighbor's wife, or male or female slaves, or ox or ass, or anything that is your neighbor's" (Exodus 20:14). This commandment is phrased slightly differently *(Lo Titaveh)* in Deuteronomy 5:18.

Many other biblical passages reinforce the notion that a person should not covet. "Do not envy a lawless person, or choose any of that person's ways" (Proverbs 3:31), even though "the eyes of a person cannot be satisfied" (Proverbs 27:20).

Prophets such as Micah and Habakkuk consider envy and greed to be at the root of social injustice. Kohelet makes the point that one who loves money "never has one's fill of money, nor a lover of wealth one's fill of income" (Ecclesiastes 5:9).

According to the Talmud, the tenth commandment summarizes all of the previous ones because envy leads to other sins (*Pesachin* 107a). A desire for something could lead to covetousness, which might lead to robbery, and then to tyranny. The twentieth century theologian Hermann Cohen warned of a similar progression from greed to envy to hate to war.

In the *Mishnah* we read: Who is rich? "One who is content with one's portion" (*Pirke Avot* 4:1). The only instance in which envy is tolerated is when it might promote learning, for example when one person is envious of another's knowledge (*Baba Batra* 21a).

Maimonides derived two separate negative Mitzvot from the tenth commandment, based upon the two different Hebrew words: *tachmod*, usually translated "covet," and *titaveh*, usually translated "desire." The former expression connotes an actual planning to acquire another's property, while the latter refers even to desiring something that belongs to someone else. To desire an object is forbidden because, according to Maimonides, "one's love for the object will become stronger until one devises some scheme to obtain it" (*The Commandments*, vol. 2, p. 251). Maimonides cites the story of Ahab and Naboth (I Kings 21) as an example. Other medieval biblical commentators did not ascribe different meanings to the two Hebrew words.

In the Catholic version of the Ten Commandments, two distinct commandments are derived from this biblical verse: "You shall not covet your neighbor's wife" and "You shall not covet your neighbor's house." (The first and second commandments as Jews number them are combined in the Catholic version in order to allow for this "extra" commandment.)

In the eighteenth century, Elijah Gaon wrote in a letter to his wife: "Do not take your daughter to the synagogue where she will see girls of her age dressed in finery of which she is deprived. This may produce envy and gossip" (Letter of Elijah Gaon of Vilna" in *Hebrew Ethical Wills* edited by Israel Abrahams, p. 321). In modern times covetousness remains a serious problem, particularly in materialistic societies. Perhaps in recognition of this inevitability, Jewish tradition holds that envy will only cease in messianic times.

ACTIVITIES

Primary

1. Bring a package of healthy cookies to class. Give some students five cookies. To other students give fewer, and to a few students give none. Make sure the students are aware of what the others have. Observe and record what the children say and do. Use this material as a basis for discussion. A few points to raise: Who shared? Who hoarded? Who felt envious (in other words, who wanted what the others had)? Discuss feelings with the class and relate to the Mitzvah of *Lo Tachmod*.

2. To emphasize the positive aspects of human relationships, make a sharing quilt with the class. One simple method is for each student to draw a picture using fabric crayons on squares of muslin. Ask that they incorporate something about the Mitzvah of Not Coveting. Follow the directions on the crayon box for making the color permanent. Machine stitch the pieces together and then quilt.

3. Discuss with students the difference between things we need and things we would like to have, giving a few examples of each. Place a large sheet of butcher paper on the wall. Divide it in half, labeling one half "Things We Need," and the other half, "Things We Want." Students then go through magazines, cut out pictures of various products, and paste them under the appropriate heading. Discuss how this activity is related to *Lo Tachmod*.

4. Write a song about sharing and Not Coveting. Use the melody of a popular children's song, such as "Old McDonald Had a Farm" or "Pop Goes the Weasel" and write new lyrics.

5. Discuss envy and jealousy between brothers and sisters and brainstorm a list of suggestions for parents to reduce these problems.

6. Read "You Shall Not Covet . . . The Peach, the Pitcher and the Fur Coat" from *Who Knows Ten* by Molly Cone. The accompanying Teacher's Guide provides excellent background and discussion material to be used with this age group.

7. Bring a beautifully wrapped box to class. Set the box in a prominent location in the classroom. Make no comment about the box until the students begin asking questions. Use a tape recorder to capture their comments. After a short period of time, play the tape and discuss. Ask: Did you want to know what was in the box? Did you covet the box or its contents? Is it hard not to covet?

Intermediate

1. Read the story of Joseph and his brothers (Genesis 37:1-11). With the students discuss the relationship Joseph had with his brothers. Consider the following questions: In what ways did the brothers covet Joseph's possessions? In what ways did they covet the relationship Joseph had with their father, Jacob? Issues to raise: Do you know anyone who is like Joseph (singled out for special treatment)? How do you get along with your brothers and sisters? How is your relationship to them like Joseph and his brothers? How is it different?

2. Ask the students to think about a time when they purposely tried to make someone envious. Who was it? What did they try to make the person jealous about? Why did they want to make the person jealous? Write a poem about this experience.

3. There is a quote from *Pirke Avot* (5:13) which reads: "There are four types of people: One who says 'What is mine is mine and what is yours is yours' is a neutral character. . . . One who says 'What is mine is yours and what is yours is mine' is a boor. One who says, 'What is mine is yours and what is yours is yours' is a saint. One who says, 'What is yours is mine and what is mine is mine' is a wicked person." Write each statement on a piece of large poster board. Take an orange and divide it up into segments. Using these as the property, have students create four skits which illustrate each of the four statements. They can then perform each skit in front of the appropriate statement.

4. Provide a moral to a story and have the students write a story about envy, jealousy, or covetousness that fits one of the following morals:
   a. "The grass is always greener on the other side" (Folk saying).
   b. "Envy and anger shorten life" (*Ben Sira* 30:24).
   c. "Who sows envy, reaps regret" (Immanuel, *Mahberot*, chapter 9).
   d. "The ear of the jealous will hear everything" (*The Wisdom of Solomon*).

5. To demonstrate to the students how they covet material objects, divide the students into three or four groups. Give each group $100 of play money. Hold an auction of 5-8 items that the students would want, such as bubble gum, comic books, a food item, etc. After the auction discuss why some items were sold for more than others. What makes something valuable? Why did some groups bid on some and not on others? How did a group feel after running out of money?

6. Read "A Tale of Three Wishes" from *Stories for Children* by Isaac Bashevis Singer. Discuss: What did Shlomah, Moshe, and Esther each desire? How did they "waste" their wishes? The Watcher in the Night said to the children, ". . . try to deserve by effort what you wanted to get too easily." What did he mean? Give a personal example of this statement.

7. Listen to and discuss the story "Shrewd Todie and Lyzer the Miser" from the recording *Eli Wallach Reads Isaac Bashevis Singer*. (If the record is not available, the story may be found in *When Shlemiel Went to Warsaw and Other Stories* by Isaac Bashevis Singer.) This story is a delightful tale that cleverly combines nonsense, treachery, and covetousness.

Some questions to consider with the students: How did Lyzer's greed get him into trouble? Did Lyzer enjoy his wealth? Who did the greater wrong, Todie or Lyzer? Why? Are you satisfied with the Rabbi's decision? How did the townspeople feel? If you were the Rabbi, how would you respond to this case? How does each of the character's behavior relate to the Mitzvah of Not Coveting? How did Lyzer's covetousness get him into trouble?

Secondary

1. Discuss: Have you ever been chosen for a special award or responsibility? How did you feel? How did others feel about you? Were they jealous? Did they covet what you received? Is it acceptable to covet an award if it motivates you to work for it?

2. Read Micah 2:1-4 and Habbakuk 2:9-10. In modern terms one might say the prophets were like whistleblowers. They called attention to the evil and wrongdoings of their time. In these two passages, the prophets have called attention to the sin of covetousness. They chastise the people for plotting to gain and make profit from others. Discuss to which recent situations Micah and Habbakuk might be responding.

3. *Baba Batra* 21a says "Envy is tolerated because it promotes knowledge." Create two lists. On one side list things which one should not envy under any circumstances. On the other side list things that might be proper for one to envy.

4. There is an old saying: "How're you going to keep them down on the farm after they've seen Paree [Paris]?" Discuss the meaning of this saying. How does the environment in which a person is raised affect how jealous the person is of what others have? Is it true that the more material goods a person has, the more the person desires? Or is the opposite true?

5. Some private schools insist that their students all wear the same uniform. Discuss reasons for this and how such a dress code relates to the Mitzvah of *Lo Tachmod*.

6. Read the story of Ahab and Naboth from I Kings 21. Discuss how transgressing the commandment "you shall not covet" leads one to transgress other commandments.

ALL-SCHOOL PROGRAMS

1. Divide students into groups of 6-10 students of mixed grade levels. Give each group a paper bag with a variety of objects. Give the groups 15 minutes to use the objects and put together a skit on the theme of "You shall not covet." The skits are then performed for the other groups.

2. Each class will write and display a poem with the title, "You shall not covet." Write the title on large sheets of paper, distributing one to each class. Write the finished poems on the large sheets and hang in the halls or on the walls of the social hall.

3. Hold a mock T.V. game show, with teachers or older students playing the roles. The host introduces the show and describes the prize (a new car, an exotic vacation, a stereo, etc.). The first contestant is introduced and told what the prize is. This contestant really wants the prize and says how great it is over and over again. The contestant is asked a series of questions (related to a Jewish holiday or other Jewish theme or to the Mitzvah "You shall not covet"). This contestant answers all but the last one correctly, and, therefore, does not win the prize. He or she is upset and distraught. The second contestant is just the opposite: he/she is not too excited about the prize, answers all but the last question correctly, but is not disappointed about not winning. After the presentation classes can break up into small groups to discuss the different responses of the contestants.

RESOURCES

For the Teacher

Glustrom, Simon. *The Language of Judaism.* Northvale, NJ: Jason Aronson, 1994, pp. 43-44.

Gross, Florence, and Dulcy Wilets. *Teacher's Guide to Who Knows Ten.* New York: UAHC Press, 1968, pp. 38-40.

Leibowitz, Nehama. *Studies in Shemot (The Book of Exodus).* Jerusalem: The World Zionist Organization, 1976, pp. 342-351.

Maimonides, Moses. *The Commandments.* New York: The Soncino Press, 1987, vol. 2, pp. 250-252.

Stern, Jay. *Syllabus for the Teaching of Mitzvah.* New York: United Synagogue Commission on Jewish Education, 1986, pp. 164-167.

Zipperstein, Jay; Leo Jung; and Aaron Levine. *Business Ethics in Jewish Law.* Rockaway Beach, NY: Hebrew Publishing Co., 1987.

For the Students

Baum, Eli. *Mitzvot Bein Adam Lachaveiro.* New York: KTAV Publishing House, Inc., 1980, pp. 19-21. (Grades 3-6)

Cone, Molly. *Who Knows Ten?* New York: UAHC Press, 1965, pp. 83-92. (Grades K-3)

Fox, Marci. *The Ten Commandments.* Instant Lesson. Los Angeles: Torah Aura Productions. (Grades K-2)

Getzel. *The Stonecutter Who Wanted To Be Rich.* Lakewood, NJ: C.I.S. Publishing, 1990. (Grades PK-2)

Hautzig, Esther. *Riches.* New York: HarperCollins Children's Books, 1992. (Grades 3-6)

Karkowsky, Nancy. *The Ten Commandments.* West Orange, NJ: Behrman House, 1988. (Grades 3-4)

Singer, Isaac Bashevis. *Stories for Children.* New York: Farrar, Straus and Giroux, 1994. (Grades 6 and up)

————. *When Shlemiel Went to Warsaw and Other Stories.* New York: Farrar, Straus and Giroux, Inc., 1986. (Grades 4 and up)

Ten Times Ten. Instant Lesson. Los Angeles: Torah Aura Productions. (Grades 6-adult)

Topek, Susan. *Ten Good Rules.* Rockville, MD: Kar-Ben Copies, Inc., 1992. (PK-1)

Audiovisual

More. A 3 minute animated film about the desire for material things. Films Incorporated. (Grades 4 and up)

The Seven Wishes of a Rich Kid. In this 30 minute video, a boy has everything money can buy, except friends. Board of Jewish Education of Greater New York. (Grades 4-8)

Keeping One's Word
נְדָרִים

OVERVIEW

Within the Jewish value system, there has always been a concern over abuse of spoken language. This is most evident in the attitudes toward slander and gossip (see *Lashon Hara*, Unit 18), and toward vows and oaths.

A vow (*neder* in Hebrew) was usually a self-imposed obligation to do or not to do a certain thing. An oath (*shevua* in Hebrew) could be similar to a vow, but more often would be used in a judicial setting. The main purpose of making an oath or vow was to lend additional credence to one's statement. According to *Pirke Avot* 3:17 vows are an aid to self-control.

One who makes a vow to God or who takes an oath imposing an obligation on oneself is commanded not to break that pledge, but to carry out what has been said (Numbers 30:3). Another passage states: "When you make a vow to the Lord your God do not put off fulfilling it; for the Lord your God will require it of you, and you will have incurred guilt; whereas you incur no guilt if you refrain from vowing. You must fulfill what has crossed your lips and perform what you have voluntarily vowed to the Lord your God, having made the promise with your own mouth (Deuteronomy 23:22-24).

The third commandment, which reads in part "You shall not utter the name of the Lord your God in vain" (Exodus 20:7), has been interpreted to mean that one should not casually make a vow or an oath. The more one swore by God's name, the less meaningful making a vow became.

The Bible contains numerous examples of oaths. Abimelech has Abraham swear that he will not deal deceitfully with him (Genesis 21:22-24). Abraham has his senior servant swear that he will not take a wife for Isaac from the Canaanite people (Genesis 24:1 ff). Israel is reported to have taken an oath at Mizpah not to give a daughter in marriage to a Benjaminite (Judges 21:10). Elijah swears to Ahab that there will be no dew or rain, except at the prophet's bidding (I Kings 17:1).

A special vow to abstain from wine and other intoxicating beverages, from cutting one's hair, and from touching a corpse was known as a Nazirite vow (Numbers 6:11). Such a vow was often taken to express thanks to God. One could be a Nazirite for life, as was the case with Samuel and Samson, or for a specified period of time. The Bible permits the voiding of the vow of an unmarried woman by her father, and the voiding of the vow of a married woman by her husband. Vows or oaths made by male children under the age of 13 and female children under the age of 12½ are not valid.

Despite its widespread practice, the taking of oaths was not encouraged by the Rabbis. "It is better to make no vows at all than to make them even if one is certain of fulfilling them" (*Chullin* 2a). "A person who takes a vow is likened to a person who builds a forbidden altar" (*Nedarim* 60b). Since it would have been futile to prohibit the making of vows, the tradition attempts to impose strict control over them. An entire tractate of the Talmud, *Nedarim*, deals with vows; another, *Shevu'ot*, with oaths. The chapter pertaining to vows in the *Shulchan Aruch* begins with a lengthy admonition against making vows.

If one is to make a vow or take an oath, it should be for a worthy purpose, such as giving a person added incentive to perform a Mitzvah or to refrain from committing a transgression. For example, one might vow to set aside a certain time each day for Torah study. When one wished to be released from a vow, it could be done before a *Bet Din* of three Rabbis or learned Jews.

Concern about unfulfilled vows was likely an important factor in the emergence of the *"Kol Nidre"* as a significant Yom Kippur ritual. *"Kol Nidre"* states that all vows that one makes unwittingly, rashly, and unknowingly should be null and void. While *"Kol Nidre"* originally applied to vows made during the past year, medieval sages changed it to apply to the year ahead, which is the form that is used most widely today. Although *"Kol Nidre"* was only valid with regard to oaths between a person and God, and not between one person and another, it was used by some in the non-Jewish community to assert that the oath of a Jew was worthless. For this reason and others, some Rabbis in the Middle Ages condemned it and removed it from usage. However, by the eleventh century, it was a standard part of the liturgy. In 1844, a Reform synod in Germany recommended that it be removed; from some prayerbooks it was, in others it was changed. However, recent prayerbooks have included it.

The custom of taking the Torah scrolls from the Ark while reciting *"Kol Nidre"* on Yom Kippur is based on the tradition that oaths were taken holding the Torah (*Shevuot* 38b). Traditionally, *"Kol Nidre"* was read or chanted before sundown, since it was deemed inappropriate to ask for oaths to be annulled on Yom Kippur.

In the Middle Ages, Jews were often compelled to take what was called an *Oath More Judaico* in lawsuits with non-Jews. Both the oath itself and the accompanying ceremony were often degrading for the Jew, indicating a lack of trust between Jews and non-Jews and pointing up the inferior status of Jews at that time.

ACTIVITIES

Primary

1. Many organizations have oaths or promises that the members pledge. Find examples of these (Girl Scouts, Boy Scouts, Campfire Girls, etc.). Share these with your students. Read each and discuss their meaning.

2. Pose the following questions to your students: Did you ever make a promise you knew you could not keep? Did you ever make a promise you wanted to keep, but could not? How did you feel? What happened to the others involved?

3. New Year's resolutions are a type of vow. Assign your students to create their own resolutions. Read these over together. Discuss how they are like vows and how they are not.

4. On the blackboard write the following promises:

I promise always to tell the truth.
I promise to keep my room clean.
I promise to try hard in school.
I promise to do all my chores.
I promise not to tell on my friends.
I promise to be kind to animals.

Read each of the promises to the children. Discuss whether these are promises they might make. Point out that Jewish people are asked to make only those promises which they can keep.

5. Make paper weights to help remind students about keeping promises. Find smooth rocks, one for each student. Students choose a saying such as "Keep your word," "Don't take promises lightly," "A promise is for keeping," or make up one. Use acrylic paints for the sayings and for added decoration.

6. In Genesis God promised that the world would never again be destroyed by flood. Read aloud Genesis 9:1-17 so that the students have a clear understanding of this story. As a class write an acrostic-style poem using the word "promise" for the initial letters of each line. The poem may reflect the general theme of promise or relate. specifically to the promise God made to Noah. If desired, illustrate the poem with a rainbow and clouds.

Intermediate

1. Ask each student to write his/her own oath or promise for the kind of Jewish life he/she wants to lead.

2. Allow students to debate whether one should/should not make vows. If this is their first debate, help them organize their views and ideas in writing. You may want to set this up as a team debate, allowing a set period of time for presentation of ideas and rebuttal. Afterward, discuss the debate and relate the discussion to Jewish teachings about vows.

3. With your students read the *"Kol Nidre"* in English from the *Machzor* used by your synagogue. Find one or more variations in other prayerbooks. Discuss the meaning of the prayer.

4. Have your students listen to *"Kol Nidre"* sung by your Cantor or on a recording. While listening students can make abstract pastel drawings reflecting how the music makes them feel. Ask the students: What message does the music give? Is the message the same one that the words give or a different one?

References: *Kol Nidre* by Richard Tucker; *Jan Peerce Sings Hebrew Melodies* by Jan Peerce.

5. Ask your students to give you examples of everyday vows that people make (e.g., to diet, to practice music, to do homework, etc.). Follow up by asking what the results are when one does not keep the vow or promise.

6. Invite a lawyer or judge to come and speak to your class on the subject of perjury. Instruct the guest to emphasize the importance of truthful testimony and the potential destructiveness of lying. Discuss how Judaism's attitude toward vows relates to testifying in court.

7. Read together the section on vows and oaths on pp. 51-54 of the *Code of Jewish Law: Kitzur Shulchan Arukh*, vol. 2, by Rabbi Solomon Ganzfried. What attitude is expressed toward the taking of vows?

Secondary

1. Read over a traditional Jewish marriage ceremony and compare it with a Reform ceremony. Discuss differences and similarities. What role do formal spoken vows play in each ceremony?

   References: *Rabbi's Manual* (Reform); *A Rabbi's Manual* edited by Jules Harlow (Conservative).

2. Assign the students to keep a journal for one week's time in which they record any types of oaths, vows, or promises that they either hear or make themselves. They should also record their reactions when they hear someone making a promise (e.g., Do they think it will be kept? Why or why not?). Ask: Do you think that everyone is too casual with promises? How can this be changed? Discuss whether or not the prevailing attitude toward making promises is the same or different from the Jewish attitude.

3. For insight into the concept of the Nazirite, read the story of Samson and Delilah in Judges, chapter 16, and show the animated film *Samson and Delilah*. With the students determine what constitutes a Nazirite vow. Did Samson make his own vow? If not, why did he have to keep it? Could someone live as a Nazirite today?

4. Learn to chant the *"Kol Nidre."* Invite the Cantor or Rabbi to serve as a resource.

5. Research the *Oath More Judaico*. Create a short dramatic presentation based upon the research. Discuss how it might have felt to be a Jew or a non-Jew in such a situation. How would experiencing this affect one's attitude toward Jews or non-Jews?

Reference: "Oath More Judaico" in *Encyclopaedia Judaica*, vol. 12, cols. 1302-1304.

6. Ask your students to write a contemporary statement like *"Kol Nidre,"* which absolves them of unfulfilled oaths. Also, have them include ways to rectify past behaviors. Remind the students that these are oaths between the individual and God.

7. Set up a mock trial revolving around one of the following issues:
   a. The Rabbi of a certain synagogue has removed the *"Kol Nidre"* from the High Holy Day liturgy, but the Ritual Committee wants to retain it. Put the Rabbi on trial.
   b. An individual in the Jewish community has pledged a large sum of money to the synagogue. For no apparent reason the person reneges. The Board of Trustees of the synagogue decides to sue for the money based on breach of promise. Defense and prosecution should use material from the Overview in presenting their cases.

ALL-SCHOOL PROGRAMS

1. Hold a special service with the theme of "Promises, Oaths, and Vows." Include *"Kol Nidre"* and material from the Jewish tradition found in the Overview section above. Students who belong to such organizations as Boy Scouts or Girl Scouts can recite the group's promise and state what it means to them. Some teachers or older students may wish to prepare a skit on a related theme, such as what happens when one does not keep promises.

2. *"Kol Nidre"* releases one from vows, oaths, and promises that were made under duress and that one is not able to fulfill. To symbolize this concept, give each student a 3″ x 5″ card and ask them to write one promise or vow that they made during the past year that they were unable to keep. Teachers will need to do the writing for younger children. Attach each card to a helium balloon and release the balloons all together.

3. To emphasize the importance of keeping promises, take the students on a guided fantasy. Begin the fantasy with someone making a promise to them about something they would really want. Ask them how they feel about it. Build up

their anticipation, and then disappoint them by revealing that the person cannot keep his/her promise. Again, ask how they feel. Repeat this two or three times, but the last time, have the person keep the promise. After the guided fantasy, break up into groups by age and discuss. Suggested questions: What is it like when a promise is broken? How does a broken promise affect one's trust in the person who has made the promise? Why do you think the tradition discouraged Jews from making vows, and taught that if one did make vows, they must be kept?

RESOURCES

For the Teacher

Bloch, Abraham P. *A Book of Jewish Ethical Concepts.* New York: KTAV Publishing House, Inc., 1984, pp. 248-250.

Ganzfried, Solomon. *Code of Jewish Law: Kitzur Shulhan Arukh.* rev. ed. Hyman E. Goldin, trans. Rockaway Beach, NY: Hebrew Publishing Company, 1991, vol. 2, ch. 67, pp. 51-54.

Maimonides, Moses. *The Commandments.* New York: The Soncino Press, 1967, vol. 1, pp. 107-109; vol. 2, pp. 198-199.

"Oath More Judaico." In *Encyclopaedia Judaica,* vol. 12, cols. 1302-1304.

For the Students

Cone, Molly. *Who Knows Ten?* New York: UAHC Press, 1965. (Grades K-3)

Harlow, Jules, ed. *A Rabbi's Manual.* New York: The Rabbinical Assembly, 1965. (Grades 7 and up)

Isaacs, Ronald H., and Kerry M. Olitzky. *Doing Mitzvot: Mitzvah Projects for Bar/Bat Mitzvah.* Hoboken, NJ: KTAV Publishing House, Inc., 1994, pp. 102-111. (Grades 6-8)

Neusner, Jacob. *Learn Mishnah.* New York: Behrman House, 1978, pp. 64-74. (Grades 5-8)

———. *Learn Talmud.* New York: Behrman House, 1979, pp. 44-84. (Grades 6-9)

Rabbi's Manual. New York: Central Conference of American Rabbis, 1961. (Grades 7 and up)

Topek, Susan. *Ten Good Rules.* Rockville, MD: Kar-Ben Copies, Inc., 1992. (PK-1)

Audiovisual

"Kol Nidre." On the sound recording *Jan Peerce Sings Hebrew Melodies.* Tara Publications. (Grades 4 and up)

Kol Nidrei. A sound recording by Richard Tucker of the songs of the High Holy Days. Tara Publications. (Grades 4 and up)

Not Bearing False Witness

עֵד שָׁקֶר

OVERVIEW

In the Ten Commandments we read: "You shall not bear false witness against your neighbor" (Exodus 20:13 or 16, see also Deuteronomy 5:17 or 20). Maimonides lists seven different Mitzvot related to testifying. These are: the obligation to testify in court, to examine witnesses carefully, and condemn witnesses who testify falsely. In addition, one is prohibited from: bearing false witness, receiving testimony from a wicked person, receiving the testimony of a litigant's relative, and convicting on the testimony of a single witness (*The Commandments* (vol. 1, pp. 191-194 and vol. 2, pp. 266-268).

The severity of breaking the ninth commandment is reflected in this statement from a *midrash* that "One who bears false witness against one's neighbor commits as serious a sin as if one had borne false witness against God, saying that God did not create the world" (*Mechilta* to Exodus 20:13). In fact, if one has been discovered to have given false testimony, the Torah says, "You shall do to him as he schemed to do to his fellow" (Deuteronomy 19:19). Maimonides explains: "If their testimony was calculated to occasion a monetary loss, we are to inflict upon them a loss of equal value; if it was calculated to cause death, they are to suffer the same kind of death" (*The Commandments*, vol. 1, p. 193).

Failing to testify when one is aware of evidence is also considered by some sources to be a serious sin. In *Sefer Hachinuch* one who suppresses testimony is compared to one who stands idly by the blood of one's neighbor (vol. 2, p. 77). The Talmud, however, states that one who fails to testify is not punished by an earthly court, but by God alone (*Baba Kama* 55b-56a). Furthermore, in criminal cases, one is required to come forward on one's own, whereas in civil cases, one need testify only when summoned to do so (*Yad Hazakah, Eidut* 1:1).

In order to determine the veracity of testimony received, judges were given the responsibility of examining witnesses thoroughly. "We must exercise the most scrupulous care, so as not to give an ill-considered and hasty decision, and so harm the

innocent" (*The Commandments*, vol. 1, pp. 192-193). This Mitzvah is based on Deuteronomy 13:13-15, which requires one to investigate carefully a report that someone is trying to persuade others to worship false gods.

Not everyone is considered a competent witness. Among those not qualified according to Maimonides are women, slaves, minors, lunatics, deaf, blind, wicked, the contemptible, relatives and other interested parties (*Yad Hazakah, Eidut* 9:1). According to the Talmud, a woman's place is in the home, not in the court. Maimonides bases the prohibition of women testifying on the fact that the Bible uses the masculine form when speaking of witnesses; Joseph Karo, however, points out that the masculine form is used throughout the Torah. The *Tur*, an important medieval code of Jewish law compiled by Rabbi Jacob ben Asher, omits women from its list of incompetent witnesses. In practice, the testimony of women was admitted when there were no other witnesses available.

Relatives disqualified to testify before a *Bet Din* (Jewish court) are listed in *Sanhedrin* 27b. However, the legal principle *dina demalchuta dina*, the law of the land is the law, would apply with regard to testifying against relatives in a secular court.

While Jewish courts today are involved in a relatively small number of cases, the regulations pertaining to witnesses are still followed in these courts.

ACTIVITIES

Primary

1. Discuss the difference between a tattletale and a witness.

2. Set up a tour of a courthouse for your class. Give students an opportunity to sit in the judge's seat, the jury box, and the witness stand. Discuss what it would be like to testify during a trial. Have the students create a photo journal essay of their trip.

3. Explain to the class the crucial role of honest testimony in the process of justice. Display a

rendition of the scales of justice for your students to examine and discuss. Using self-hardening clay, have students create their own representations of justice.

4. Write a group story about a person who bears false witness. Create the story's introduction for the students to add on to. Call on different students to continue the story, having the students describe the event, the consequences of bearing false witness, and how the situation is resolved. You may wish to record the story on paper and have students illustrate it.

5. Share the following situations with the class:
   a. You are spending the afternoon at your friend Sarah's house. She wants to play with her brother's new radio. You heard both her mother and her brother tell her to leave it alone. Sarah takes you to her brother's room and turns on the radio anyway. She accidentally pulls off a knob. She tries to put it back, but she hears her brother's footsteps. The two of you run out of the room. The brother discovers the broken radio, and accuses you and Sarah. She denies everything. What do you do?
   b. You and your sister are doing a painting project in the kitchen. You forgot to spread newspaper over the tablecloth. The jar of paint spills and makes a great big stain. What do you do? Your sister wants to take the cloth and put it in the washer or stuff it in the clothes hamper. What may happen when your mother or father asks where the tablecloth is?
   c. You see someone take a pack of gum from the candy counter at the supermarket. No one else saw this. What do you do?
      Discuss these situations. Utilize materials from the Overview to include Jewish attitudes in cases such as these.

6. Ask students to research the requirements and duties of a member of a *Bet Din*. Then tell them to imagine that they are functioning as such a person. Have them write a letter or journal entry in which they describe one day's events.

Intermediate

1. Invite an attorney and someone familiar with Jewish law to visit your class. Ask them to make a presentation about being a witness in a court case and being a witness in a case before a Jewish court. Afterward, ask students if the criteria for being a witness in a Jewish court is different from doing so in a civil court. Which is more demanding? Why?

2. In many cities the police department sponsors a crime prevention program. This type of program encourages people to come forward with information relating to crimes they have witnessed. Have class members interview a representative of this organization. Brief the person to emphasize the important role that students' testimony can play in the criminal justice system.

3. The transmission of tradition and learning from one generation to the next is central to Judaism. In a very real sense, previous generations of Jews become witnesses to subsequent generations.
   a. Invite a Holocaust survivor, a freed Soviet Jew, or Ethiopian Jew to share his/her memories and experiences.
   b. Ask your students how they will be witnesses to the next generation of Jews. Each student should write a personal statement (testimony) on this topic.

4. Create a class court to deal with situations, such as name-calling and other disruptive behaviors. Establish rules for testimony, using the Jewish tradition as a guideline (see Overview above, or *Code of Jewish Law*, edited by Solomon Ganzfried, vol. 4, pp. 67-71).

5. The results of someone making false accusations can be serious. Ask students to write an ending to the following incomplete story:

   Anne is a new girl in town. She is from a small farming community and has come to spend the summer with her aunt. Anne is invited to a party to meet other thirteen-year-olds. At the party she begins to make many friends, but one girl, Andrea, becomes very jealous. At one point during the party, the guests take turns playing the piano. Andrea takes off a ring and bracelet to make it easier to play. She sets them on the edge of the piano and forgets them. When she returns to the piano, they are missing. She announces the loss and turns accusingly toward Anne and says, _____.

Read the endings students write and discuss the importance of not bearing false witness.

6. Ask students to think of a situation in which they saw someone do something wrong (cheat on a test, shoplift, etc.). Based on the Mitzvah of *Ayd Shahkeyr*, not giving false testimony, what should a witness do? Use material from the Overview section above to help form a plan of action.

Secondary

1. Distribute copies of the Overview section to each student. Tell them to imagine that they are anthropologists sent to study a group of people which observes the Mitzvah of *Ayd Shahkeyr*. The students are to write a field diary that describes what the values of the culture are (i.e., what is important to them). Remind the students to include biblical and Rabbinic material to support their conclusions.

2. The Rabbis were very concerned about individuals making accusations based on false testimony. Read the following passage from *Sanhedrin* 37b to the class:

What is meant by "based on circumstantial evidence"? The judge says to the witness: "Perhaps you saw a man pursuing his fellow into a ruin. You followed him and found him with sword in hand and blood dripping from it, while the smitten man lay writhing in pain. If this is what you saw, you saw nothing."

Discuss this text. Generate a list of possible scenarios for what really happened. If desired, students can role play the criminal action and then discuss how they might testify.

3. To help students understand the role that testimony plays in the judicial system, arrange a tour to a court which is in session. Request an attorney or other court official to explain the proceedings.

4. Prior to the class session, visit the public library to gather materials on the trials of Nazi war criminals which were conducted a long time after the events occurred (e.g., Eichmann, Demjanjuk, Barbie, etc.). Try to find a different article for each student. Distribute the articles and ask students to summarize them for the rest of the class. Have them also offer their personal comments regarding the accused, the witnesses, and the attorneys. Once each student has made a presentation, hold an open forum discussion on the following issues: Are the witnesses getting too old to testify? Are the defendants too old to prosecute? Can the accused be accurately defended?

5. The novel *The Fixer* by Bernard Malamud is a fictional account of the famous case of Mendel Beilis who was wrongfully accused of blood libel charges. Read and discuss the novel. View the film *The Fixer*. Consider the following questions: What role does false testimony play in the story? Why is the testimony believed?

6. According to Jewish law, among those unfit to serve as witnesses are the blind and the deaf. Contact local agencies who deal with the blind and the deaf to do some awareness programs with your students. Discuss whether or not those who are deaf or blind should be excluded from offering testimony in all cases, or only in certain cases. Write a set of guidelines.

All-School Programs

1. At an assembly, ask students if they think it is difficult to be a witness. Take a vote by show of hands. Arrange for two or three individuals to put on a short role play which contains elements of disagreement and controversy. Instruct students to watch the role play and, when the scene is over, to write down what they witnessed. Ask for volunteers to read what they wrote. Discuss similarities and differences in the compositions. Take another vote on the initial question: Is it difficult to be a witness?

2. Invite a police investigator or a defense attorney or a prosecuting attorney to function as a panel of experts to discuss circumstantial evidence and other types of courtroom evidence.

3. Organize a *Bet Din*. Invite three Rabbis to sit as the judges. Each class (from Grade 3 up) writes a scenario of a case. Then assign parts to class members, who present their case to the *Bet Din*.

The other classes may sit as interested community members until their respective cases are called. The Rabbis render judgments utilizing Jewish sources. (If you live in a community with only one Rabbi, ask the Rabbi to recommend other qualified individuals to participate on the *Bet Din*.)

RESOURCES

For the Teacher

Ganzfried, Solomon. *Code of Jewish Law: Kitzur Shulhan Arukh*. rev. ed. Hyman E. Goldin, trans. Rockaway Beach, NY: Hebrew Publishing Co., 1991, vol. 4, ch. 181, pp. 67-81.

Leibowitz, Nehama. *Studies in Shemot (The Book of Exodus)*. Jerusalem: The World Zionist Organization, 1976, pp. 334-341.

Maimonides, Moses. *The Commandments*. New York: The Soncino Press, 1967, vol. 1, pp. 191-194, vol. 2, pp. 266-268.

"Witness." In *Encyclopaedia Judaica*. Jerusalem: Keter Publishing House Jerusalem Ltd., 1972, vol. 16, cols. 584-590.

For the Students

Malamud, Bernard. *The Fixer*. New York: Viking Penguin, 1994. (Grades 9 and up)

Bet Din: *The Jewish People's Court*. Los Angeles: Torah Aura Productions, 1984. (Grades 6 and up)

Audiovisual

The Demjanjuk Trial: A Moment in History. A 15 minute video of the trial of John Demjanjuk, who was accused of hiding his Nazi past. Anti-Defamation League. (Grades 7 and up)

The Fixer. A 132 minute film which is a fictional account of the case of Mendel Beilis, who was wrongfully accused of blood libel charges in Russia. Facets Multimedia, Inc. (Grade 7 and up)

Kitty: Return to Auschwitz. An 82 minute film about a survivor of Auschwitz who returns 35 years later with her son to serve as a witness to him about her experience. Simon Wiesenthal Center. (Grades 7 and up)

UNIT 18

Not Gossiping

לְשׁוֹן הָרַע

OVERVIEW

According to the Talmud, *Lashon Hara* harms three persons: the speaker, the listener, and the person spoken about (*Arachin* 15b). *Lashon Hara* (literally the evil tongue) refers to a broad range of spoken comments, including both slander and gossip. Jewish writings from the biblical period and onward strongly condemn *Lashon Hara*. The Bible states: "You must not carry false rumors" (Exodus 23:1) and "You shall not go about as a talebearer among your people" (Leviticus 19:16).

The Rabbis point to a number of examples of *Lashon Hara* in the Torah. These include the serpent which urged Eve to eat of the fruit of the tree of knowledge of good and evil (Genesis 3:4-5); Sarah, when she spoke about Abraham's advanced age and laughed at the thought of him fathering a child (Genesis 18:12-15); Joseph bringing evil reports about his brothers to their father (Genesis 37:2); and Miriam and Aaron speaking against Moses because of his Cushite wife (Numbers 12:2). In addition, according to the Talmud, the generation of the Exodus was doomed because its members listened to slander — the reports of the ten spies who warned against entering the land of Canaan.

The Psalmist cautions us: "Keep your tongue from evil and your lips from speaking guile" (Psalms 34:14). Biblical and post-biblical wisdom literature depicts the influence of language: "Death and life are in the power of the tongue" (Proverbs 18:21); "If you hear something said, let it die with you" (*Ben Sira* 19:10); "Many have fallen by the edge of the sword, but not so many as have fallen by the tongue (*Ecclesiasticus* 28:18).

The Rabbis use especially strong language in speaking against *Lashon Hara*, considering it equivalent in malevolence to idolatry, incest, and murder. A person who engages in it is comparable to one who denies the fundamental principles of Judaism (*Arachin* 15b). To emphasize just how far a rumor can spread, a *midrash* teaches, "What is spoken in Rome, may kill in Syria" (*Beresheet Rabbah* 98:23). Indeed, the Rabbis go so far as to declare that the destruction of Jerusalem resulted from false charges brought to the Roman authorities by a disgruntled individual who was insulted by his neighbor (*Gittin* 65a).

Perhaps for such a reason, the Rabbis taught that among those who engaged in *Lashon Hara*, an informer was considered the most wicked. As if to discover or at least to counteract the informers, a nineteenth blessing was added to the *Amidah*. Still recited in synagogues throughout the world, this blessing was directed against Jewish sectarians in the generation after the destruction of the Second Temple. It reads in part: "Slanderers shall not have hope, and may all who do evil perish in an instant, let all of them quickly be cut off [from the Jewish people]." As if to lend additional emphasis, another prayer related to this theme follows the *Amidah*. It reads: "My God, guard my tongue from (speaking) evil and my lips from speaking falsely. And to those who curse me, may my soul be silent" (*Berachot* 17a).

In addition to condemning *Lashon Hara*, the Talmud offers advice on how to avoid it: don't socialize with friends who gossip; study Torah and examine your own faults. Maimonides said that one should not speak disparagingly of anyone, even if what one says is true. *The Code of Jewish Law*, vol. 1, pp. 97-98 lists a number of examples of *Lashon Hara*:

Saying that a person did an evil thing.
Saying that a person's ancestors were non-Jews.
Saying "I have heard this about him."
Saying "I don't want to discuss what happened to him."
Praising a person in the presence of his enemies (because the latter would be tempted to respond with slander).

In the modern era, Rabbi Yisrael Meir Kahan wrote extensively on the subject. His work entitled *Chafetz Chaim* (to cherish life), covering the laws of evil gossip and slander, made such a profound impact on its readers that the author has since been known as the Chafetz Chaim.

ACTIVITIES

Primary

1. Play "telephone" to demonstrate how gossip can start. With students sitting in a circle, whisper a statement to the person to your left. Each person in turn whispers what he/she heard to the next person. The last person then announces aloud what he/she heard. Discuss what happened to the information. Why did it happen? What happens in real life situations when information gets passed from one person to the next? Listen for the students to identify things such as exaggeration, forgetting important facts, misinformation, etc. Explain the Jewish commandment not to gossip.

2. Provide the students with pieces of felt in a variety of colors. Have them make book marks which will remind them not to gossip or slander others.

3. Read Genesis, Chapter 37, the story about Joseph to the students. They will learn that when Joseph was 17 years old, he helped his brothers watch the sheep. Joseph often gave his father Jacob bad reports about his brothers. Point out that the Torah does not tell us whether or not Joseph was telling the truth about his brothers. The Torah does tell us that Jacob loved Joseph more than his other sons, and that, therefore, the brothers were unfriendly toward Joseph. Ask the following questions: How do you think the brothers felt? Whether or not the reports were true, should Joseph have spoken badly about his brothers? Are you ever in a situation when you could bring bad reports about someone they know to a teacher, parent, or others? When is it appropriate and when should you keep silent? Should Joseph have kept silent? If he had kept silent, might things have been better between his brothers and himself? Do you ever keep silent about certain situations in order to keep friendships?

4. Ask the students how they feel when someone says something about them that isn't true. Give examples, such as "You hit someone" or "You were talking when you were supposed to be quiet." Ask: What should one do if this happens?

5. Read to your class "The Gossip" from *Who Knows Ten?* by Molly Cone. Questions to

discuss: What did the woman do that was wrong? How were people hurt by what she said? What did the Rabbi tell her to do? How were the feathers in the pillow like the woman's gossip?

6. Read "Yossel and the Tree" in *Lessons from Our Living Past* by Jules Harlow. Discuss the questions at the end of the story. Also discuss how Yossel's behavior reflects the Mitzvah of Not Gossiping.

Intermediate

1. An actual event often provides the basis for a story which is told and retold. In the retelling facts get changed and information gets added. Provide students with the kernel of an idea. In order to make a whole story, each student must imagine the details that have not been included. Use this idea or one of your own:

    The police receive a call that there is a robbery in progress at the local grocery store. They race to the store where they find the janitor apparently emptying out one of the cash registers.

    Give students a few minutes to complete the story. Have some or all of the students read their stories aloud. Point out how significant differences emerge from the same story. Relate this to gossip and discuss.

2. Based on the students' understanding of *Lashon Hara*, have each create an artistic interpretation of it. Let them illustrate the idea of *Lashon Hara* in clay. Use a self-hardening type available in most art supply stores.

3. Direct the students to write a Public Service Announcement which is a statement against *Lashon Hara*. This might become a part of a radio show broadcast the students put on for the religious school.

4. Convene a session of a "Jewish Congress" at which student delegates create anti-*Lashon Hara* legislation.

5. Have the students think of situations in which they or someone they know slandered another person. Instruct each student to write about what happened, using a pseudonym for the person. Ask them to include how they would change the

circumstances and the results. Also, if faced with the same situation, find out what others in the class would do.

6. Help the students to understand the differences between rumor, gossip, and slander. After briefly explaining each word, read the following examples and ask the class to identify (by a show of hands) whether each is rumor, gossip, or slander.
   a. A friend tells you that she thinks another student in the class has a crush on you. (gossip)
   b. A newspaper falsely reports that a politician has been stealing money. (slander)
   c. Three students tell you there is going to be a surprise spelling test. (rumor)
   d. Although he has not eaten at the restaurant, a man says that the food there is awful. (slander)
   e. You overhear that someone got in trouble and you tell three friends. (gossip)
   f. Your mother says she heard that the circus is coming to town. (rumor)

7. Ask students to write a description from two points of view, negative and positive, about someone they know, either a family member, a friend, or an acquaintance. Discuss and evaluate the descriptions. Ask how one's point of view may color one's feelings about someone. How might one's attitude lead to gossip or slander?

Secondary

1. Bring to class a copy of the daily newspaper and copies of weekly magazines such as *People, Time,* and *Newsweek,* a biography of a notable individual, a copy of the *National Enquirer,* etc., enough so that each class member has a different source. Have the students read their sources and find an article which contains an example of *Lashon Hara.* Discuss the following issues: Is it possible to publish print materials like these and not slander or gossip about an individual? Should people, particularly those in the public eye, simply accept things like this as part of modern day life? Should the media control what is written?

2. Extend activity #1 by tracing the same story in a variety of print sources. Compare how different publications treat the same story. Could *Lashon Hara* be more harmful depending on the writer's

outlook or the publishing style of a magazine or newspaper?

3. Read through the prayer directed at slanderers found as part of the weekday *Amidah.* If necessary, call upon the Rabbi, Cantor, or Director of Education to help you find it. Read it in both Hebrew and English if possible. Discuss the theme of this prayer.

4. Extend activity #3 by having the students create their own prayer of repentance regarding gossip or slander.

5. Our tradition says that when one hears gossip, one should bury it seven fathoms deep. Brainstorm with the students ways they might respond to hearing *Lashon Hara.*

6. Present the following situation to the class: Your school has a school newspaper and your class has the responsibility to write the gossip column. When the first column is written, and it is obvious that some people's feelings are going to be hurt and that some other people are going to be embarrassed. Discuss whether or not the column should run in the paper. Then tell the students that the decision is not to run the column and that they need to compose an article explaining why, according to Jewish tradition, such a column is inappropriate. The article can be written individually or in small groups.

ALL-SCHOOL PROGRAMS

1. One of the greatest slanders against the Jewish people in modern times was the "Zionism is Racism" resolution passed by the United Nations General Assembly in 1975. The American section of the International Association of Jewish Lawyers and Jurists began Project CASAZ (Combat Anti-Semitism and Anti-Zionism) in order to work toward the repudiation of this resolution. Obtain information about Project CASAZ from P.O. Box 65784, Washington, D.C. 20035. Develop a program to inform your congregation about this project.

2. Establish a *Bet Din* to try the case of a gossiper. Students create the scenario and take the parts of the accused, the accuser, the three Rabbis of the *Bet Din,* the defense attorney, and prosecutor.

3. Hold a *kibbutz*-style town meeting to deal with the following make-believe situation. On *Kibbutz Rodef Yirakot*, there is a disgruntled member, Yosi, who feels that his fellow *kibbutzniks* do not treat him with enough respect. Yosi recently lost the election for treasurer of the *kibbutz*, so he started a rumor that the *kibbutz* water supply is contaminated. The rumor spread rapidly. The *kibbutz* council calls a general meeting to try and get to the bottom of this. Role play and discuss the situation and its resolution. Did the commandment not to gossip come into play in the decision making process?

4. Several films use the theme of the destructive power of rumor, slander, and gossip. View and discuss one or more of those films listed below:

References: *Rumor; Three Sovereigns for Sister Sarah; Gentleman's Agreement.*

RESOURCES

For the Teacher

Bloch, Abraham P. *A Book of Jewish Ethical Concepts.* New York: KTAV Publishing House, Inc., 1984, pp. 148-152.

Goldberger, Moshe. *A Review Guide to the Laws of Proper Speech Based on Sefer Chofetz Chayim.* New York: Eichler Publications, 1986.

"Lashon Hara." In *Encyclopaedia Judaica.* Jerusalem: Keter Publishing House Jerusalem Ltd., 1972, vol. 10, cols. 1432-1433.

Maimonides, Moses. *The Commandments.* New York: Soncino Press, 1967, vol. 2, pp. 239, 280.

"Shofar." *Encyclopaedia Judaica.* Jerusalem: Keter Publishing House Jerusalem Ltd., 1972, vol. 14, cols. 1651-1652.

Stern, Jay B. *Syllabus for the Teaching of Mitzvah.* New York:United Synagogue Commission on Jewish Education, 1986, pp. 148-154.

Telushkin, Joseph. *Words That Hurt, Words That Heal.* New York: William Morrow, 1996.

Wylan, Stephen M. *Gossip: The Power of the Word.* Hoboken, NJ: KTAV Publishing House, Inc., 1993.

For the Students

Artson, Bradley Shavit. *It's a Mitzvah: Step-by-Step to Jewish Living.* West Orange, NJ: Behrman House and New York: The Rabbinical Assembly, 1995, pp. 148-157. (Grades 8-adult)

Baum, Eli. *Mitzvot Bein Adam Lachaveiro.* New York: KTAV Publishing House, Inc., 1980, pp. 48-50. (Grades 3-6)

Cone, Molly. *Who Knows Ten?* New York: UAHC Press, 1971. (Grades K-3)

Harlow, Judes, ed. *Lesson from Our Living Past.* West Orange, NJ: Behrman House, 1972. (Grades K-4)

Kaye, Joan S.; Jan Rabinowitch; and Naomi F. Towvim. *Why Be Good? Sensitivities and Ethics in Rabbinic Literature.* Boston: Bureau of Jewish Education of Greater Boston, 1985, pp. 57-67. (Grades 7 and up)

Prager, Janice, and Arlene Lepoff. *Why Be Different? A Look into Judaism.* West Orange, NJ: Behrman House, 1986, pp. 60-65. (Grades 6-8)

Sugarman, Morris. *Ethical Literature.* West Orange, NJ: Behrman House, 1987, pp. 11-14.

Audiovisual

For Goodness Sake! A 29 minute video in which Dennis Prager speaks about the fact that people are not always good and considers how some people include goodness in their lives. Ultimate Issues. (Grades 7-adult, includes teacher guide)

Gossip. In this 17 minute video, two teens see two other teens hugging and assume they are romantically involved. They spread the "gossip" and have to come to terms with what they said. Filmfair Communications. (Grades 7-10)

Jacob the Liar. A 95 minute German film with English subtitles about a rumor that spreads throughout the ghetto that Russian forces will soon liberate Warsaw. Facets Multimedia, Inc. (Grades 9 and up)

Rumor Clinic. A 5½ minute trigger film that traces the course of a rumor. Anti-Defamation League. (Grades 3 and up)

School Ties. A 107 minute study of persecution of a teenage boy by his peers. Rated PG for profanity. Available from video stores. (Grades 7 and up)

Studying Torah

תַּלְמוּד תּוֹרָה

OVERVIEW

Jews have been referred to as the "People of the Book," a term which reflects the centrality of the Torah to Judaism. In fact, it has been said that Judaism was the first religion to make the knowledge of sacred scripture the responsibility of everyone, rather than of religious leaders only. It should then come as no surprise that *Talmud Torah*, the study of Torah, is a Mitzvah. Actually, *Talmud Torah* refers not only to the study of the Torah, but to all Jewish study. The following *Mishnah* indicates the importance of *Talmud Torah*.

"These are the things whose fruits a person enjoys in this world while the capital remains for the person in the world to come: honoring father and mother, acts of lovingkindness . . . making peace between a person and one's friend. But the study of Torah is equal to them all" (*Peah* 1:1).

One reason that *Talmud Torah* was considered so significant was that it would lead a person to observe other Mitzvot. The Rabbis of the Talmud considered the question: "Which is greater, study or practice?" Rabbi Tarfon answered that practice is greater. But Rabbi Akiba insisted that study is greater, because it leads to practice. The majority agreed with Rabbi Akiba.

The *Beit Hamidrash* (house of study) is considered to be of greater sanctity than the *Beit Haknesset* (synagogue). In reality, the house of study and the synagogue were often one and the same. A group could move from study to prayer with minimal interruption. The worship service itself contains both prayer and study. One of the best known prayers, the *Kaddish*, was first used at the end of study sessions.

The scriptural basis for the Mitzvah of *Talmud Torah* is the first paragraph of the *Sh'ma* which commands us to teach the words of Torah to our children, and to speak of them in our homes, and on our way, upon rising in the morning, and before going to bed.

The Pharisees, the forerunners of Rabbinic Judaism about 2000 years ago, are credited with introducing universal Torah study into Judaism and making it central. During the first five centuries of this era, great academies were established at such places as Yavneh and the Galilee in Palestine, and Sura, Nehardea, and Pumbedita in Babylonia.

In the Middle Ages, Western Europe became the center of Jewish scholarship, with important academies in Paris, Troyes, Narbonne, Metz, Worms, Speyer, Altona, Cordoba, Barcelona, and Toledo. Beginning in the sixteenth century, the migration of Jews to Eastern Europe led to the establishment of many important academies there. During much of this period, *Talmud Torah* as conducted in the academies was primarily the study of Talmud, particularly its legal intricacies. The ideal approach to study was referred to as *Torah Lishmah*, study for its own sake.

Traditionally, it is the responsibility of the father to teach his son Torah, but usually a *melamed* (teacher) was hired or students were sent to *cheder* (a one room school). According to the Talmud, one was not supposed to move to a town that did not have a teacher.

In Eastern Europe particularly, the beginning of one's Jewish education was a special occasion. "A boy's first visit to a classroom and the first lessons he received were traditionally enveloped in emotion and ceremony. Dressed in new clothes, the child was carried to the schoolroom by a Rabbi or learned man. There he received a clean slate on which letters of the Hebrew alphabet or a simple biblical verse had been written in honey. The child licked off the slate while reciting the name of each letter, and afterward he ate treats of honey cake, apples, and nuts — all aimed at making his introduction to his studies sweet and tempting" (*Voices of Wisdom: Jewish Ideals and Ethics for Everyday Living* by Francine Klagsbrun, p. 245).

During the Enlightenment period in Germany, a new approach to study was introduced — *der Wissenschaft des Judentums*, the Science of Judaism. Using insights from such fields as archaeology and linguistics, the Bible and other texts were looked at in a new light. While most traditional Jews rejected this approach to study, it remains a widely used approach in the non-Orthodox community.

ACTIVITIES

Primary

1. To reinforce the value of study, teach your class the song "People of the Book" by Cantor Jeffrey Klepper. Find it on the album *To See the World Through Jewish Eyes*, Volume II.

2. A popular Hebrew song (based on a saying from *Pirke Avot*), "Al Shelosha Devarim" translates as: "The world stands on three things: On Torah, on worship, and on deeds of lovingkindness."
   a. Discuss with the students how each of these elements serves as a foundation for our Jewish world.
   b. Work with the Cantor or song leader to learn the song. (It can be found in many Hebrew songbooks.)
   c. Have students write a skit or play about the Mitzvah of *Talmud Torah* using this song as a jumping-off point.

3. Have each student design a cover for a *Chumash* (Pentateuch in book format). Suggest that they use pictures and words which relate to the Mitzvah of *Talmud Torah*. The theme for the book covers could be: "We Are the People of the Book." If funds are available, small size Bibles or other appropriate books of your choice can be issued to each student and their book covers would then be designed to fit these books.

4. Have each student start a word bank consisting of words about Judaism and the importance of study to Jews. To help them begin, discuss the students' past Jewish experiences. Provide pencils, index cards, and a box or other container for their cards.

   One engaging way to utilize the words in the word bank is to make peek-a-boo cards. Use the cards for several sessions or throughout the school year, encouraging students to add (make deposits) to their word banks on a regular basis.

   Materials needed: 5" x 8" index cards.

   Procedure: Fold the index cards in half. On the outer front flap, write a brief description of a Jewish practice, ritual object, or value. On the inside flap, write a matching description. Have the students test each other's "Jewish I.Q." using these cards. (Example: On the front of the card write "Havdalah candle." On the inside write "Many wicks are twisted together.")

5. There is a well known saying from Proverbs 3:18 which reads: "It [the Torah] is a tree of life to those who hold fast to it, and all of its supporters are happy." This may be a difficult image for the students to understand. Create your own tree of life with your class.

   Materials needed: Large sheet of paper, tempera paints, pens.

   Procedure: Draw a tree with many branches on the sheet of paper. The trunk can take the shape of a Torah scroll. Create leaves by using tempera paint to make handprints on the branches. On each child's handprint, write his or her Hebrew and English name. Learn and sing the song "The Torah" on the album *To See the World Through Jewish Eyes*, Volume II.

6. Create a bulletin board which will convey and reinforce the message that Jewish learning is the key to fulfilling the Mitzvot.

   Materials needed: Construction paper, felt markers.

   Procedure: Make a door out of construction paper and tack it on one side of the bulletin board. Make sure the knob and key hole are prominent. Cut out several pieces of brightly colored construction paper in the shape of keys. One the keys write important Jewish teachings and sayings. Place the keys on the bulletin board opposite the doorway.

7. Invite the Rabbi to visit your classroom for a study session (on a predetermined topic) and/or an "Ask the Rabbi" period. Discuss with the Rabbi why study is a Mitzvah.

Intermediate

1. Following are citations for quotes from *Pirke Avot* on the subject of education: chapter 1, sections 4, 6, 12, 13, 15, 16; chapter 2, sections 2, 5, 9, 17, 19; chapter 3, section 21; chapter 4, section 6; chapter 5, section 18. Using these quotations as a basis, have students create a poster series for display in the synagogue.

   Reference: *As a Tree by the Water: Pirkey Avot* by Reuven P. Bulka. (Note: Other versions of *Pirke Avot* may number the sections differently, so you may need to read through the material to find those with references to education.)

2. Help students to understand that the concept of *Talmud Torah* came into being about 2000 years

ago. Utilize maps to identify those locations where Jewish academies were established during the first five centuries of the Common Era (see Overview section above). Find out if those cities still exist, what their modern names are, and if they still have significant Jewish populations.

Reference: *Atlas of Jewish History* by Martin Gilbert.

3. The *Sh'ma* and *V'ahavta* contain the scriptural basis for study. Have students learn to read or chant this prayer in Hebrew or English.

Reference: *Hebrew Prayers Ditto Pak* by Frances Borovetz, pp. 10-12.

4. Tell students that they have been asked by the Board of Trustees of the synagogue (1) to improve the image of their Hebrew School/Religious School and (2) to help others to understand that, as students of Judaism, the religious school students are performing the Mitzvah of *Talmud Torah*. Their first assignment is to design a school T-shirt. Suggest they use Jewish sources for ideas (Torah, *Pirke Avot*, Jewish quotation books, etc.). Select the best design, or create a composite of one or more designs. Have T-shirts made and then sell them to the students. (The shirts may be made by a local T-shirt imprinting company, or the designs can be silkscreened onto plain colored shirts by the students themselves with help from someone who knows how.)

   Brainstorm with students other ways to carry out their charge from the synagogue Board.

5. There are many notable Jewish teachers who have made significant contributions to Jewish life and practice. Have students create a reference kit on all-star Jewish teachers. Include a short biography of each person and, when possible, pictures, copies of their books, and a listing of their accomplishment. A few suggestions are: Moses, Yochanan ben Zakkai, Joseph Caro, Maimonides, Nachmanides, Rashi, Penina Moise, Nahama Leibowitz, and your own Rabbi and Director of Education.

6. Have students create an illustrated banner utilizing the quotation from *Peah* in the Overview section above, "These are the things whose fruits . . ."

Secondary

1. Have the students reenact the debate described in the Overview section above between Rabbi Tarfon and Rabbi Akiba over the question: Is study or practice the greater Mitzvah?

2. Direct the students to create a skit which exemplifies the ideas in the quotation "These are the things whose fruits . . . ." The complete quote may be found in the Overview section above.

3. Assign the students to interview professionals in the Jewish community (i.e., individuals who work for a synagogue, Jewish Community Center, Federation, Jewish Family Service, etc.) to find out what course of study is required for their particular job. The students can also inquire about the Jewish backgrounds of these individuals and find out what led them to work for the Jewish community.

4. Have the students research which colleges offer courses in Jewish studies by writing for information from various schools. (The reference listed below will be of invaluable assistance.) Using the information and materials they collect, create a display for the hallway of the religious school. This kind of information can play a big part in a high school senior's choice of colleges.

Reference: *Jewish Life on Campus*, published by B'nai B'rith Hillel Foundation.

5. Sometimes the best way to learn something is to teach it to someone else. Assign each student as an aide to a teacher in your religious school. The aide's job is to find out what the class is studying, pick one aspect of it to teach (in consultation with the teacher of the class he/she will teach), create a lesson plan (with your help), and carry it out. Discuss the experience in a follow-up session, asking how it felt to be the facilitator for others as they are involved in *Talmud Torah*.

6. With the students create a curriculum of age-appropriate study for today's religious school based on the following quote from *Pirke Avot* 5:21. "Judah ben Tema used to say: 'The age of readiness for the study of scripture is five years; for the study of *Mishnah*, ten years; for fulfilling

the Mitzvot, 13 years, for the study of 'Talmud, 15 years . . . .'" Students can create a list of possibilities for a curriculum of age-appropriate studies and then divide up the subjects and assign age groups to them. Encourage the students to remember what interested them at each particular age, as well as what can be understood by students at that age.

ALL-SCHOOL PROGRAMS

1. Plan a special recognition for the teachers in the Hebrew and Religious School of your synagogue. This might include a worship service, special awards or presentations, and/or a *Seudah Mitzvah,* a celebratory feast.

2. At an assembly program, teach the song *"La'asok B'divre Torah"* by Kol B'Seder and *"Talmud Torah K'neged Kulam"* by Craig Taubman. Both may be found on the audiocassette *American Nusach Concert.*

3. Plan a sweet welcome for students on the first day of school by greeting each of them with a basket or bag of sweets, fruit, and nuts. As these are handed out, tell the students you hope their year of study will be as sweet as these treats. If desired, a more elaborate welcome assembly can be planned in addition. Later, in class, explain that, traditionally, honey was put on the page to make learning sweet for young beginning learners. Brainstorm with the class other ways of making the Mitzvah of *Talmud Torah* sweet.

RESOURCES

For the Teacher

"A Love for Learning." In *Kings and Things: 20 Plays for Jewish Kids from 8 to 18* by Meridith Shaw Patera. Denver: A.R.E. Publishing, Inc., 1996.

"An Old Young Student." In *Lively Legends — Jewish Values: An Early Childhood Teaching Guide* by Miriam P. Feinberg and Rena Rotenberg. Denver: A.R.E. Publishing, Inc., 1993.

Gilbert, Martin. *Atlas of Jewish History.* New York: William Morrow, 1993.

"The Good Teacher." In *Lively Legends — Jewish Values: An Early Childhood Teaching Guide* by Miriam P. Feinberg and Rena Rotenberg. Denver: A.R.E. Publishing, Inc., 1993.

Hertz, Joseph H. *Pirke Aboth: Sayings of the Fathers.* West Orange, NJ: Behrman House, 1945.

Jacobs, Louis. West Orange, NJ: Behrman House, 1987, pp. 4-11.

Loeb, Sorel Goldberg, and Barbara Binder Kadden. *Teaching Torah: A Treasury of Insights and Activities.* Denver: A.R.E. Publishing, Inc., 1984.

Strassfeld, Sharon, and Michael Strassfeld, comps. and eds. *The Second Jewish Catalog.* Philadelphia: The Jewish Publication Society of America, 1976, pp. 176-261.

"Study." In *Encyclopaedia Judaica.* Jerusalem: Keter Publishing House Jerusalem, Ltd., 1972, vol. 15, cols. 453-460.

For the Students

Artson, Bradley Shavit. *It's a Mitzvah: Step-by-Step to Jewish Living.* West Orange, NJ: Behrman House and New York: The Rabbinical Assembly, 1995, pp. 158-173. (Grades 8-adult)

Bogot, Howard I., and Daniel B. Syme. *Books Are Treasures.* New York: UAHC Press, 1982. (Grades PK-2)

Borovetz, Frances. *Hebrew Prayers Ditto Pak.* Denver: A.R.E. Publishing, Inc., 1980. (Grades 4-7)

Cone, Molly. *About Learning.* New York: UAHC Press, 1972. (Grades 1-3)

Gersh, Harry. *Midrash: Rabbinic Lore.* New York: Behrman House, 1985. (Grades 9 and up)

Isaacs, Ronald H., and Kerry M. Olitzky. *Doing Mitzvot: Mitzvah Projects for Bar/Bat Mitzvah.* Hoboken, NJ: KTAV Publishing House, Inc., 1994, pp. 63-74. (Grades 6-8)

Kippur, Leonore C., and Bogot, Howard I. *The Alef-Bet of Jewish Values: Code Words of Jewish Life.* New York: UAHC Press, 1985, pp. 42-43. (Grades 3-6)

Audiovisual

The Mitzvah Machine. A 10 minute animated film centering around the Bar/Bat Mitzvah ceremony that deals with the nature of Mitzvah in Jewish life. United Synagogue Commission on Jewish Education. (Grades 6 and up)

To See the World through Jewish Eyes, Volume II. Sound recording. Includes songs on Torah, God, and prayer. UAHC Press. (Grades 1-3)

Yentl. A 134 minute video about a girl who disguises herself as a boy in order to enter the world of Jewish study. Available at many video stores. (Grades 7 and up)

OVERVIEW

The word *Tzedakah* is difficult to translate precisely. Many use the word charity, but that is from the Latin word *caritas*, meaning love or dearness, whereas *Tzedakah* is a religious duty. Similarly, the word philanthropy is from two Greek words meaning "love of man." The Hebrew root of *Tzedakah* means justice and righteousness. *Tzedakah* is not something one does out of the goodness of one's heart, but rather out of one's sense of responsibility toward God and toward one's fellow human beings.

We are taught that because God created the world, everything ultimately belongs to God. We are caretakers of what we possess (even our own bodies) and, therefore, are not permitted to do whatever we wish with our possessions. Every human being, as a person created in God's image, is entitled to have his or her basic needs met. If one cannot meet those needs, then it is the community's responsibility to help out. A person who has been blessed by God with more than enough to meet one's own needs is obligated to share that blessing with others. *Tzedakah* is required even of the poorest of persons, so that all might enjoy the satisfaction of fulfilling this Mitzvah.

A number of provisions for the practice of *Tzedakah* are delineated in the Torah. For example, the corners of one's field and the gleanings thereof are to be left for the poor and the stranger (Leviticus 19:9-10, see chapter 21, "Leaving the Gleanings"). During the *shmitah* (sabbatical year), the land was to lie fallow and the needy were permitted to eat from it (Exodus 23:10-11). In addition, debts were cancelled and land was to be returned to its original owner in order to prevent indebtedness. The Torah commands that "you open your hand to the poor and needy kinsman in your land" (Deuteronomy 15:11).

The prophets developed the theme of helping the poor. In a passage read as the Haftarah on Yom Kippur, Israel is told that the fast God desires "is to share your bread with the hungry, and to take the wretched poor into your home; when you see the naked, to clothe them . . . ." (Isaiah 58:7). Isaiah and Ezekiel insist that *Tzedakah* is necessary for a life of piety. And, in the Book of Proverbs, a woman of valor is one who "stretches forth her hand to the poor" (31:20).

The Rabbis spoke of *Tzedakah* in the highest terms. It is as important as all of the other Mitzvot combined and atones for sin (*Baba Batra* 9a). It hastens redemption (*Baba Batra* 10a), and can even save one from death. "One who gives even a *prutah* to the poor is privileged to sense God's presence" (*Baba Batra* 10a). The Talmud also contains guidelines for contributing *Tzedakah*. Giving one-tenth of one's income is average, one-twentieth miserly; no one should give so much as to become impoverished. How one gives is also important. For example, one shouldn't give in a way that would shame the recipient.

Maimonides developed an elaborate schema delineating eight levels of *Tzedakah*: The highest level is to give a person a job or enter into a business partnership with the person so that he or she will be able to do without the need for receiving *Tzedakah*. The second highest level is to give to the poor in such a way that neither the donor nor the recipient knows the identity of one another. Third, the donor knows the recipient, but the recipient does not know the donor. Fourth, the recipient knows the donor, but the donor does not know the recipient. Fifth is giving directly to a poor person without being asked. Sixth is giving after being asked. Seventh is giving cheerfully but less than one should. The eighth and lowest level of *Tzedakah* is giving grudgingly. (Maimonides, *Yad Hazakot, Matnot Aniyim* 10:7-14).

Other guidelines regarding *Tzedakah* are found in the works of Maimonides, in the *Shulchan Aruch*, and in other collections of Jewish literature. Among them are: Give to the non-Jewish poor as well as to the Jewish poor in order to preserve good relations; a *Bet Din* can compel a person to give *Tzedakah*; in receiving *Tzedakah* women take precedence over men, relatives over strangers, the poor of one's own town over the poor of another town, and the poor of the land of Israel over all other lands.

Maimonides points to the pervasiveness of this Mitzvah by noting that he had not heard of a Jewish community without a charity fund. Such a fund was often called a *kuppah*, and was run by charity wardens who would go door to door just prior to Shabbat. It is a tradition to put *Tzedakah* coins in a *pushke* before Shabbat or a holiday.

Another tradition is to give money to someone going on a trip as *Tzedakah* to donate at their destination. This practice may have originated because of the belief that God would watch over one who was traveling to perform a Mitzvah.

Within the last century, we have seen the emergence of social welfare agencies and centralized fund-raising in Jewish communities throughout the world. Professional fund-raisers are responsible for raising millions of dollars to aid Jews in local communities as well as in Israel and around the world. Jews are often disproportionately represented in fund-raising efforts to benefit the general welfare. While the methods for raising *Tzedakah* have changed in our time, the practice of *Tzedakah* remains central to the Jewish experience.

ACTIVITIES

Primary

1. Encourage families to give *Tzedakah* each week prior to lighting Shabbat candles. Students can construct their own *Tzedakah* boxes, decorating a box or container with a slit cut for dropping in coins.
   Reference: *100+ Jewish Art Projects for Children* by Nina Streisand Sher and Margaret Feldman.

2. Many organizations have established food pantries and soup kitchens for the needy. One area is often neglected: the giving of personal toiletries. Generate a list of personal care items that an individual might need. Brainstorm how students might be able to acquire these supplies to donate to a shelter for the homeless. Once a course of action is decided upon, follow through with the collection and donation.

3. The giving of *Tzedakah* consists of more than supplying food and clothing to the less fortunate. The students can make tray favors and deliver them to a nursing home. The favors might be for a specific holiday or celebration.
   Reference: *100+ Jewish Art Projects for Children* by Nina Streisand Sher and Margaret Feldman.

4. It your synagogue has not begun a canned food drive, organize one with your students. The

giving of an item of food each week may be in addition to the collection of *Tzedakah* money.

5. Conduct a "Proud Whip" with your students. Each student, in turn, should complete the following statement: "When it comes to *Tzedakah*, I am proud that _____."

6. Tell your students the following story.

A New Song
It was the custom among a group of Chasidim to learn a new song each year. They sang their new song while celebrating the holiday of Simchat Torah. One year a storekeeper said that he had learned a new melody. Everyone wanted to hear how he had learned it. The Rabbi told him to share his story. So the storekeeper began.

"One day a peasant came to my store. He had bought things from me before, but on that day I hardly recognized him. He told me his crops had failed, that his wife had recently had a baby, and that his family was hungry. He had no one left to ask for help except me. The peasant asked if he could have half a sack of flour. He hoped he could repay me by the end of the summer. I said of course, and measured out a half a sack of flour. The peasant thanked me and left. I thought over the situation. Why hadn't I given him a full sack? So I decided to give him the rest. I ran after him and, as I approached him, he was singing a beautiful, joyful tune. I gave him the flour and he was overcome with happiness. I left him the flour, but the melody stayed with me. This is the Simchat Torah song I want to share with you."

Discuss the following questions: What was the storekeeper's payment for giving the flour? The melody stayed with the storekeeper. What kind of feeling do you think this gave him? How do you feel when you give *Tzedakah*? How did the rest of the Chasidim benefit from the peasant's act of *Tzedakah*?

Intermediate

1. Invite as a guest speaker a local social services official or other knowledgeable person to inform the students about what your community does for the needy.

2. Organize students for a letter writing campaign. Identify individuals and corporations known for

giving large sums of money in support of various causes. Create a questionnaire asking how and why they are involved in *Tzedakah*. Ask the individuals or companies to write a personal statement regarding their *Tzedakah* activities.

3. Assign each student to create his/her own *Tzedakah* contract. Each student should choose how he/she wishes to give *Tzedakah*, when to give it, and to whom. Include provisions for changing and updating the contracts when necessary.

4. Maimonides described eight levels of *Tzedakah*. These may be found in the Overview section above. Write each level out on a large index card. Shuffle the cards and give each student an opportunity to place the cards in order. Discuss whether or not they agree with the order set out by Maimonides.

5. Another way to learn about the eight levels of *Tzedakah* is for the students to dramatize each level of *Tzedakah* with a skit.

6. Each student can create a list of five positive outcomes for observing the Mitzvah of *Tzedakah*.

Secondary

1. Invite a number of individuals involved in various philanthropic organizations to be a part of a community forum to discuss what their groups do for the less fortunate in your community. Introduce the program with a discussion of the Mitzvah of *Tzedakah*.

2. In most communities there are soup kitchens and dining halls for the needy. Call one such organization and arrange for your students to help serve and/or prepare a meal. Jewish individuals might be especially welcome on such holidays as Christmas to fill in for Christians who want to spend the holidays with their families.

3. Create a slide-tape show of a *Tzedakah* project. Include the fund-raising aspects, how the money was allocated, and possibly some historical background on the *Tzedakah* recipients.

4. Organize a tour for students of one or more agencies funded by the Jewish Federation. Ask a Federation representative to make a presentation, providing background of each agency, its function, and how it is funded.

5. Your Rabbi may know of a needy family within the community who could benefit from *Tzedakah* given by your class. To preserve the dignity of the family, let the Rabbi serve as intermediary to ascertain the family's needs. To the extent that they are able, have the students work to fulfill some or all of the family's needs.

6. Assign each student to carry out his or her own personal *Tzedakah* project. Options may include tutoring someone who is learning to read, accompanying a senior citizen to the store or physician's office, helping at a community center, etc.

7. Study the food shortage in various regions and the surpluses in other areas. Discuss possible solutions to the imbalance. Show the film *And Who Shall Feed This World?* in conjunction with this activity.

ALL-SCHOOL PROGRAMS

1. There is a Jewish tradition of giving a traveler *Tzedakah* money to donate upon reaching his/her destination. Such donations are said to help ensure a safe trip. Establish a synagogue fund to provide *Tzedakah* money to congregants who are traveling. When the travelers return, they can describe in the congregation's bulletin the recipients they chose, and any interesting experiences they had while making the donations.

2. Hold a Havdalah service and discussion one Saturday evening. Base the discussion on the song "*Shavua Tov*" (A good week, a week of peace . . .). Ask: How can we live our lives differently this week by including acts of *Tzedakah*? Follow up on the discussion at an Erev Shabbat congregational dinner.

3. Start a *Tzedakah* Cooperative in the synagogue. Individuals and families pool their donations and then decide how to distribute the money. Participants research and make presentations on possible recipients, as well as discuss the Jewish requirements for *Tzedakah*.

4. Hold a *"Tzedakah Fair"* for your school or congregation. Invite representatives from local charities to have a booth with information and activities. Every student should be given a list of questions, and should be directed to find the answers at the booths.

Reference: "Tzedakah Fair" in *Learning Together,* edited by Janice Alper, chapter 31.

5. This program may be used as part of a worship service or in connection with a *Tzedakah* appeal. If the latter, have students choose where they want their *Tzedakah* monies sent at the end of the school year prior to the assembly.
   a. Opening song: *"Hiney Ma Tov."*
   b. Torah Reading: Leviticus 19:9-18.
   c. Present two short skits based on the Torah reading: (1) You shall leave them for the poor and for the stranger, and (2) You shall love your neighbor as yourself. (One or two classes can be assigned responsibility for these.)
   d. A representative from each class announces the recipients of its *Tzedakah* funds and why each group was chosen.
   e. Closing song: *"Im Eyn Ani Li Mi Li."*

RESOURCES

For the Teacher

Alper, Janice. *Learning Together: A Sourcebook for Jewish Family Education.* Denver: A.R.E. Publishing, Inc., 1987, chapters 30, 31.

Bikurim: Tzedakah Programs That Work. New York: Coalition for the Advancement of Jewish Education, 1987.

"Charity." In *Encyclopaedia Judaica.* Jerusalem: Keter Publishing House Jerusalem Ltd., 1972, vol. 5, cols. 338-353.

Eckstein, Abraham, and Azriel Eizenberg. *Tzedakah: A Source Book of Caring and Sharing.* New York: Bureau of Jewish Education of Greater New York, 1982.

Goldin, Barbara Diamond. *Creating Angels: Stories of Tzedakah.* Northvale, NJ: Jason Aronson Inc., 1995.

"Little Becomes Much." In *Lively Legends — Jewish Values: An Early Childhood Teaching Guide* by Miriam P. Feinberg and Rena Rotenberg. Denver: A.R.E. Publishing, Inc., 1993.

Neusner, Jacob. *Tzedakah: Can Jewish Philanthropy Buy Jewish Survival?* Atlanta, GA: The Scholar's Press, 1990.

Siegel, Danny. *Gym Shoes and Irises (Personalized Tzedakah).* New York: The Town House Press, 1982.

Strassfeld, Sharon, and Michael Strassfeld, comps. and eds. *The Third Jewish Catalog.* Philadelphia: The Jewish Publication Society of America, 1980, pp. 12-91.

"Three Loaves." In *Lively Legends — Jewish Values: An Early Childhood Teaching Guide* by Miriam P. Feinberg and Rena Rotenberg. Denver: A.R.E. Publishing, Inc., 1993.

Riemer, Jack, and Nathaniel Stampfer, eds. *So That Your Values Live On: Ethical Wills and How To Prepare Them.* Woodstock, VT: Jewish Lights Publishing, 1991.

Sher, Nina Streisand, and Margaret Feldman. *100+ Jewish Art Projects for Children.* Denver: A.R.E. Publishing, Inc., 1996.

For the Students

Bush, Lawrence. *Emma Ansky-Levine and Her Mitzvah Machine.* New York: UAHC Press, 1981. (Grades 3-5)

Fox, Marci. *Making the World Better.* Instant Lesson. Los Angeles: Torah Aura Productions. (Grades K-2)

Grishaver, Joel Lurie, and Beth Huppin. *Tzedakah, Gemilut Chasadim and Ahavah.* Denver: A.R.E. Publishing, Inc., 1983. (Grades 6 and up)

In God's Image. Los Angeles: Torah Aura Productions, 1987. A board game. (Grades 4 and up)

Isaacs, Ronald H., and Kerry M. Olitzky. *Doing Mitzvot: Mitzvah Projects for Bar/Bat Mitzvah.* Hoboken, NJ: KTAV Publishing House, Inc., 1994, pp. 41-50. (Grades 6-8)

Rabinovich, Jan. *Tzedakah Workbook.* Los Angeles: Torah Aura Productions, 1986. (Grades 3-5)

Rosenberg, Amye. *Tzedakah.* New York: Behrman House, 1979. (Grades K-3)

Tzedakah Lotto Game. Los Angeles: Torah Aura Productions, 1984. (Grades 2-6)

Warmflash, Philip. *Remember Me.* Instant Lesson. Los Angeles: Torah Aura Productions. (Grades 6-adult)

Zwerin, Raymond A. *For One Another: Jewish Organizations That Help Us All.* New York: UAHC Press, 1975. (Grades 6 and up)

Audiovisual

For Goodness Sake. In this 24 minute video, Hollywood celebrities show why it is important to be good to each other and convey a message of personal responsibility. CRM Films. (All ages)

Profiles in Chesed. Eight 5 minute slide-tape shows about people and institutions helping each other. Torah Aura Productions. (Grades 4 and up)

Tzedakah Media Kit. Contains a filmstrip entitled *The Art of the Tzedakah Box* and a radio play of the story "The Secret." Torah Aura Productions. (Grades 4 and up)

Tzedakah: The Road to Dignity. In an 18 minute slide-tape show, four outstanding models of righteousness are introduced. Torah Aura Productions. (Grades 4 and up)

Leaving the Gleanings
פֵּאָה, לֶקֶט, שִׁכְחָה

OVERVIEW

The Torah contains a number of Mitzvot designed to allow the poor to be the beneficiaries of the agricultural yield of landowners.

"When you reap the harvest of your land, you shall not reap all the way to the edges of your field or gather the gleanings of your harvest. You shall not pick your vineyard bare, or gather the fallen fruit of your vineyard; you shall leave them for the poor and the stranger" (Leviticus 19:9-10).

Another passage states that one should not turn back to pick up a sheaf that has been forgotten. Rather, "it shall go to the stranger, the fatherless, and the widow — in order that the Lord your God may bless you in all your undertakings" (Deuteronomy 24:19).

Maimonides derives nine separate Mitzvot from these verses — four positive and five negative. The first of these is known as *Peah*, meaning corner. One is to leave the four corners of one's fields unharvested. The second tractate of the *Mishnah* is entitled *Peah*, and includes the laws pertaining to this practice. According to the Rabbis, this should equal a minimum of one-sixtieth of the field. One should add to this amount based upon the size of the field, the number of the poor, and the yield of the harvest. Rabbi Simeon explains that the corners were chosen in order to assure that the owners were being honest, and so as not to waste the time of the poor. The poor were not allowed to use a scythe or spade, but rather had to pick the crop with their hands to prevent injuring each other.

A second provision, called *Leket*, requires that the gleanings — those crops which fall to the ground during the harvest — be left on the ground for those in need. An example of this procedure is found in Ruth, when Ruth gleans in the fields belonging to Boaz. While in ancient times it was common to leave sheaves in the field in order to placate the spirits, the Torah is careful to emphasize the ethical motivation of this precept.

A person is also enjoined from returning to pick up sheaves that were forgotten (*Shich'chah*) the first time. The *Tosephta* points out that this is a Mitzvah that is observed not on purpose, but by forgetting.

Similarly, when harvesting grapes one is required to leave for the needy bunches of grapes that were misformed, as well as those grapes which fall to the ground.

The Rabbis interpreted that these laws apply outside of the Land of Israel, as well as within it. And although they apply specifically to the Jewish poor, in the interests of peace, they are extended to the poor and needy of all peoples.

According to *Sefer HaChinuch*, these laws are to keep us from becoming selfish. Samson Raphael Hirsch explains that they serve to remind the owner of the field that all the produce has been given him in trust, so that he should not believe that it is all his.

In some agricultural communities in the United States, groups have been allowed by the owners to glean the produce left by professional harvesting crews and machines. The gleanings are then distributed to the poor through food banks.

It is also informative to know that the side curls worn traditionally by Jewish men are known as *peah* (plural, *payot* or, in Ashkenazic pronunciation, *payos*). These sidelocks are grown because of the prohibition in the Torah that "You shall not round off the side-growth on your head" (Leviticus 19:27). While this prohibition represents the primary reason for leaving side locks, it is also possible that these *payos* are a reminder to leave unharvested a portion of what we have.

ACTIVITIES

Primary

1. Take your class on a field trip to a farm. If possible go at a time of year when the children can harvest some produce (apples and pumpkins in the fall, berries in the late spring, etc.). Have students prepare some food for themselves, and donate the leftover uncooked produce to a food bank. Discuss how the latter relates to the Mitzvah of Leaving the Gleanings.

2. Children like to know that their efforts are appreciated and, at this young age, a tangible

reward is very effective. To motivate your class to participate in a food drive for needy persons, each student will receive a "Sharing Our Harvest" cloth patch. These are available from Joycrest, Inc., P.O. Box 2245, Westminster, CA 92684 at a nominal cost. If you prefer, create paper certificates to distribute.

Suggest that students make posters to advertise the food drive and that they also place a notice in the synagogue bulletin. In all the publicity, have them include references to the Mitzvah of *Peah*. Set up a collection point in your classroom or in the synagogue's entry way as a reminder to the congregation. If possible, take your class to the food bank so they can *see* where their donations go. Ask the food bank director to discuss with the class the significance of sharing their harvest.

3. Read the story of Ruth to your class. Utilize a flannel board and make cut-outs from felt of Ruth, Naomi, Boaz, and the wheat field. In this way the students will be able to retell the story themselves, using the flannel board figures as prompters.

4. Read the class the story *From Grain to Bread* by Ali Mitgutsch. This story will help students understand how wheat becomes bread. With the students, list the steps for making bread. Ask the students what the farmer would need to do in order to fulfill the Mitzvot of *Peah, Leket, and Shich'chah*.

5. The Mitzvot of *Peah, Leket,* and *Shich'chah* are important within the context of our agricultural heritage. To help the students understand the importance of seeds as a source for food, do the following activities:
   a. Place some seeds on a wet sponge to see how the seeds germinate. Use grass seed and make sure the sponge is sitting in a dish with shallow water.
   b. Study food packages to see how many items derive from seeds. Remember that flour comes from seeds, as do popcorn, nuts, beans, etc. Have the students create a display of these packages.

Reference: *Food Plants* by Jennifer Cochrane.

6. Have students design a bumper sticker which states the need for sharing one's harvest with others.

Intermediate

1. With your class, grow a small garden and, when it is time to harvest, follow the Mitzvah of *Peah*, and the other Mitzvot in this unit. This long-term project will give the students an excellent chance to put these Mitzvot into practice.

2. Have the students create a Righteous Action Cube based on these Mitzvot. Paint or cover the outside of a cardboard box. On each side of the box glue, draw, or paint pictures and phrases appropriate to the theme of *Peah* and gleanings.

3. The following project can be done very simply, or it may be as elaborate as the students desire. The students will observe and record the amount of food wasted in their homes or in the school cafeteria. Students will have to position themselves near the trash cans at school to observe, or they may conduct interviews. At home, they may want to weigh and record the food items thrown out. Set a time frame for observation (three days, one week, etc.). Students then share the recorded data. Discuss the results. See if students have suggestions to remedy this wasteful situation. Ask: How can you apply the Mitzvot of *Peah, Leket,* and *Shich'chah* to this situation?

4. *Birkat HaMazon* (blessing after meals) contains the following: "Blessed are You, O Eternal, our God . . . You give food to all living things . . . You never let us lack for food . . . Blessed are You, O Eternal, Who feeds everyone." Discuss with the class: Are these statements true? Does God feed everyone? Why do we need the laws of *Peah*? How far does human responsibility go in feeding the world?

5. As a possible outgrowth of activity #4, the students might participate in the stocking of shelves at a local food pantry.

6. Have each student or pair of students write a personal statement about the need to feed the hungry. The students can share these statements with their families. Families can then be encouraged to help solve the dilemma of the

hungry in our nation of plenty. (See activity #1 under All-school Programs below.)

Secondary

1. Tell your students to imagine that they are farmers and that they allow gleaners in their land. Have them write an ethical will to their children encouraging them to continue this practice.

   References: *So That Your Values Live On: Ethical Wills and How To Prepare Them*, edited by Jack Reimer and Nathaniel Stampfer; *Ethical Wills: Handing Down Our Jewish Heritage* by Barbara Binder Kadden and Bruce Kadden.

2. The Jewish tradition ensured that farmers would provide sustenance for the hungry. This Mitzvah evolved in an agricultural society. Direct your students to create guidelines for other professions (physicians, attorneys, business owners) similar to those required by this Mitzvah. For example, a lawyer might be required to donate a certain number of hours of legal services for the poor each year.

3. There is a Jewish tradition of providing holiday packages for the needy. At Passover this is called *Maot Chittim,* at Chanukah and Purim, *Shalach Manot.* With your students choose a Jewish holiday for which to provide provisions. Ask the Rabbis or a Jewish social service agency to help distribute these packages.

4. Read together the book of Ruth. Then have a "Blackboard Press Conference." Draw a circle face of Ruth on the blackboard and introduce her to the class: "This is Ruth. You have read her story. Now what questions do you have for her?" Write on the board the questions suggested by the students. After five or six questions, ask for a volunteer (or volunteers) to speak for Ruth and answer the questions that have been raised. Be non-judgmental about the answers to the questions, but point out any incorrect facts later in the discussion.

   Reference: *Values Education.*

5. Have students write for information from local and national organizations which help feed the hungry. After receiving the information, create a display for the congregation on the theme of hunger. Some suggested national organizations are:

American Jewish World Service
15 W. 26th St., 9th Floor
New York, NY 10010

Jewish Fund for Justice
35 W. 44th St.
New York, NY 10036

Mazon: A Jewish Response to Hunger
12401 Wilshire Blvd., Suite 303
Los Angeles, CA 90025

Oxfam America
26 West St.
Boston, MA 02111

6. Produce a mini-documentary about Mitzvot related to *Peah.* One student can serve as a reporter and others role play the scenario. Scenes should include: leaving the corners of the fields, gleaning, and not returning to pick up the forgotten produce.

ALL-SCHOOL PROGRAMS

1. Invite a guest speaker from the welfare system to learn how our government helps the needy. In a follow-up discussion, compare the Jewish tradition for feeding the hungry by means of the Mitzvot of *Peah, Leket,* and *Shich'chah* with governmental programs. Discuss: What types of programs might be developed that reflect these Mitzvot? (For example, large farms might be encouraged to give away excess produce to poor people.)

2. Mazon is a national Jewish organization which offers a Jewish response to hunger. It is suggested that three percent of the cost of the food at a *simcha* (B'nai Mitzvah, wedding, etc.) be donated to Mazon. This organization, in turn, distributes grants to a variety of organizations which fight hunger. Create an ongoing committee to distribute Mazon materials to individuals and families in the congregation who are celebrating *simchas.* (See Secondary activity #5 above for the address of Mazon.)

3. The following is an exercise in selfish versus unselfish behavior. This will also test the participants' ability to share resources. The organizers of this activity will need to create a menu of foods which the participants will be able to purchase. Each participant will be given printed

money or tokens. The "money" is distributed *unevenly*, so that some participants will be able to purchase a full meal, while others will be able to purchase only crackers and water. After distributing the money (making clear that some have much more than others), tell students they are free to purchase their meal. It is best to do this at a regular meal time, and indicate that this is all that they will get. Allow this to go on for at least 10 minutes. Then stop and discuss behavior attitudes, reactions, and feelings. What was it like having only enough for a little food, when others could afford a lot? Who shared? Who did not? Why not? Point out that the Mitzvah of *Peah* obligated a farmer to share his/her produce with the poor.

4. Research resources in the community that distribute meals or packaged foods to the poor. Choose one organization and become regular contributors to their program. For example, the school might make 100 sandwiches once a month to be distributed at a certain soup kitchen, or collect canned goods for a particular food bank.

RESOURCES
For the Teacher

Birnbaum, Philip, ed. *Maimonides' Mishneh Torah (Yad Hazakah)*. Rockaway Beach, NY: Hebrew Publishing Co., pp. 153-159.

Hawley, Robert C. *Value Exploration through Role Playing*. New York: Hart Publishing Co., Inc., 1975.

Kroloff, Charles. *When Elijah Knocks: A Religious Response to Homelessness*. West Orange, NJ: Behrman House, 1992.

Leibowitz, Nehama. *Studies in Devarim (Deuteronomy)*. Jerusalem: The World Zionist Organization, 1980, pp. 243-249.

"Leket, Shikhhah, and Peah." In *Encyclopaedia Judaica*. Jerusalem: Keter Publishing House Jerusalem Ltd., 1972, vol. 11, cols. 3-4.

For the Students

Cochrane, Jennifer. *Food Plants*. Chatham, NJ: Rawtree Steck Vaughn Publishers, 1990. (Grades 5-9)

Gersh, Harry. *Mishnah: The Oral Law*. New York: Behrman House, Inc., 1984, pp. 19-22. (Grades 7 and up)

Glosser, Joanne; Beth Huppin; and Bill Kunin. *Feed the World: Hazan Et Hakol*. New York: Coalition for the Advancement of Jewish Education, 1986. (Grades 7 and up)

Mitgutsch, Ali. *From Grain to Bread*. Minneapolis: Carolrhoda Books, Inc., 1981. (Grades K-3)

Syme, Deborah Shayne. *Partners*. New York: UAHC Press, 1990. (Grades K-3)

Values Education. 2d ed. Center for Learning, 1992. Distributed by Social Studies School Service. (Grades 6-12)

Audiovisual

The Bible According to Kossoff: The Story of Ruth. A 20 minute video that portrays Ruth as a symbol of loyalty and devotion. Her loyalty is repaid by the kindness of a kinsman. Films for the Humanities and Science. (Grades 7-adult)

Ruth: Esther. A 45 minute video that tells the story of each woman in separate segments. Christian Publishers. (Grades 4-6)

UNIT 22

Being Kind to Animals

צַעַר בַּעֲלֵי חַיִּים

OVERVIEW

The Mitzvot which deal with the treatment of animals come under the category of *Tza'ar Ba'alei Chayim*, literally "the suffering of living beings." By observing these Mitzvot, we prevent or minimize the suffering of animals and encourage humane treatment. We are taught that animals may be used by human beings for our benefit in a variety of ways, but they must be treated kindly, because they, too, are God's creations.

The Bible contains a number of explicit injunctions relating to the treatment of animals. "When you see the ass of your enemy lying under its burden and would refrain from raising it, you must nevertheless raise it with him" (Exodus 23:5; also see Deuteronomy 22:4). According to a *midrash*, this means that a person should help unload an animal without remuneration. This injunction is codified by Maimonides as both a positive and a negative Mitzvah.

The Torah also forbids plowing with an ox and an ass yoked together (Deuteronomy 22:10). According to most authorities, the purpose of this Mitzvah is to prevent the suffering which could occur if animals of unequal strength plowed together. Furthermore, one is forbidden to "muzzle an ox while it is threshing" (Deuteronomy 25:4). It would be unkind to prevent an animal from eating produce amidst which it is walking.

The commandment pertaining to the Sabbath observance explicitly specifies that one's ox, ass, and cattle should not do any work on that day (Deuteronomy 5:14).

The Torah displays a particular sensitivity to the parent-offspring relationship among animals. For example, an ox, sheep, or goat could not be taken away from its mother to be sacrificed until it was eight days old (Leviticus 22:27). This passage continues by prohibiting the sacrifice of an animal and its young on the same day (Leviticus 22:28). Maimonides explains that "the pain of the animals under such circumstances is very great," comparable to how a human being would feel (*Guide for the Perplexed*, 3:48). Similar sentiments are expressed in the verses which instruct a person not to take both a mother bird and her eggs or fledglings, but

to let the mother go free (Deuteronomy 22:6-7). The thrice repeated prohibition against boiling a kid in its mother's milk (Exodus 23:19, 34:26, Deuteronomy 14:21) may reflect a similar sensitivity.

Besides the extensive legal material which legislates kindness toward animals, various narratives reflect the idea. Balaam, for example, is condemned for striking his ass (Numbers 23:32-33). And who can forget the surprising ending to the book of Jonah when God rhetorically asks the prophet, "Should not I care about Ninevah, that great city, in which there are more than 20,000 persons who do not know their right hand from their left, and many beasts as well" (Jonah 4:11)?

Rabbinic literature reflects a similar attitude toward the treatment of animals. A story is told of Rabbi Judah HaNasi who saw a calf being led to slaughter. When the animal thrust its head into the Rabbi's sleeve and began crying as if begging for mercy, he responded, "Go! For you were destined for this." Whereupon Rabbi Judah was afflicted with a painful illness. Then one day he stopped his servant from sweeping a litter of kittens from the house, and he was cured (*Baba Metzia* 85a).

According to another *midrash*, Moses and King David were chosen to be leaders of the Jewish people only after they showed compassion toward their sheep.

Other legal matters assuring the proper treatment of animals were also introduced by the Rabbis. A person is supposed to feed one's animal before eating (*Berachot* 40a); and, one is prohibited from buying an animal unless one can feed and care for it properly.

The laws pertaining to the Sabbath specify that certain acts normally forbidden are permitted in order to relieve an animal's pain. For example, one is permitted to assist an animal in the process of giving birth. Also, if an animal falls into a ditch, provisions for its sustenance must be provided. And one may untie bundles of sheaves if they are to be used for animal fodder (*Shabbat* 128b).

Additionally, the extensive laws pertaining to the proper slaughtering of animals and fowl seem to reflect a concern that their death be as quick and as painless as possible. For example, the knife is to be sharp and free of nicks and the slaughterer is not to pause during the act of *shechitah*. These laws also served to shape a negative attitude toward hunting. Ishmael, Esau, and Nimrod, all of whom are cast in a negative light in the *midrashim*, were hunters.

Rabbinic literature contains the germ of an idea that originally and ideally human beings were to be vegetarians. This conclusion is based upon Genesis 1:29 wherein God gives humankind plants and fruit for food. Only after the flood does God say to Noah, "Every creature that lives shall be yours to eat" (Genesis 9:3). Rabbi Abraham I. Kook, former Chief Rabbi of Palestine and one of the most respected Rabbis of modern times, explained that the permission to eat meat was a concession to human beings after the flood because of the moral deterioration of humanity. Since human beings were not able to refrain from eating meat as God's original plan called for, a compromise was instituted allowing for the eating of meat, but only in accord with restrictive dietary laws. Rabbi Kook, who was a vegetarian, taught that humankind would again not eat meat in the world to come.

The question of using animals in research is dealt with in recent legal literature. The consensus is that animals may be used in research which might lead to the cure and/or prevention of human disease. Even as research animals, they are to be treated with the greatest possible care and regard.

With such a compassionate attitude toward the treatment of animals, it should come as no surprise that the first humane society was founded in England in the 1800s by a Jew, Lewis Gompertz.

ACTIVITIES

Primary

1. Visit a local zoo with your class. Each student or pair of students may be detectives, investigating the kind of enclosure in which a particular animal lives. Invite a parent to accompany each pair of students to help record observations. Afterward, discuss whether or not the zoo management is abiding by the Mitzvah of *Tza'ar Ba'alei Chayim*.

2. Have students write stories about their pets. Possible first sentences are: My pet is important to me because _____. I love my pet because _____. Have them include a sentence or two about how they carry out the Mitzvah of Being Kind to Animals.

3. Hold a general discussion with the class about the care and feeding of their pets and why the Mitzvah of *Tza'ar Ba'alei Chayim* is so important.

4. Extend activity #3 by inviting a veterinarian or a veterinarian's assistant to talk about animal care.

5. Visit your local public library to gather materials about endangered animals. Show pictures of these animals to the class and give brief explanations about their plight. Have each student write a poem (or write a class poem) describing one or more of these animals, how the students feel about the situation, how saving these animals is performing the Mitzvah of being kind to animals, and how he/she would like to help.

6. Tell students to imagine that they are someone's pet. Ask: How would they like to be treated?

Intermediate

1. Invite an animal expert to speak to your class about the physical needs of various animals and how they need to be treated in captivity. Following this, the students may construct model enclosures for zoo animals that would be in keeping with the Mitzvah of *Tza'ar Ba'alei Chayim*.

2. To help students develop an empathetic attitude toward animals, pose the following question: Do animals have feelings? Direct your students to observe their own pet or a friend's pet over a three or four day period at different times of day. The student observers should record date, time, and behavior, and report back to the class. Discuss how knowing that animals have feelings leads one to treat them in a more kindly way.

3. Tell the students to imagine that their pet can talk. Have them write an imaginary conversation with their pet. Suggest they include comments about the pet's care, food, feelings, etc., as well as about the importance of *Tza'ar Ba'alei Chayim*.

4. Assign students various organizations to contact regarding the well-being of the nation's wildlife. The following organizations can provide materials free or at little cost:

Environmental Protection Agency
1129 20th Street
Washington, DC 20460

National Wildlife Federation
1400 Sixteenth St., NW
Washington, DC 20036

Keep America Beautiful, Inc.
9 W. Broad St.
Stamford, CT 06902

National Park Service
U.S. Department of the Interior
Washington, DC 20240

U.S. Forest Service
Department of Agriculture
Washington, DC 20250

The National Audubon Society
700 Broadway
New York, NY 10003

Canadian Wildlife Federation
2740 Queensview Drive
Ottawa, Ont.
Canada K2B 1A2

Ministry for Conservation
240 Victoria Pde E
Melbourne, Australia

a. Discuss how these materials reflect the Mitzvah of *Tza'ar Ba'alei Chayim.*
b. Using the materials you receive, create a display for the school or synagogue.

5. Ask students to design commemorative coins honoring the concept of *Tza'ar Ba'alei Chayim.* Remind them that they have two sides of the coin to design, and that they should utilize aspects of Jewish tradition in their work.

6. Share this story with the class:

Moses and the Lamb

When Moses fled Egypt, he went to Midian and became a shepherd for his father-in-law, Jethro. One day, Moses saw a small lamb run away from the flock. Concerned that it would perish in the desert, Moses chased after it. He saw the lamb stop at a stream and drink from it. Moses realized that the lamb had run away because it was thirsty. Moses asked the lamb to forgive him. If he had known why the lamb was running away, he would not have chased it. He felt very sorry for chasing the lamb and making it thirstier and tired.

After the lamb was finished drinking, Moses lifted it up on his shoulder and carried it back to the rest of the flock. Because of the compassion Moses showed the little lamb, he was found worthy of leading God's flock, the people of Israel, out of slavery in Egypt.

Some questions for discussion: Does the way someone treats animals indicate how he or she treats people? How does this story show that Moses is qualified to lead the Israelites?

Secondary

1. Have students conduct a debate on whether zoos should exist and whether or not zoos can foster the Mitzvah of *Tza'ar Ba'alei Chayim.* They can interview animal experts for background information. These might include veterinarians, zoo officials, SPCA officials, animal rights activists, etc.

2. Invite a speaker from a research facility which uses animals in their laboratories to discuss the use of animals in research. Discuss whether this use is acceptable when considering the Mitzvah of *Tza'ar Ba'alei Chayim.*

3. Invite an animal rights activist (from Greenpeace, Save the Whales, or a similar organization) to make a presentation prior or subsequent to the speaker suggested in activity #2 immediately above. If the situation can be handled, you might bring in the speakers at the same time and have a panel presentation.

4. Many individuals choose to live as vegetarians. One reason some give as a basis for their eating style is that they do not want to kill another living thing in order to eat. Contact one of the following groups to gather information about vegetarianism. Study and discuss the materials with your class.

Jewish Vegetarians of North America
c/o Israel Mossman
6938 Relance Rd.
Federalsburg, MD 21632

The Jewish Vegetarian Society
210 Riverside Drive
New York, NY 10025

5. A sensitive understanding of *Kashrut* is found in the book: *The Jewish Dietary Laws* by Samuel H. Dresner, Seymour Siegel, and David M. Pollock. Read selections from the essay "Their Meaning for Our Time," which relate to the treatment of animals. Discuss the essay, focusing on the question of whether or not the dietary laws reflect the Mitzvah of *Tza'ar Ba'alei Chayim*.

6. To extend activity #5, direct your students to do further research on the laws of *Kashrut*. Focus in particular on how the requirements of *Kashrut* were designed to ease the suffering of animals, and therefore fulfill the Mitzvah of *Tza'ar Ba'alei Chayim*. If possible, invite a *shochet* (ritual slaughterer) or a kosher butcher as a resource.

ALL-SCHOOL PROGRAMS

1. Hold a teach-in during which experts speak about the issue of animal rights. Include activities for all age groups and invite parents. Discuss the Mitzvah of *Tza'ar Ba'alei Chayim*. Create a resolution regarding the humane treatment of animals.

2. Contact an organization which works for the survival of endangered species, such as Save the Whales. Invite a guest speaker from the group and/or set up a display in your synagogue or school. Provide educational materials to distribute. For a listing of these organizations in your community, check with your public library or contact the local zoological association.

3. Have students organize themselves into a "World Congress" whose purpose is to help ensure the rights of animals on a world-wide scope, thereby fulfilling the Mitzvah of *Tza'ar Ba'alei Chayim*. Students should represent various animal rights groups (e.g., S.P.C.A., Save the Whales), religious organizations, the scientific and medical groups (which want to use animals for experiments), anti-vivisection groups (which oppose using animals for experiments), vegetarians, furriers, etc. Each group should study the issue from its perspective and make a presentation. Follow up with a question and answer period.

RESOURCES
For the Teacher

Dresner, Samuel H.; Seymour Siegel; and David M. Pollock. *The Jewish Dietary Laws.* New York: The Rabbinical Seminary of America, 1982.

"The Bell of Justice." In *Lively Legends — Jewish Values: An Early Childhood Teaching Guide* by Miriam P. Feinberg and Rena Rotenberg. Denver: A.R.E. Publishing, Inc., 1993.

Glustrom, Simon. *The Language of Judaism.* Northvale, NJ: Jason Aronson, 1994, pp. 16-18.

Leibowitz, Nehama. *Studies in Devarim (Deuteronomy).* Jerusalem: The World Zionist Organization, 1980, pp. 135-142, 217-22.

Schochet, Elijah Judah. *Animal Life in Jewish Tradition: Attitudes and Relationships.* New York: KTAV Publishing House, Inc., 1984.

"The Stolen Donkey." In *Lively Legends — Jewish Values: An Early Childhood Teaching Guide* by Miriam P. Feinberg and Rena Rotenberg. Denver: A.R.E. Publishing, Inc., 1993.

Strassfeld, Sharon, and Michael Strassfeld, comps. and eds. *The Third Jewish Catalog: Creating Community.* Philadelphia: The Jewish Publication Society of America, 1980, pp. 288-297.

For the Students

Artson, Bradley Shavit. *It's a Mitzvah: Step-by-Step to Jewish Living.* West Orange, NJ: Behrman House and New York: The Rabbinical Assembly, 1995, pp. 196-217. (Grades 8-adult)

Girion, Barbara. *Misty and Me.* New York: Charles Scribner's Sons, 1979. (Grades 5-8)

Isaacs, Ronald H., and Kerry M. Olitzky. *Doing Mitzvot: Mitzvah Projects for Bar/Bat Mitzvah.* Hoboken, NJ: KTAV Publishing House, Inc., 1994, pp. 7-19. (Grades 6-8)

Sequoia, Anna. *67 Ways To Save the Animals.* New York: Harper Perennial, 1990. (Grades 7 and up)

Audiovisual

Bip Hunts Butterflies. A 10 minute film featuring Marcel Marceau in pantomime interacting with a dying butterfly. University of Minnesota. (Grades K-6)

Daisies and Ducklings. An audiocassette by Fran Avni containing cheerful songs about animals and the environment. Lemonstone Records. Available from A.R.E. Publishing, Inc. (Grades PK-3)

Noah's Ark. A 30 minute video of the story of Noah told in cartoon form. Three young visitors go time traveling. Hanna-Barbera Productions. (Grades K-3)

Noah's Ark Video. Well animated 27 minute video narrated by James Earl Jones. Available at video stores. Lightyear Entertainment. (Grades K-3)

UNIT 23

Redeeming Captives
פִּדְיוֹן שְׁבוּיִים

OVERVIEW

Our experiences as an oppressed minority have no doubt contributed to the significance in Jewish life of the Mitzvah of *Pidyon Shevuyim*, Redeeming Captives. According to Maimonides, this Mitzvah supercedes that of charity to the poor. Money set aside for the poor or for the building of a synagogue may be used instead to ransom a captive. A delay in fulfilling this Mitzvah was considered tantamount to transgressing the commandment, "You shall not stand idly by the blood of your neighbor" (Leviticus 19:6).

In the Rabbinic era, the major concern was to ransom Jews captured by robbers, Jews who were kidnapped and sold into slavery, and Jews who have been imprisoned unjustly. There is the Talmudic account of Rabbi Joshua ben Hananiah who heard that a young man was imprisoned in Rome. He went to the prison and declared that he would not move until the young man was ransomed. The captive later became a great Jewish scholar, Rabbi Ishmael ben Elisha.

The Talmud also contains discussions about priorities with regard to ransoming captives. If a person, his father, and a teacher are all captives, the person may have himself ransomed first, the teacher has the next priority, and lastly the father. One's mother would have priority over all of them. A scholar takes precedence over even a king of Israel, since a king can be replaced by anyone, but it might be impossible to find as learned a scholar.

The Rabbis recognized that their concern for ransoming captives could lead to exorbitant demands. Therefore, they said that one should not pay too high a ransom — not more than the person's value as a worker.

In a very famous case, Rabbi Meir of Rotenberg refused to allow the community to ransom him, choosing instead to spend the last seven years of his life in prison.

In the middle of the seventeenth century, the Jewish community of Venice established a *Chevrat Pidyon Shevuyim*, a society devoted to ransoming Jews who were captured. In other well established European communities, it was not uncommon for one person to be appointed collector of ransom funds.

In more recent history, the Mitzvah of *Pidyon Shevuyim* came into consideration during the Holocaust. In 1943 the Rumanian government apparently offered to cooperate in moving 70,000 Jews from Transnistria to any place of refuge chosen by the Allies in return for transportation and expenses. One Jewish group took out a three-quarter page ad in *The New York Times* with the headline: "FOR SALE TO HUMANITY: 70,000 Jews Guaranteed; Human Beings at $50 Apiece." There were no responses from the world community! Most of those Jews died in death camps.

An even more bizarre scenario occurred in May of 1944 when Adolph Eichmann apparently offered to release one million Hungarian Jews in exchange for 10,000 trucks and sizable amounts of coffee, tea, cocoa, soap, and foreign currency. The plan was seen by some as "blackmail"; others claimed it was merely a ploy to disrupt the war effort by sending out a flood of refugees. However, certain persons were able to keep the negotiations open long enough to save the lives of a small number of those Jews.

Also under the category of *Pidyon Shevuyim* are the remarkable rescue operations associated with Israel during the last half of the twentieth century:

- In 1950 tens of thousands of Jews were brought out of Yemen — that land on the southern end of the Arabian peninsula — in "Operation Magic Carpet."

- On July 4, 1976, the 200th anniversary of United States Independence, dozens of sky-jacked American citizens were rescued from Entebbe Airport in Uganda by an Israeli special forces team led by Yonatan Netanyahu. All of the captives were saved by the daring night rescue. However, during the rescue the Israeli Commander was killed by a stray bullet. The daring feat, first called "Operation Thunderbolt," was renamed "Operation Yonatan" after him.

- In the 1980s, "Operation Moses" and "Operation Solomon" were initiated to save the Jewish remnant of Ethiopia. Jewish communities all over the world contributed funds to help in the rescue and resettlement of the Beta Yisrael community. Some 30,000-40,000 of these Jews, who trace their lineage back to the son of King Solomon and the Queen of Sheba, were ultimately airlifted to Israel where they could begin life anew.

- From 1964 and continuing through the late 1980s, through the tireless efforts of Jews in the free world, hundreds of thousands of Soviet Jews were enabled to leave the oppression and injustice of that totalitarian regime. The Soviet Union had refused to allow its citizens to emigrate, and had imposed particularly harsh measures on Jews who attempted to practice Judaism or who applied to leave. Many "Refuseniks," Jews who applied to leave but were refused permission, became the focal point of efforts to free Soviet Jews. Pressure by Israel, the U.S. government, and the North American Jewish community resulted in limited success, until the late 1980s, when significant political changes allowed many Jews to leave for Israel and other countries. The enormous task of resettling these new immigrants was accepted by Jewish communities everywhere and carried out with caring sensitivity. The Mitzvah of *Pidyon Shevuyim* was thus blended with the Mitzvah of *Hachnasat Orchim,* Welcoming the Stranger.

ACTIVITIES

Primary

1. Read and discuss My Name Is Rachamim by Jonathan P. Kendall. Questions to consider: How do you know Rachamim and his family are Jewish? How is your Jewish life like/unlike Rachamim's? Why did Rachamim and his family have to leave their home? How did Rachamim feel when he found out there were other Jews in the world? What happened to Rachamim and his people when they arrived in Israel? How does Rachamim's experience reflect the Mitzvah of Pidyon Shevuyim?

2. Learn about "Operation Magic Carpet," the airlifting of Yemenite Jews to Israel in 1950. Create a bulletin board display about this rescue.

   Reference: *Israel: Covenant People, Covenant Land* by Seymour Rossel, pp. 166-167.

3. Briefly introduce the students to the information about Jews who were not allowed to leave the Soviet Union and Ethiopia as presented in the Overview and other resources. Brainstorm all the ways that the children could have helped Jews who were not allowed to leave their country. Allow each student in turn to complete the sentence: To help these Jews, I would . . .

4. Arrange for your class to be pen pals with Ethiopian Jewish children who are now in Israel or with Jewish children from the former Soviet Union. If your school is on-line, you may be able to make these connections through the Internet. Other resources are: North American Conference on Ethiopian Jewry, 165 E. 56th St., New York, NY 10022; Bay Area Council for Jewish Rescue and Renewal, 106 Baden St., San Francisco, CA 94131; or a local organization which works in these areas.

5. To introduce the idea of being a captive, discuss situations when students have been temporarily confined to one place (e.g., grounded in their room, stuck in an elevator, forced to stay inside when the weather is bad, etc.). Ask what it feels like to be in such situations. Does it help to know that it is only temporary? Emphasize that Jews who were captive in communities such as the former U.S.S.R., Ethiopia, and Arab lands did not know when or if they would be free.

6. Read to the class *On Eagles' Wings and Other Things* by Connie Colker Steiner. Compare Avraham's journey to Israel with the journeys of the other children in the story. On a map locate each of the places from which the children in the story come, then determine who traveled the furthest to Israel and who traveled the shortest distance.

7. Introduce students to the Talmudic saying *Kol Yisrael Arayvin Zeh BaZeh* — All Israel is responsible for one another. Write this saying on the board in Hebrew and English. Ask students what this means and have them give examples of how they show responsibility for other Jews. Relate this saying to the Mitzvah of *Pidyon Shevuyim.*

Intermediate

1. Assign your students to collect newspaper and magazine articles about captive/refugee issues in such places as Rwanda, Bosnia, Afghanistan, etc. Share and discuss these, and brainstorm ways that the students might help work for the safe repatriation of these people.

2. Research what life was like for Ethiopian Jews before they left for Israel. Each group of students should choose or be assigned a different area, such as Shabbat and holiday observance, language, dress and housing, family.

References: *K'lal Yisrael: Our Jewish Community* by Ann Ricki Hurwitz and Sue Hurwitz; *A Young Person's History of Israel* by David Bamberger, pp. 150-152.

3. The Rabbis of the Talmud laid down the laws for ransoming captives:
   a. Women captives should usually be given precedence before male captives.
   b. A person captured together with his father and his teacher may ransom himself first. He is then bound to ransom his teacher and only thereafter his father. A scholar should be given preference even to a king of Israel.
   c. The court (bet din) has the power to force a husband to ransom his wife.
   d. Money set aside for charity purposes or for the building of a synagogue may be used to ransom captives.
   e. A person who delays the fulfillment of this duty and causes an undue prolongation of his fellow Jew's imprisonment is regarded as if he has spilled his blood (i.e., as a murderer).
   Discuss these rules and decide what, if any, revisions, students would make in them.

4. Listen to the song "Leaving Mother Russia" on the audiocassette *The Bridge* by Kol B'Seder. List all the information about the situation of the Jews in the former Soviet Union that you learn about from the song. If possible, invite a person who was active in working for the freedom of Soviet Jews to speak about what he or she did to help.

5. Choose one of the stories listed below to read aloud to your students. Questions to consider: Why were the people compelled to leave their countries? What kind of help do they get from others? What is their reception in their new communities? What would it be like to go through such an experience? How does the story illustrate or relate to the Mitzvah of *Pidyon Shevuyim*?

References: *Call Me Ruth* by Marilyn Sachs; *Manya's Story* by Bettyanne Gray; *Behind the*

Border: Memories of a Russian Girlhood by Nina Kossman; *Hanna, The Immigrant* by Jan Siegel Hart; *L'Chaim: The Story of a Russian Emigre Boy* by Tricia Brown; *One Foot Ashore* by Jacqueline Dembar Greene (on the Spanish Inquisition).

6. Invite a speaker knowledgeable on the subject of Jews in the U.S.S.R./C.I.S. to class. He/she can speak about the positive results of the efforts by Jews around the world to redeem the Jews in the former U.S.S.R. and about the current situation of Jews in the C.I.S., where there was a resurgence of anti-Semitism in the 1990s. Remind the speaker to keep the presentation simple and to allow ample time for questions and discussion.

Secondary

1. Use a discussion or debate format to deal with the following issue: Should the Jewish responsibility to redeem captives extend to non-Jewish groups?

2. During the Holocaust there were a number of failed attempts to rescue large numbers of Jews. Assign students to research the Rumanian offer and Eichmann's offer to sell Jews. The research may take the form of written reports, recreated newspaper accounts, or radio show presentations. Discuss how these offers were attempts to fulfill the Mitzvah of *Pidyon Shevuyim*.

Reference: *The Abandonment of the Jews* by David S. Wyman.

3. During 1986, an American, Jonathan Pollard, was convicted of spying for Israel and is now in an American prison. Many American and Israeli leaders have campaigned for his release. In fact, Israel awarded him citizenship in 1995. Should Israel attempt to redeem this captive? Have your students research this event using newspaper and magazine accounts available at the public library. They might also interview the editor of the local Jewish newspaper and/or Federation and synagogue leaders to ascertain their views. After the students have analyzed the material and the interviews, hold "public interviews." Each student presents his/her views and is questioned by the rest of the class. You might take an opinion poll prior to the public interviews and again afterward to see if students change their views.

4. Have students put on the play "The Passover of Hope" in the book *Kings and Things: 20 Jewish Plays for Kids 8 to 18* by Meridith Shaw Patera for parents or another group of students. This moving play is based on the story "The Last Passover in the Warsaw Ghetto" by Wladyslaw Pawlak and deals with the observance of Passover while under German attack.

5. Enable students to understand what it might be like to be a captive. Use large cardboard boxes or tri-wall to simulate a jail cell. Ask students what graffiti they would write on the walls if they were prisoners. Assign different historical situations (e.g., the former Soviet Union, Holocaust, Inquisition, Cyprus Internment Camps, etc.) and ask students to write graffiti which reflects their assigned historical period.

6. There are many folk songs which reflect the Mitzvah of *Pidyon Shevuyim.* One of these is "Go Down Moses." This song may be found in many folk song collections. Learn and perform this and others of these songs with your class.

Reference: *Manginot: 201 Songs for Jewish Schools,* edited by Stephen Richards.

7. Watch and discuss a video of Steven Spielberg's film *Schindler's List.* Consider the following questions: What might have prompted Oscar Schindler to begin to rescue Jews? Did his motives change as the war progressed? How does what he did compare to the Mitzvah of *Pidyon Shevuyim?*

8. Each student should list 10 Jewish activities they enjoy doing. Ask them which they would have to abandon if they were taken captive and were either living in a repressive society or having to stay in jail. They might also rank order the 10 items to determine which Jewish activity they would miss most. Given that they live in a free society, ask how they could enhance those activities which mean the most to them.

9. Show and discuss one of the films about the 1976 rescue by Israeli commandos of the 104 hijacked Jewish passengers in Entebbe, Uganda. Discuss why Jews feel a responsibility to rescue other Jews whose lives are in danger. Share with students the biblical verse, "You shall not stand idly by the blood of your neighbor" (Leviticus 19:6) and the blessing from the morning liturgy, "Blessed are You, Adonai our God, Sovereign of the world, Who brings freedom to the captives." To what lengths should Israel and the Jewish community go to help rescue Jews?

References: *Operation Thunderbolt, Raid on Entebbe.*

ALL-SCHOOL PROGRAMS

1. Establish a task force to identify disadvantaged refugee groups living in your community. Do an assessment to determine what needs exist. Make a plan for synagogue members to help those individuals and families. Discuss whether or not this help falls under the rubric of *Pidyon Shevuyim.*

2. Create a campaign to redeem a fictional Jewish community. Write a brief description of the community, its predicament, and what needs to be done to help redeem them. Divide the students into groups to create: a television advertisement, petitions to political leaders, guerilla theater, posters, songs, etc. Hold a rally to present all the creations.

3. Invite a speaker to an assembly for students and parents to talk about the previous rescue of Jews from the Soviet Union, Ethiopia, and/or Arab lands. Be sure to brief the speaker to include a discussion of the Mitzvah of *Pidyon Shevuyim.* To find a speaker, contact your local Federation, JCRC, or American Jewish Congress.

4. Create a newspaper about the rescue of Ethiopian Jews. Provide students with a variety of resources (see below) or have teachers, other adults, or older students who have been properly prepared play the roles of Ethiopian Jews, political leaders, etc. Younger students can draw pictures. Older students can write news or feature articles, editorials, or cartoons.

5. Divide students into groups and assign each group a different historical rescue to research. Include: leaving Egypt, Operation Magic Carpet, Operation Moses/Operation Solomon (Ethiopian Jews), Soviet Jews. Each group should then create a panel of a mural that will represent the Mitzvah of *Pidyon Shevuyim* throughout Jewish history.

RESOURCES

For the Teacher

"Captives, Ransoming of." In *Encyclopaedia Judaica*. Jerusalem: Keter Publishing House Jerusalem Ltd., 1972, vol. 5, cols. 154-155.

Davids, Ronn S. "Our Duty to Rescue Political Hostages." In *Reform Jewish Ethics and Halakhah: An Experiment in Decision Making*. West Orange, NJ: Behrman House, 1994, pp. 367-412.

The Gathering. New York: Coalition for the Advancement of Jewish Education, 1988.

Glustrom, Simon. *The Language of Judaism*. Northvale, NJ: Jason Aronson, 1994.

Patera, Meridith Shaw. *Kings and Things: 20 Plays for Jewish Kids 8 to 18*. Denver: A.R.E. Publishing, Inc., 1996.

Rapoport, Louis. *Redemption Song: The Story of Operation Moses*. New York: Harcourt, Brace, Jovanovich, 1986.

Richards, Stephen, ed. *Manginot: 201 Songs for Jewish Schools*. New York: Transcontinental Music Publications and New Jewish Music Press, 1992.

Ross, Lillian. *The World of Soviet Jewry*. Miami: Central Agency for Jewish Education, 1982.

Steiner, Connie Colker. *On Eagles' Wings and Other Things*. Philadelphia: The Jewish Publication Society of America, 1987.

Wyman, David S. *The Abandonment of the Jews*. New York: Pantheon Books, 1984, pp. 82ff, 243-251.

For the Students

Artson, Bradley Shavit. *It's a Mitzvah: Step-by-Step to Jewish Living*. West Orange, NJ: Behrman House and New York: The Rabbinical Assembly, 1995, pp. 108-117. (Grades 8-adult)

Bamberger, David. *A Young Person's History of Israel*. 2d ed. West Orange, NJ: Behrman House, 1994. (Grades 5-7)

Brown, Tricia. *L'Chaim: The Story of a Russian Emigre Boy*. New York: Henry Holt, 1994. (Grades 2-4)

Gray, Bettyanne. *Manya's Story*. New York: Lerner Group, 1995. (Grades 6 and up)

Greene, Jacqueline Dembar. *One Foot Ashore*. New York: Walker and Co., 1994. (Grades 3-6)

Grishaver, Joel Lurie. *Schindler's List. P'shat vs. Drash as Truth about the Holocaust*. Instant Lesson. Los Angeles: Torah Aura Productions. (Grades 6-adult)

Hart, Jan Siegel. *Hanna, the Immigrant*. Austin, TX: Eakin, 1991. (Grades 3-6)

Hurwitz, Ann Ricki, and Sue Hurwitz. *K'lal Yisrael: Our Jewish Community*. West Orange, NJ: Behrman House, 1991. (Grades 5-6)

Kendall, Jonathan P. *My Name Is Rachamim*. New York: UAHC Press, 1987. (Grades 1-4)

Kossman, Nina. *Behind the Border: Memories of a Russian Girlhood*. New York: Lothrop, 1994. (Grades 3-6)

Kushner, Arlene. *Falasha No More: An Ethiopian Child Comes Home*. New York: Sure Sellers, 1986. (Grades 3-6)

Levitan, Sonia. *The Return*. New York: Atheneum, 1987. (Grades 4-7)

"Pidyon Shevuyim." In *Gemilut Hasadim*, vols. 1 and 2. Baltimore: Bureau of Jewish Education, 1983. (Grades 7-9, has accompanying book for teachers)

Rossel, Seymour. *Covenant People, Covenant Land*. New York: UAHC Press, 1985. (Grades 7 and up)

Sachs, Marilyn. *Call Me Ruth*. New York: Doubleday and Co., Inc., 1982. (Grades 4 and up)

Stein, Glenn. *Operation Solomon: Rescuing the Jews of Ethiopia*. Instant Lesson. Los Angeles: Torah Aura Productions. (Grades 4-adult)

Audiovisual

Again — The Second Time. A 19 minute documentary on the May 24, 1991 airlift, Operation Solomon, by Israel of over 14,000 Ethiopians in 36 hours. Ergo Media Inc. (Grades 7 and up)

Dosvedanya Means Good-bye. A 30 minute video about Tamara Okun, a Russian Jew who waited eight years to receive her exit visa. As the years passed, her sense of Jewish identity grew stronger and more profound. The film follows Tamara and her family as they journey from Leningrad to Vienna and to their new home in Washington, D.C. Ergo Media Inc. (Grades 9 and up)

The Falashas. A 27 minute classic film study of Ethiopian Jewry by Meyer Levin in 1973. Describes Jewish ritual and practices as observed for generations in isolation. Ergo Media Inc. (Grades 7 and up)

Freedom to Hate: Anti-Semitism in Russia. A 58 minute video describes the virulent anti-Semitic organization Pamyat. Dated but pertinent to the topic of redeeming captives. Filmakers Library. (Grades 10 and up)

Operation Moses: A Documentary. A 27 minute video containing the story of the rescue, immigration, and absorption of Ethiopian Jewry. Ergo Media Inc. (Grades 7 and up)

Operation Thunderbolt. This 124 minute feature film on video is a dramatization of the July 4, 1976 rescue of the 104 hijacked airplane passengers in Entebbe, Uganda. Available in some video stores. (Grades 7 and up)

Raid on Entebbe. A 150 minute video made for TV about the Israeli commando assault on the Entebbe airport in Uganda to rescue the Jews held hostage by Arab terrorists. Available at some video stores. (Grades 7 and up)

Sousa. A 30 minute video about a group of Jews who fled the Nazis and found a haven in the Dominican Republic. Ergo Media Inc. (Grades 7 and up)

"We Are Leaving Mother Russia." On the audiocassette *The Bridge* by Jeffrey Klepper and Daniel Freelander. Available from A.R.E. Publishing, Inc. (Grades 3 and up)

UNIT 24

Welcoming the Stranger
הַכְנָסַת אוֹרְחִים

OVERVIEW

The literal meaning of the term *Hachnasat Orchim* is "bringing in of guests." Providing hospitality to strangers is a tradition which has its roots in earliest biblical times. Abraham is the first person to perform this Mitzvah when he greets three visitors who approach his tent: "My lords, if it please you, do not go on past your servant. Let a little water be brought; bathe your feet and recline under the tree. And let me fetch a morsel of bread that you may refresh yourselves" (Genesis 18:3-5). Abraham prepares a meal for his visitors, who have come to inform him that his wife Sarah will soon bear a son. It is Lot, Abraham's nephew, who next performs the Mitzvah when he offers hospitality to two angels who come to Sodom to destroy the evil city (Genesis 19:1-3).

Abraham sends his servant Eliezer to Haran in order to find a wife for Isaac. At the well, Eliezer meets Rebekah, who draws water for him and his camels and offers a room for him to spend the night. Taking him to her home, he meets her family members who also greet him warmly. Then, on behalf of Abraham, Eliezer offers to take Rebekah to Isaac. The match is made because of *Hachnasat Orchim*. (Genesis 24:28ff)

Another exemplar of hospitality in the Bible is Jethro. Upon hearing that an Egyptian rescued his seven daughters from wicked shepherds, Jethro invites the stranger in to break bread (Exodus 2:20). He then rewards the Egyptian, who turns out to be Moses, by giving his daughter Zipporah for a wife.

These examples led one writer to conclude that "In ancient Israel, hospitality was not merely a question of good manners, but a moral institution which grew out of the harsh desert and nomadic existence led by the people of Israel" (*Encyclopaedia Judaica*, vol. 8, col. 1030).

The Rabbis cited these biblical precedents as a basis for practicing hospitality. They wrote that Abraham and Job left open the flaps on all four sides of their tents in order to welcome guests. Rabbi Huna's famous statement, "Let all who are hungry enter and eat" (*Ta'anit* 20b) became a central theme of the *Seder*. In *Pirke Avot* 1:5 we are taught: "Let your house be opened wide and let the poor be members of your household." According to the *Talmud*, hospitality to the wayfarer is one of the pleasures enjoyed in this world and which is also rewarded in the world to come (*Shabbat* 127a). So important is this Mitzvah that, if necessary, it was permitted to clear a warehouse full of straw on Shabbat in order to make room for guests (*Shabbat* 126b).

The Rabbis established guidelines for both the host and the guest. For example, the host was expected to wait on guests, responding to their needs, but the host was forbidden to watch the guests too closely lest they refrain from eating their fill. The guests, on their part, were to show ample gratitude and to avoid overstaying their welcome.

In Jerusalem it was customary to display a flag in front of one's door to indicate that guests were welcome to come in for a meal (*Baba Batra* 93b). The Middle Ages saw this custom become formalized in some communities through the establishment of a *Chevra Hachnasat Orchim*, a group of people who would help visitors to a town find meals and lodging. It was during this period that the custom of reciting *Kiddush* at the synagogue on Erev Shabbat developed in order to accommodate visitors who might otherwise not have an opportunity to bless and drink Sabbath wine. For a similar reason, a communal *sukkah* was erected at some synagogues.

In Germany and Poland, it was considered a special privilege to invite *yeshivah* students to one's home for a meal or an extended stay, a practice which became known by the Yiddish phrase *essentag*.

Hospitality continues to be an important Mitzvah today. Attending a Shabbat service away from home will often lead to an invitation for a meal. In Jerusalem some Jews will seek out Shabbat guests at the Western Wall. Many communities arrange to invite military personnel and college students to holiday meals and celebrations. Most synagogues make a special effort to welcome newcomers to the community.

Perhaps as much as any other Mitzvah, *Hachnasat Orchim* exemplifies the saying: "All Israel is responsible for one another" (*Shevuot* 39a).

ACTIVITIES

Primary

1. Build a diorama with a desert theme, depicting Abraham's tent with the flaps open in all four directions. Then have an individual dressed as Abraham make a surprise visit to your classroom. He can explain the reasons for having a tent with four doorways and why welcoming strangers was so important to Abraham. Invite the children to ask questions of your biblical guest on other topics as well.

2. Make a welcome mat for your religious school classroom. Use an unfinished piece of artist's canvas and stencil a welcome greeting on it with permanent acrylic paint. Include the Hebrew phrase for welcome — *Baruchim Haba'im.*

3. Make cards of welcome for new children in the synagogue. Use themes related to the Mitzvah of *Hachnasat Orchim.*

4. Discuss how the students like to be treated when they are in a new place, and how they think newcomers should be treated.

5. Learn the song *"Shalom Chaverim."* The music can be found in many Jewish songbooks. The students can sing this song whenever a guest comes to their classroom.

6. Read the story *The Magician* by Uri Shulevitz. Discuss using the following questions: What makes this individual magical to the townspeople? To the elderly couple? What kind of "person" was the magician? Did he seem harmful to the townspeople? To the elderly couple? Did the magician make good magic or evil magic? What was the Rabbi's reply? Could this really happen? How does the appearance or behavior of a stranger affect how you perform the Mitzvah of *Hachnasat Orchim*? What are some of the good deeds you perform that demonstrate the Mitzvah of *Hachnasat Orchim*? What kind of rewards do you expect to receive for these deeds?

Intermediate

1. Take an oral history of an immigrant. Take care to note how he or she was welcomed, what made him/her feel a part of the new country, etc.

2. Create a ritual in which you welcome newcomers to your synagogue. It might take the form of a special service. Include references to the Mitzvah of *Hachnasat Orchim.*

3. In most communities, there is a group called Welcome Wagon. Its function is to welcome new individuals and families to the community. Invite a representative of Welcome Wagon to speak to your class or group to explain what it is that they do for newcomers. Relate the activity of Welcome Wagon to the Mitzvah of *Hachnasat Orchim.*

4. Listen to the song *"Shalom, Shalom"* from the musical *Milk and Honey.* Discuss the various uses of the word *shalom.* Also investigate the Hebrew root of the word *shalom* in *Your Jewish Lexicon* by Edith Samuel, pp. 26-29.

5. Create a tile mosaic with the word *shalom* in Hebrew or English. Embellish it with some designs. Use books on Jewish and Israeli art, such as those listed below, to provide the basis for some unique designs to copy.

   References: *Jewish Art* by Grace Cohen; *Jewish Art Masterpieces* by Iris Fishof; *Jewish Symbolic Art* by Abram Kanof.

6. Read the story "Hershele and Hanukkah" by Isaac Bashevis Singer found in *The Power of Light: Eight Stories for Hanukkah.* Ask students to list some of the good deeds Reb Berish did. How do his actions demonstrate the Mitzvah of *Hachnasat Orchim*? How is he rewarded? Point out the special role that Elijah plays in the story.

Secondary

1. Read excerpts of diaries by people who immigrated to America or Israel, paying specific attention to how these individuals were welcomed. What else might have been done to fulfill the Mitzvah of *Hachnasat Orchim*?

2. As a means of fulfilling the Mitzvah of *Hachnasat Orchim*, adopt and befriend a Soviet Jewish family or other recent immigrant family. Contacts can be made through the local Soviet Jewry Office, Jewish Family Service, Catholic Social Service, or other agencies which help resettle immigrants.

3. In most major airports and train terminals, there is an organization called Travelers Aid. Do some research on this group. If such an organization exists in a local transportation center, invite a guest representative to explain its function. Relate the activities of this organization to the Mitzvah of *Hachnasat Orchim*.

4. Assemble "Shalom Baskets" for newcomers to your synagogue. Suggestions of items to include: A Jewish calendar, *challah*, small bottle of wine, Shabbat candles, a guide to Jewish facilities in your community (if available), a roster of synagogue members. Through discussion generate an expanded list of items to include.

5. Read the story "Eating Days" by Lamed Shapiro found in *A Treasury of Yiddish Stories*, edited by Irving Howe and Eliezer Greenberg. Discuss how the practice of *essentag* is an example of the Mitzvah of *Hachnasat Orchim*.

6. In order to enable students to practice the Mitzvah of *Hachnasat Orchim*, have them role play some or all of the following scenarios:
   a. You and a friend are eating at a restaurant when you see a new kid from the synagogue who is sitting alone.
   b. A teen-age relative from Israel is visiting your family for the first time. You don't know how to speak Hebrew and your Israeli relative doesn't speak English. You want to take him/her to a school dance.
   c. Your divorced mother is bringing home a new date for you and your siblings to meet.

ALL-SCHOOL PROGRAMS

1. Sponsor a Shabbat or holiday dinner for new members of the synagogue. Be sure that new and old members are interspersed at the tables.

2. Plan a Shabbat service and special *Oneg Shabbat* to welcome new members and introduce them to other congregants. The theme of the service

could be "*Hachnasat Orchim* as a Jewish Value." Invite someone who is knowledgeable about the congregation to give a brief history of the congregation and/or the Jewish community.

3. Establish a host-family program in your congregation. Recruit members who are interested in serving as hosts to new members. You might want to match new members to hosts based on common interests, similar aged children, geographic location, etc. In the recruitment literature, explain the Mitzvah of *Hachnasat Orchim*. The hosts might invite the new members for a Shabbat or holiday meal, sit with them at services, and introduce them to other members.

4. To enable students to experience the Mitzvah of *Hachnasat Orchim*, hold a "Cavalcade of Holidays." Each class is responsible for preparing a display about a Jewish holiday. Invite classes from church schools to learn about Judaism. Begin at an assembly, with the Rabbi welcoming the guests and the students singing "*Shalom Chaverim*." The guests rotate to each of the displays to learn about the holiday. Class members should be at each booth to explain the display and to answer questions.

RESOURCES

For the Teacher

Bloch, Abraham P. *A Book of Jewish Ethical Concepts*. New York: KTAV Publishing House, Inc., 1984, pp. 161-165.

Fishof, Iris. *Jewish Art Masterpieces*. New York: H.L. Levin Associates, 1995.

Glustrom, Simon. *The Language of Judaism*. Northvale, NJ: Jason Aronson, 1994, pp. 27-28.

Goodman, Jerry. "Protecting Human Rights Around the World." In *Olam/World Repair Manual: Jewish Civics: A Tikkun* by Mark Gopin, Mark H. Levine, and Sid Schwartz. New York: Coalition for the advancement of Jewish Education and Rockville, MD: The Washington Institute of Jewish Leadership and Values, 1994.

Grossman, Grace Cohen. *Jewish Art*. New York: Hugh Lauder Levin Associates, 1995.

"Hospitality." In *Encyclopaedia Judaica*. Jerusalem: Keter Publishing House Jerusalem Ltd., vol. 8, cols. 1030-1033.

Kanof, Abram. *Jewish Symbolic Art*. Hewlett, NJ: Gefen Publishing House, 1992.

Streisand, Nina Sher, and Margaret Feldman. *100+ Jewish Art Projects for Kids*. Denver: A.R.E. Publishing, Inc., 1996.

For the Students

Artson, Bradley Shavit. *It's a Mitzvah: Step-by-Step to Jewish Living*. West Orange, NJ: Behrman House and New York: The Rabbinical Assembly, 1995, pp. 74-83. (Grades 8-adult)

Feinberg, Miriam P. *Just Enough Room*. New York: United Synagogue, 1991. (Grades PK-3)

"Hachnasat Orhim — Hospitality." In *Gemilut Hasadim*, vols. 1 and 2. Baltimore: Bureau of Jewish Education, 1988. (Grades 1-3, has accompanying book for teachers)

Isaacs, Ronald H., and Kerry M. Olitzky. *Doing Mitzvot: Mitzvah Projects for Bar/Bat Mitzvah*. Hoboken, NJ: KTAV Publishing House, Inc., 1994, pp. 29-40. (Grades 6-8)

Rosenberg, Amye. *Mitzvot*. New York: Behrman House, 1984, pp. 8-9. (Grades K-2)

Shapiro, Lamed. "Eating Days." In *A Treasury of Yiddish Stories*. Irving Howe and Eliezer Greenberg, eds. New York: Viking Penguin, 1990, pp. 449-471. (Grades 7 and up)

Singer, Isaac Bashevis Singer. *The Power of Light*. New York: Farrar, Straus and Giroux, Inc., 1980. (Grades 4-6)

Audiovisual

American Jews: Introductory Video (The Golden Land on the Silver Screen). Six selected films which focus on the American Jewish experience are reviewed, then followed by questions and thoughts about American Jewish life. Ergo Media Inc. (Grades 10 and up)

An American Tail. An animated, full-length video that features the adventures of Feivel, a Jewish mouse, who comes with his family to America. Available at video stores. (Grades K-6)

The Good Hearted Ant. A 10 minute video in which a good hearted ant, angry because his father turned away a starving cricket, refuses to do his work until the cricket is found. International Film Bureau. (Grades K-3)

Journey to America. A 60 minute overview of the immigrant experience using oral interviews and archival material. PBS. (Grades 10-adult)

Present Memory. This 88 minute video encourages an understanding of many facets of Jewish life in America as it looks at both ethnic and cultural life. Filmakers Library. (Grades 7-adult)

To Jew Is Not a Verb. In a 15 minute video, David is accused of "jewing" another boy while trading baseball cards. A lesson about stereotyping is the result. Beacon Films Inc. (Grades 4-9)

West of Hester Street. A one hour film which depicts the efforts of American Jewish leaders to settle new immigrants in Galveston during the years 1881 to 1914. Media Projects. (Grades 4 and up)

UNIT 25

OVERVIEW

"Thus Abraham and his son Ishmael were circumcized on that very day; and all his household, his homeborn, slaves and those who had been bought from outsiders, were circumcized with him. And the Lord appeared to him by the terebinths of Mamre" (Genesis 17:26-18:1).

In the Talmud the comment on these verses teaches, "God visited the sick, as it is written, 'And the Lord appeared to him by the terebinths of Mamre.' So you must visit the sick" (*Sota* 14a). By performing the Mitzvah of *Bikur Cholim*, Visiting the Sick, we imitate God, as it were, who visited Abraham when he was recovering from his circumcision.

Many Talmudic statements indicate the centrality of this Mitzvah. Visiting the Sick is considered a religious duty without limit (*Shabbat* 127a). A person is rewarded both in this world and in the world to come for Visiting the Sick. "Whoever visits a sick person helps him to recover" (*Nedarim* 40a). Rabbi Akiba went so far as to say that not visiting a sick person could be considered as if one sheds blood (*Nedarim* 40a).

There are specific guidelines for Visiting the Sick. So that visits will be beneficial, and not burdensome, to the patient: One should not stay too long on any one visit so as not to tire the patient; one may make frequent visits, but not during the first three hours of the day, when the patient is likely to be feeling better and the visitor may, therefore, find no need to offer a prayer; neither should one visit during the last three hours of the day, when the illness is worse, and a visitor might lose all hope. When talking to a sick person, a visitor should be careful not to give the person false hopes or cause the person despair.

There are two basic reasons for Visiting the Sick: to look after his or her needs and to offer prayers on his or her behalf. Jewish tradition has special prayers for the bedside and for the synagogue. At the bedside one may recite, "May God have mercy upon you among the other sick of Israel," and in the synagogue the "*Mi Shebeyrach.*" The recitation of certain Psalms is always appropriate.

ACTIVITIES

Primary

1. As a group list and discuss the ways one can help out at home if a parent is ill in order to perform the Mitzvah of *Bikur Cholim*.

2. To extend activity #1, have the group role play the suggestions they brainstormed. Costumes and props will give a realistic effect. Take still photos of the role plays. Create a bulletin board display of the photos with accompanying descriptions.

3. Make up a packet of activities for a friend who is home sick and in bed. Have the students think of quiet activities, such as crossword puzzles, word jumbles, dot-to-dot pictures, simple origami (paper folding), etc. If the class is thinking of packets for friends who are Jewish, they could include material and activities for an upcoming holiday. Discuss how this fulfills the Mitzvah of *Bikur Cholim*.

4. To enable students to participate in *Bikur Cholim*, make paper flower bouquets or get well cards for Jewish patients in a local hospital. Ask the Rabbi or other synagogue personnel for a current list of congregants in the hospital. The local public library will have several arts and crafts resource books which will describe card and flower making.

5. Interview the Rabbi, a doctor, a nurse, and a hospital volunteer. Prepare interview questions in advance on how visiting helps a sick person and on what the students can do to help a sick person, thereby performing the Mitzvah of *Bikur Cholim*.

6. After a session immediately prior to this activity, send home a note with the students asking that each bring a doll from home. After summarizing the material from the Overview section above, set

up a hospital ward with dolls as patients. Assign students to play the roles of doctor, nurse, visitor, relative, member of a *Bikur Cholim* society, and Rabbi to visit and care for the patients.

Intermediate

1. Read through the *Code of Jewish Law* by Solomon Ganzfried, vol. 4, pp. 87-89, which contains guidelines created by the Rabbis for Visiting the Sick. Consider the following questions: Are the guidelines adequate? Do they need to be changed? Reworded? Added to? Using these as a basis, write a series of contemporary guidelines for Visiting the Sick.

2. As a way to involve students in the *Bikur Cholim*, put together holiday boxes for Jewish patients at a local hospital. Choose an upcoming holiday (include Shabbat among your choices). Generate a list of items which would allow the hospital-bound patient to celebrate and enjoy the holiday. Check hospital safety regulations (some may not permit candles to be lit). Make or collect the items, place them in a decorated box, and deliver them to the hospital.

3. There is a tradition in Jewish folklore which teaches that when a Jewish individual becomes seriously ill, it may be possible to change that person's fate by changing his/her Hebrew name. According to superstition, this change confuses the Angel of Death who therefore may not be able to find that Jewish soul. To learn more about this tradition, see the reference listed immediately below.

   Reference: *Jewish Magic and Superstition* by Joshua Trachtenberg, pp. 204-206.

4. Come up with a plan to raise funds or use monies from the weekly *Tzedakah* collection to purchase games, books, and/or toys to donate to the children's ward of a local hospital. Brainstorm other ways to fulfill the Mitzvah of *Bikur Cholim*.

5. If there is a Jewish hospital in your community, research its history. Create a visual display based on your research to be shown at the hospital itself or in your synagogue or school.

6. Arrange a tour of a local hospital for your class. Ask the tour leader to emphasize hospital

guidelines and suggestions for visiting patients, as well as opportunities for young people to volunteer.

7. Very often we fear what we do not understand. This relates directly to Visiting the Sick. Contact a local children's hospital. Request a pediatric nurse or hospital volunteer to make a presentation explaining such medical procedures as tonsillectomies and appendectomies. Ask that they use the dolls which are specially designed as an aid for such talks.

Secondary

1. Judaism considers prayer an important part of the healing process. One of the traditional prayers recited for the sick is a *"Mi Shebeyrach"* (see *The Authorized Daily Prayerbook* by Joseph H. Hertz, pp. 492-93). Additionally there is a prayer called *Birkat HaGomel* recited by one who has recovered from a serious illness or has been delivered from peril (*ibid.*, pp. 486-87). Read these prayers in Hebrew and English and discuss their contents. You may wish to invite the Rabbi or Director of Education to add some insights to these prayers.

2. View *Echoes of a Summer*, a film about a terminally ill youth. Discuss how the Mitzvah of *Bikur Cholim* relates to someone who is terminally ill.

3. Invite a speaker from a local hospice society to discuss appropriate attitudes and behavior when dealing with a terminally ill person.

4. Investigate the Jewish attitude toward euthanasia. Then debate one of the following:
   a. It is right to withhold medical treatment from a seriously ill patient who has no chance of recovery.
   b. A terminally ill patient should have the right to stop medical treatment which might hasten his/her death.
   c. It is right to pray for someone to die.

   References: *Modern Medicine and Jewish Ethics* by Fred Rosner, chapters 15-16; *Jewish Bioethics* by Fred Rosner and J. David Bleich, chapters 15-16; *Bioethics: A Jewish View* by James L. Simon, Raymond A. Zwerin, and Audrey Friedman Marcus, pp. 2-7.

5. Doctors play a critical role in the Mitzvah of *Bikur Cholim*. Upon graduation from medical school, doctors recite the Hippocratic Oath which is a summary statement of a doctor's responsibilities. An alternative oath called "The Physician's Prayer," is attributed to the medieval Jewish scholar Maimonides, who was a physician; it is used by a few medical schools. Compare the two oaths and identify their similarities and differences. "The Physician's Prayer" can be found in *Medicine in the Bible and the Talmud* by Fred Rosner, pp. 136-138. The article on pp. 125-136 discusses the origin of the prayer. Both oaths appear in *Bioethics: A Jewish View* by James L. Simon, Raymond A. Zwerin, and Audrey Friedman Marcus, p. 21.

6. The novel *Alan and Naomi* by Myron Levoy deals in part with the concept of *Bikur Cholim*. Read those parts of the novel which deal directly with *Bikur Cholim* and use this as a basis for an opening discussion with the class.

ALL-SCHOOL PROGRAMS

1. Organize a "Mitzvah Meals" program for your synagogue, providing food to families during the illness of a family member. Make reference to the Mitzvah of *Bikur Cholim* in the publicity.

2. Create a booklet comprised of Psalms, prayers, poems, and other inspirational readings to be distributed to congregants who are ill. Write an introduction that discusses *Bikur Cholim*.

3. Many individuals play vital roles in the Mitzvah of *Bikur Cholim*. Invite a doctor, nurse, Rabbi, and a hospital volunteer to an assembly. Divide the students into four groups. Have the speakers rotate from group to group, discussing briefly his or her role in the healing process. Be sure to leave time for questions. Bring the students together at the end and discuss the importance of each person's role in the healing process.

RESOURCES

For the Teacher

Ganzfried, Solomon. *Code of Jewish Law: Kitzur Shulhan Arukh.* rev. ed. Hyman E. Goldin, trans.

Rockaway Beach, NY: Hebrew Publishing Co., 1991, vol. 4, ch. 193, pp. 87-89.

Hertz, Joseph H. *The Authorized Daily Prayer Book.* New York: Bloch Publishing Co., 1945.

Meier, Levi, ed. *Jewish Values in Health and Medicine.* Lanham, MD: University Press of America, 1991.

Rosner, Fred, et al. *Jewish Bioethics.* New York: Hebrew Publishing Co., 1979, chapters 15-16.

"Sick, Prayer for," "Sick, Visiting the," and "Sick Care, Communal." In *Encyclopaedia Judaica.* Jerusalem: Keter Publishing House Jerusalem Ltd., 1972, vol. 14, cols. 1496-1499.

Strassfeld, Sharon, and Michael Strassfeld, comps. and eds. *The Third Jewish Catalog: Creating Community.* Philadelphia: The Jewish Publication Society of America, 1980, pp. 140-145.

"Visiting a Sick Friend." In *Lively Legends — Jewish Values: An Early Childhood Teaching Guide* by Miriam P. Feinberg and Rena Rotenberg. Denver: A.R.E. Publishing, Inc., 1993.

Yurow, Jane Handler, and Kim Hetherington. *Give Me Your Hand: Traditional and Practical Guidance to Visiting the Sick.* Washington, DC: Adas Israel Synagogue, n.d.

For the Students

Artson, Bradley Shavit. *It's a Mitzvah: Step-by-Step to Jewish Living.* West Orange, NJ: Behrman House and New York: The Rabbinical Assembly, 1995, pp. 62-73. (Grades 8-adult)

Isaacs, Ronald H., and Kerry M. Olitzky. *Doing Mitzvot: Mitzvah Projects for Bar/Bat Mitzvah.* Hoboken, NJ: KTAV Publishing House, Inc., 1994, pp. 20-28. (Grades 6-8)

———. *The How-to Handbook for Jewish Living.* Hoboken, NJ: KTAV Publishing House, Inc., 1993, pp. 111-112. (Grades 7 and up)

Audiovisual

AIDS: Answers for Young People. An 18 minute film set in a classroom where teen peer educators discuss AIDS. Churchill Media. (Grades 7 and up)

The Boardwalk Club. The story in 27 minutes of an elderly couple who differ on where to spend their retirement years. The Cinema Guild. (Adult)

Complaints of a Dutiful Daughter. A 60 minute video which explores a daughter's relationship with her mother who has Alzheimer's Disease. Women Make Films. (Grades 10 and up)

The Face of Wisdom: Stories of Elder Women. A series of eight 27 minute videos, each of which focuses on a different elderly woman from a different ethnic group. Franciscan Communications. (Grades 10 and up)

"Home is Where the Heart Is." On the audiocassette *Jewish Rock and Roll Singer* by Mah Tovu. A touching song addressing the subjects of AIDS, compassion for the sick, and teaching children.

about acceptance of those with different lifestyles. (Grades 9 and up)

Meet Me in Miami. An 18 minute story of three elderly Jews who are facing the tough realities of their changing situations with dignity. National Center for Jewish Films. (Grades 8 and up)

Renewal of Spirit. Audiocassette by Debbie Friedman that contains healing prayers and songs, including *"Mi Shebeirach."* Sounds Write Productions, Inc. Available from A.R.E. Publishing, Inc.

UNIT 26

Honoring the Elderly
כִּבּוּד זְקֵנִים

OVERVIEW

"You shall rise up before the aged and show deference to the old; you shall fear your God: I am the Lord" (Leviticus 19:32). This passage expresses the Jewish ideal regarding treatment of the elderly. The Bible regards living a long life and dying in old age to be a blessing. A long life is said to be the reward for observing the Mitzvot of honoring one's parents, allowing a mother bird to go free when taking her eggs, and having accurate weights and measures in your business dealings.

The patriarchs, in particular, lived long lives: Abraham to 175, Isaac to 180, and Jacob to 147. Moses died at 120, which has become the ideal length of life as reflected in the birthday wish: "May you live to be 120." Even if these figures are not taken literally, the biblical text clearly indicates that long life is a reward for living righteously. Furthermore, Isaiah describes a corrupt generation as one in which "the young shall bully the old" (Isaiah 3:5). According to Lamentations (5:12), one of the sins which contributed to the destruction of the Temple was that "no respect has been shown to elders."

In contrast to these passages which lead one to look forward to old age, Kohelet offers a more sobering picture: "Appreciate your vigor in the days of your youth, before those days of sorrow come and those years arrive of which you will say, 'I have no pleasure in them' . . . . When the arms become shaky and the legs are bent, and the teeth, grown few, are idle, and the eyes grow dim" (Ecclesiastes 12:1-3).

The Rabbinic attitude toward the elderly reflects both the idealism of the earlier biblical passages and the realism of Kohelet. For example, "It is always the aged who uphold Israel. When does Israel stand upright? When they have their aged with them. For one who takes counsel with the old never falters" (Exodus Rabbah 38).

A person who learns from the young is compared to one who eats unripe grapes and drinks wine from a vat, whereas a person who learns from the old is compared to one who eats ripe grapes and drinks wine that is aged (Pirke Avot 4:26). Rabbi Joshua ben Levi taught that one should "honor and respect the aged and saintly scholar whose physical powers are broken" (Berachot 8b). Elisha ben Abuyah compared learning when one is old to writing on blotted out paper (Pirke Avot 4:28). The Talmud recognized that the elderly were apt to be needy. "Every profession in the world is of help to a person only in one's youth, but in one's old age, one is exposed to hunger" (Kiddushin 82b).

In his delineation of the Mitzvot, Maimonides interpreted the commandment to Honor the Elderly as referring to both the scholars and the aged, reflecting the Rabbinic notion that the two go hand-in-hand (The Commandments, vol. 1, pp. 224-226). Many medieval Jewish ethical and halachic works single out the elderly as being worthy of special charity and treatment. While it was the responsibility of a family to support its parents and other elderly relatives, the Jewish community stepped in when necessary.

To meet the need of caring for the elderly, the first Jewish home for the aged was founded in 1749 in Amsterdam. During the eighteenth and nineteenth centuries, an increasing number of Jewish foundations to care for the elderly was established. Prior to the Holocaust, Germany alone had 67 Jewish homes for the aged.

The first Jewish home for the aged in the United States was created in 1855 in St. Louis. During the next century, almost every large Jewish community in North America established a home for the aged. In recent years there has been a significant increase in the absolute number of senior citizens, as well as in their proportion of the general community. In 1982, 13 per cent of the Jews in the United States were age 65 and older. This figure is projected to increase by several per cent each decade. It has also become clear that a significant percentage of the Jewish elderly live in poverty. Taken together, these factors have influenced many synagogues, Jewish Community Centers, social service agencies, and Federations to devote more money and programming to the elderly.

ACTIVITIES

Primary

1. Visit a home for the aged. Before going on the visit, discuss with the students what they may see and hear; encourage them to share their own experiences with the elderly. You may want the visit to coincide with a holiday observance. The class might prepare greeting cards, a song, or a skit to present.

2. Have the students invite their grandparents to come to a religious school session. For those students whose grandparents are unable to attend, arrange for them to adopt a grandparent for the day. Ideas for sessions:
   a. Ask both generations to share how they celebrate a particular holiday such as Passover or Chanukah.
   b. Bake *challah* together.
   c. Have the older generation talk about growing up Jewish.
   d. Teach a song and sing it together.

3. Make holiday greeting cards for Rosh Hashanah, Chanukah, or Passover to send to grandparents or older acquaintances and friends.

4. Have students discuss a recent visit with a grandparent or older individual. Ask questions to encourage discussion, such as: What did you do? Where do you go? Did your visitor need any special help? Did you have a meal or treat?

5. Brainstorm with the students ways in which they can help the elderly. Write a list of these on a large sheet of paper or poster board and display in the classroom.

6. Read and discuss *Bubby, Me, and Memories* by Barbara Pomerantz. Ask the following questions: What are some of the things the young girl remembers about her *bubby*? How do these memories help her when her grandmother dies? What special memories do you have of your grandparents?

Intermediate

1. Have the students research significant achievements of people over the age of 65. Some suggestions are: Grandma Moses, Arthur Rubinstein, Albert Schweitzer, Golda Meir, Ben Franklin, Maggie Kuhn, George Burns.

2. View the movie *Close Harmony*, a film depicting the creation of a choir of young children and senior adults. Discuss reactions to the film.

3. Using a variety of magazines, ask the students to find examples of how the elderly are portrayed. Then take these pictures and create a collage. Discuss stereotypes, ageism, new ways in which the media presents unbiased views of older people.

4. Create a resource packet on the elderly for your synagogue or school. Include government pamphlets, available from the National Institute on Aging, 9000 Rockville Pike, Bethesda, MD 20892, or the Administration on Aging, 200 Independence Ave. S.W., Washington, DC 20201, and also the booklet *So Teach Us To Number Our Days: A Manual on Aging for Synagogue Use* by Sanford Seltzer, available from the Union of American Hebrew Congregations, 838 Fifth Ave., New York, NY 10021.

5. As a class project, develop a Mitzvah service for the elderly. Someone might need his/her windows washed, an attic cleaned, a garden trimmed and weeded, or a friendly visitor on a regular basis. (These are only a few of the possible ways students can help.) Each service can be a one-time offer of help or, if possible, an ongoing project.

6. Create a reading resource center on the aged. Each student should choose one book or story to read. After reading a book each student will illustrate on poster board an idea, a scene, or a feeling derived from the book.

References: *The Memory Box* by Mary Bahr; *Nanny's Special Gift* by Rochelle Potaracke; *Sweet Notes, Sour Notes* by Nancy Smiler Levinson; *Grandma's Latkes* by Malka Drucker.

7. Distribute plain sheets of paper and pencils to your students. Ask them to close their eyes and imagine what they will look like, what they will be doing, and who will be their friends and close family members when they are 70 years old. As they open their eyes, tell them to imagine that

the paper before them is a mirror. Have them draw their 70-year-old reflection. At the bottom of the picture, they can record what they do, the names of their friends and close family members, and what their lives are like.

Secondary

1. Invite a speaker to make a presentation on Alzheimer's Disease.

2. Have the students keep a television log in which they record portrayals of the elderly for one week's time. Students should record the kinds of roles and situations in which elderly people find themselves. Discuss: Do these television depictions reflect real life? Are television portrayals of the elderly a positive or negative influence on how the students respond to older people in day-to-day life?

3. Discuss and critique the following quotations from *Pirke Avot*:

   "Elisha ben Abuya said: 'One who learns when a youth is similar to ink written on new paper. One who learns when old is similar to ink written on erased paper'" (4:25).

   "Rabbi Yosi bar Yehuda of K'far Hababli said: 'One who learns from the young is similar to one who eats unripe grapes and drinks wine from his wine press. One who learns from the old is similar to one who eats ripe grapes and drinks old wine'" (4:26).

   Have students write their own contemporary statements about learning from the young and learning from the old.

4. View the film *Number Our Days*. Ask students to imagine and describe what they think their lives will be like when they reach 80.

5. View the trigger films *Tagged* and *To Market, To Market*. Share reactions and discuss how the situations portrayed can be improved.

6. Help your students develop a new dimension in their relationships with elderly individuals by making them collectors of stories, folktales, and personal histories. The students will need tape recorders and a list of questions for their interview subjects. The questions may be prepared by the teacher or by the students themselves.

ALL-SCHOOL PROGRAMS

1. Have a few individuals made up to look elderly. See and discuss the physical transition in going from a young person to an old person.

2. Organize a Grandparents' Shabbat service for your congregation. Grandparents and grandchildren can participate in the service, and some could speak about their relationships with each other in place of a sermon.

3. Plan a multi-generational weekend retreat. The theme might be the Jewish attitude toward the elderly or another theme that is appropriate for all ages.

4. After viewing the movie *Close Harmony*, create an intergenerational choir at your synagogue. Or, create a children's choir and, as was done in the film, sing with members of a home for the aged.

5. Organize a Jewish Film Series on the theme of the Aged. Among the titles to consider including are *Brighton Beach*, *Close Harmony*, *Lies My Father Told Me*, *Miracle of Intervale Avenue*, *Number Our Days*, *A Private Life*, *The Story of Esther*, *Tell Me a Riddle*, and *Yudie*.

RESOURCES

For the Teacher

"Age and the Aged." In *Encyclopaedia Judaica*. Jerusalem: Keter Publishing House Jerusalem, Ltd., 1972, vol. 2, cols. 343-348.

Myerhoff, Barbara. *Number Our Days*. New York: Simon and Schuster, 1978.

For the Students

Bahr, Mary. *The Memory Box*. Salt Lake City, UT: Whitman Associates, 1992. (Grades 1-4)

Baum, Eli. *Mitzvot Bein Adam Lachaveiro*. New York: KTAV Publishing House, Inc., 1980, pp. 30-32. (Grades 3-6)

Drucker, Malka. *Grandma's Latkes*. Orlando, FL: Harcourt Brace and Co., 1992. (Grades 2-5)

Fox, Mem. *Wilfred Gordon McDonald Partridge*. Brooklyn, NY: Kane/Miller Book Publishers, 1985. (Grades PK-2)

Herman, Dorothy C. *From Generation to Generation*. Miami: Central Agency for Jewish Eduation, 1985. (Grades 7 and up)

"Hidur P'nei Zaken." In *Gemilut Hasadim, vols. 1 and 2.* Baltimore: Bureau of Jewish Education, 1983. (Grades 4-6, has accompanying book for teachers)

Isaacs, Ronald H., and Kerry M. Olitzky. *Doing Mitzvot: Mitzvah Projects for Bar/Bat Mitzvah.* Hoboken, NJ: KTAV Publishing House, Inc., 1994, pp. 112-123. (Grades 6-8)

Kaye, Joan S.; Jan Rabinowitch; and Naomi F. Towvim. *Why Be Good? Sensitivities and Ethics in Rabbinic Literature.* Boston: Bureau of Jewish Eduation of Greater Boston, 1985, Unit III. (Grades 7 and up)

Levinson, Nancy Smiler. *Sweet Notes, Sour Notes.* New York: Lodestar/Dutton, 1993. (Grades 2-5)

Olitsky, Kerry M., and Lee H. Olitzky. *Aging and Judaism.* Denver; A.R.E. Publishing, Inc., 1980. (Grades 7 and up)

Pomerantz, Barbara. *Bubby, Me, and Memories.* New York: UAHC Press, 1983. (Grades K-3)

Potaracke, Rochelle. *Nanny's Special Gift.* Mahwah, NJ: Paulist Press, 1994. (Grades 1-4)

Schnur, Steven. *The Return of Morris Schumsky.* New York: UAHC Press, 1987. (Grades 4-6)

Audiovisual

The Bottom Line. A 30 minute video that looks realistically and from a Jewish perspective at issues that face many elderly people (e.g., quality/quantity of life, who lives and who dies). Ergo Media Inc. (Grades 10 and up)

Brighton Beach. A 55 minute film which portrays life in a Russian neighborhood in Brooklyn. Arthur Cantor, Inc. (Grades 7 and up)

Close Harmony. A 30 minute film chronicling the development of a choir composed of young children and elderly people. Learning Corporation of America. (Grades 3 and up)

Grandma Didn't Wave Back. A 24 minute film describing how Debbie's relationship with her grandmother changes as the older woman needs to be in a care center. Films for the Humanities and Sciences. (Grades 3 and up)

Lies My Father Told Me. A 102 minute film about the relationship between a young Jewish boy, his assimilated father, and traditional grandfather. Modern Sound Pictures, Inc. (Grades 10 and up)

Miracle of Intervale Avenue. A 65 minute documentary of a once thriving Jewish community in the South Bronx. In the midst of a decaying neighborhood, Blacks, Puerto Ricans, and Jews help and support one another. Ergo Media Inc. (Grades 7 and up)

Number Our Days. A 29 minute video which portrays an aging Jewish community in the Venice Beach area of Southern California. Direct Cinema. (Grades 7 and up)

A Private Life. A 30 minute film which explores the themes of aging, love, and immigration in the lives of two survivors of Hitler's Europe. Museum of Modern Art Circulating Film Library. (Grades 9 and up)

The Story of Esther. A 15 minute film which highlights the life of Esther Beir, an 82-year-old resident of the Lower East Side. Anti-Defamation League. (Grades 5 and up)

Tell Me a Riddle. A 90 minute film which tells the award winning story of rediscovered love between two elderly people. Orion Corporation. (Adults)

Yudie. A 20 minute film examining the life of an older Jewish woman, living independently, who speaks with candor and humor about union organizing campaigns, a marriage, a divorce, and life on the Lower East Side. New Day Films. (Grades 8 and up)

UNIT 27

Not Murdering

לֹא תִּרְצָח

OVERVIEW

The translation of a Hebrew word from the Bible can sometimes shape a great religious value. Such is the case with regard to the Sixth Commandment — *Lo Tirtzach* (Exodus 21:12 and Deuteronomy 5:17). The King James translation of the Bible, and most subsequent Christian versions, translate the Commandment: "Thou shalt not kill." Most Jewish translations, however, render the verse: "Thou shalt not murder." This is because the Hebrew root *R-TZ-CH* usually refers to a deliberate and premeditated act (murder), whereas other Hebrew roots such as *H-R-G* and *K-T-L* lack the sense of premeditation — i.e., to kill.

Furthermore, other passages in the Torah appear to indicate divine approval for certain types of killing. For example: "A person who fatally strikes another shall be put to death" (Exodus 21:12). Or, with regard to war, when a town refuses an offer of peace, "you shall lay siege to it; and when the Lord your God delivers it into your hand, you shall put all its males to the sword" (Deuteronomy 20:12-13). These passages and others indicate that, at least in the Torah, God does not forbid all killing.

The first homicide in the Torah occurs when Cain kills his brother Abel. When God inquires as to Abel's whereabouts, Cain tries to avoid responsibility by asking: "Am I my brother's keeper?" (Genesis 4:9). God responds: "Your brother's blood cries out to Me from the ground. Therefore, you shall be more cursed than the ground . . . . If you till the soil, it shall no longer yield its strength to you. You shall be a ceaseless wanderer on earth" (Genesis 4:10-12). When Cain protests that, as a wanderer, anyone who meets him might kill him, God promises that "sevenfold vengeance shall be taken on anyone who kills Cain" (Genesis 4:15). God places a mark on Cain, so no one will kill him.

Following the flood God addresses Noah with regard to murder: "Whoever sheds the blood of a man, by man shall his blood be shed" (Genesis 9:6). To refrain from shedding blood — not killing — is one of the seven laws of the sons of Noah which are considered, in the Jewish tradition, to be the minimal ethical standard incumbent upon all persons and societies.

The Torah differentiates between the accidental and the purposeful. "A person who fatally strikes another shall be put to death. If [however] the person did not do it by design, but it came about by an act of God, I will assign you a place to which the person can flee" (Exodus 21:12-13). This place was one of the six cities of refuge, which were established upon settling in the land.

In the biblical tradition, willfulness or premeditation was established by showing that a deadly instrument was used or that the suspect harbored hatred toward the victim. The Rabbis, however, made it exceedingly difficult to convict a person of murder and, therefore, to impose the death penalty. Only if the murder was premeditated and had been committed after the accused had been warned by two witnesses that such an offense was punishable by death, could the accused be put to death.

The Rabbis' emphasis on the value of life is expressed in many passages. "Whoever saves a single life, scripture regards the person as though he/she has saved the entire world, and whoever destroys a single life, scripture regards the person as though he/she destroys the whole world" (*Sanhedrin* 4:5). Furthermore, we are taught that if one sheds blood, it is as if that person had diminished God's image (*Mechilta* to Exodus 20:13).

Homicide, however, can be justified under the following conditions and situations: As an act of self-defense; to prevent a person from killing or raping another; if one should suddenly confront a burglar at night, but not during the day (Exodus 22:1-2); and as a public execution of persistent heretics. As with all capital punishment, the latter was rarely if ever carried out, for as we read in the Talmud: "A Sanhedrin which executes [a criminal] once in seven years is known as destructive. Rabbi Eleazer ben Azariah says: "Once in seventy years." Rabbi Tarfon and Rabbi Akiba say: "If we had been members of the Sanhedrin, no one would ever have been executed." Rabbi Simeon ben Gamliel says: "Rabbi Tarfon and Rabbi Akiba would have been responsible for the proliferation of murderers in Israel" (*Makot* 1:10).

The sentiment against capital punishment has prevailed since Talmudic times. The State of Israel has sentenced only two people to death, Adolf Eichmann and John Demjanjuk, for their roles in the Holocaust. In Israel, only the crimes of treason and genocide are punishable by death.

ACTIVITIES

Primary

1. Young children often do not understand that death is permanent. Begin a discussion on this issue by talking about the difference between pets sleeping and dying. Draw on the students' experiences. Talk about having to put a sick animal "to sleep." Conclude by discussing the difference between sleeping and dying for human beings.

2. Jewish tradition teaches: "Whoever saves a single life, scripture regards the person as though he/she saved the entire world; and whoever destroys a single soul, scripture regards the person as though he/she destroyed the whole world" (Sanhedrin 4:5). The following activities are based on this quote:
   a. Students paint a mural depicting individual actions which save the world.
   b. Students hold a fund-raising activity to collect money to donate to Save the Children, Mazon, or other worthwhile causes which save lives.
   c. Students hold a canned food drive with donations going to a local food pantry.

3. Read "His Name Was Hyam" from Who Knows Ten? by Molly Cone. Questions to consider: What kind of person was the man looking for? Was he disappointed to hear that Hyam was a good man? Why? What did Hyam mean when he asked the man if he was a fortune teller? When he promised little but took much? After their discussion Hyam changed his statement to "You want a lot for a little." What did he mean? Why did Hyam save the man? In your opinion was he worth saving? What Jewish saying did Hyam use to explain his actions?

4. Read and discuss The Number on My Grandfather's Arm by David A. Adler. Questions to discuss: What does the girl's grandfather have on his arm? Why did he have it on his arm? What

did the Nazis do to the girl's grandfather and to other Jews? How did the girl feel when she heard the story? How did you feel?

5. Read the story of Cain and Abel in A Child's Bible: Lessons from the Torah by Seymour Rossel, pp. 24-26. Ask: Why did Cain kill Abel? List all the reasons that the students can think of for why it is wrong to kill another person.

6. One reason that murdering is considered to be such a serious offense is that it cannot be undone. To illustrate this point to students, list the following offenses on the chalkboard: stealing, bearing false witness, taking revenge, gossiping, and murdering. Ask the students how, once a person did one of these offenses, each act could be undone. For example, a person who stole something could return it to its owner. Conclude by pointing out that because murder is irrevocable, it is a much more serious offense than the others.

Intermediate

1. Hold a discussion with your students regarding intentional versus accidental behavior. Discuss what intent means. Relate these discussions to material presented in the Overview section above.

2. Direct the students to research the Hebrew word for murder used in the sixth Commandment — tirtzach. Compare several Jewish translations with those found in Christian versions of the Bible. Discuss the differences between murder and killing.

3. Direct students to research the cities of refuge. Then, make a relief map of ancient Israel and plot out where these cities were located.

   Reference: "City of Refuge" in Encyclopaedia Judaica, vol. 5, cols. 591-594.

4. Hold an interview whip during which you elicit your students' opinions on the death penalty. In order or at random, ask the opinion of each student. The interview question may simply require a yes or no answer. In addition, you might ask the students why they support or oppose the death penalty.

5. The first homicide reported in the Bible is the killing of Abel by Cain. With your class read about this incident in Genesis 4:1-16. Ask what is missing from the narrative. If they can't discover it, point out that the text omits the conversation between the brothers (verse 8). Have each student imagine what it must have been like to be Cain. Have them write a diary entry in which they describe the conversation and the reason behind the murder.

6. Invite a lawyer to describe those instances when the death penalty would be the punishment for a crime. Have the students compare the attorney's remarks to the statement of the Rabbis regarding this punishment.

7. View and discuss one of the films on Cain and Abel listed in the Resource section at the end of this Unit. Ask: Was the film true to the text? Does the film help you to understand the story? If you were the filmmaker, what would you have done differently?

Secondary

1. There has been considerable controversy in the Jewish and secular communities over the death penalty. Assign students to collect information on this issue. They may interview attorneys, judges, human rights advocates, and clergy, and may also research newspaper articles and books on this subject. Be sure to include specifically Jewish views on the subject.

2. Present groups of upper grade students with case studies and ask them to decide how they would resolve the problems posed in each. You may author the cases or they may be written by the student groups. After discussing a case study, pass it on to the next group. Possible topics to use for the case studies include: drunk driving incident involving a fatality; handgun misuse; breaking and entering at night, etc. Refer to the Overview section above to develop further ideas.

3. Encourage the students to rewrite parts of the Cain and Abel story and change the ending. What implications does this have for their own interpersonal relationships and relationships in society at large?

4. Invite an individual who chose to be a conscientious objector to make a presentation to your class.

5. As a class read *Dawn* by Elie Wiesel, a moving story which deals with the execution of a British hostage during the fight to create a Jewish homeland in Palestine. Consider whether terrorism is *ever* justified.

6. There are several situations in the Bible which relate to the subject of murder. Read, act out, and discuss the skits in *Sedra Scenes: Skits for Every Torah Portion* by Stan J. Beiner for the following portions: *Beresheet* (pp. 1-6), *Vayera* (pp. 21-24), *Vayeshev* (pp. 49-52).

7. Extend activity #6 by reading the actual biblical stories upon which the skits in *Sedra Scenes* are based. Discuss.

ALL-SCHOOL PROGRAMS

1. Drunk drivers are responsible for many deaths of innocent victims. Invite a member of M.A.D.D. (Mothers Against Drunk Driving) or S.A.D.D. (Students Against Drunk Driving) to make a presentation at an assembly to your religious school.

2. Extend activity #1 by organizing a safe rides program for teens to use on weekends.

3. Hold a panel discussion on the theme "Violence on Television." Invite a psychologist, representatives from a television station, and the Rabbi to discuss the impact of T.V. violence on crime. You may want to follow up this program with a petition or a letter writing campaign directed at television networks.

RESOURCES

For the Teacher

Bayme, Steven. "Terrorism and Violence." In *Jewish Ethics: A Study Guide* by Joseph Lowin. New York: Hadassah The Women's Zionist Organization of America, Inc., 1986.

Birnbaum, Philip, ed. *Maimonides' Mishneh Torah (Yad Hazakah)*. Rockaway Beach, NY: Hebrew Publishing Co., 1944, pp. 233-240.

Dorff, Elliot N., and Newman, Louis E., eds. *Contemporary Jewish Ethics and Morality: A Reader.* New York: Oxford University Press. 1995.

"Homicide." In Encyclopaedia Judaica. Jerusalem: Keter Publishing House Jerusalem, Ltd., 1972, vol. 8, cols. 944-946.

Myers, Michael. *Terrorism: A Discussion Guide.* New York: Coalition for the Advancement of Jewish Education, 1987.

Stern, Jay B. *Syllabus for the Teaching of Mitzvah.* New York: United Synagogue Commission on Jewish Education, 1986, pp. 190-193.

For the Students

Adler, David A. *The Number on My Grandfather's Arm.* New York: UAHC Press, 1987. (Grades K-3)

Baum, Eli. *Mitzvot Bein Adam Lachaveiro.* New York: KTAV Publishing House, Inc., 1980, pp. 15-16. (Grades 3-6)

Beiner, Stan J. *Sedra Scenes: Skits for Every Torah Portion.* Denver: A.R.E. Publishing, Inc., 1982, *Beresheet,* pp. 1-6; *Vayera,* pp. 21-24; *Vayeshev,* pp. 49-52. (Grades 4 and up)

Cone, Molly. *Who Knows Ten?* New York: UAHC Presss, 1965. (Grades K-3)

Fox, Marci. *The Ten Commandments.* Instant Lesson. Los Angeles: Torah Aura Productions. (Grades K-2)

Gersh, Harry. *Midrash: Rabbinic Lore.* West Orange, NJ: Behrman House, 1985, pp. 11-13. (Grades 9 and up)

Karkowsky, Nancy. *The Ten Commandments.* West Orange, NJ: Behrman House, 1988. (Grades 3-4)

Rossel, Seymour. *A Child's Bible Book 1: Lessons from the Torah.* West Orange, NJ: Behrman House, 1988, pp. 24-26. (Grades 3-5)

Ten Times Ten. Instant Lesson. Los Angeles: Torah Aura Productions. (Grades 6-adult)

Topek, Susan. *Ten Good Rules.* Rockville, MD: Kar-Ben Copies, Inc., 1992. (Grades PK-1)

Wiesel, Elie. *Dawn.* New York: Avon Books, 1970. (Grades 7 and up)

Audiovisual

Cain and Abel. A 17 minute film about Genesis 4:1-5:27. The Genesis Project, which produced this film with live actors, is no longer in business. However, the film is available through many Bureaus of Jewish Education. (Grades 6 and up)

Hangman. A 12 minute animated film in which a person who has let others die to protect himself becomes the hangman's last victim. McGraw-Hill. (Grades 7 and up)

Joseph Schultz. A 14 minute video in which a Nazi soldier who refuses to follow orders and execute a group of villagers is executed with the villagers. Anti-Defamation League. (Grades 7 and up)

UNIT 28

Not Stealing
לֹא תִגְנֹב

OVERVIEW

Three times the Torah commands: "You shall not steal" (Exodus 20:13, Leviticus 19:11, Deuteronomy 5:17). The Rabbis, not accepting that all three referred to the same thing, posited this distinction: the prohibition in Leviticus is directed against stealing property; in the Ten Commandments (Exodus and Deuteronomy), the prohibition is against stealing a human being (i.e., kidnapping). This is because the commandment against stealing is listed among other crimes against persons, such as murder and adultery.

The tradition also distinguishes between stealing and robbing (Leviticus 19:13), and between a thief/burglar who steals secretly and a robber who takes openly and forcefully.

With regard to restitution, the Torah states: "When one steals an ox or a sheep and slaughters it or sells it, one shall pay five oxen for the ox, and four sheep for the sheep" (Exodus 21:37). If, however, the stolen property is still in the thief's possession, the thief need only pay double (Exodus 22:3). A person who lacked the means to make the appropriate restitution could be indentured for the theft (Exodus 22:2). However, Jewish tradition stipulated that if one admitted to the theft before witnesses testified, the only restitution required was to return what was stolen.

The Rabbinic tradition recognized seven categories of theft:

1. Deceit or fraud, which the Talmud compares to "stealing a person's mind" — g'nayvat hada'at (Chullin 94a).
2. Using false weights and measures to steal. "You shall not falsify measures of length, weight, or capacity. You shall have an honest balance, honest weights, an honest ephah [a dry measure, approximately two pecks], and an honest hin [a liquid measure, approximately one gallon]" (Leviticus 19:35-36).

    Not only was it prohibited to use these false weights and measures, but even keeping them was forbidden. These were considered to be particularly serious infractions, since restitution was bound to be difficult if not impossible.

3. Stealing something forbidden to be used or which was useless, for which no restitution is required.
4. Stealing documents or property for which simple restitution must be made.
5. Stealing animals, garments, or other possessions, which required double restitution.
6. Stealing and selling or slaughtering oxen or sheep, for which the restitution is fivefold and fourfold respectively.
7. Kidnapping, for which the punishment was death.

In addition, the Talmud considers someone who borrows an object without the owner's consent to be a thief (Baba Batra 88a). Even if one has the owner's consent to borrow an object, but changes or departs from the intended usage, one is a thief (Baba Metzia 78a).

Related to these Mitzvot are those dealing with lost property. One is forbidden to ignore lost property (based on Deuteronomy 22:1-3), and must restore it to its owner (based on Exodus 23:4 and Deuteronomy 22:1-3). The passage from Exodus specifies a possession of one's enemy, while the Deuteronomy verses refer to one's brother, which is usually interpreted as a fellow Jew.

An animal which is found must be cared for until it is claimed by its owner. The finder is obligated to advertise in order to attempt to notify the owner. Meanwhile, the finder is obligated to care for the animal. The tradition even speaks of a high rock outside of Jerusalem where people announced what they had lost or found. Finding a lost article and keeping it was tantamount to theft.

Rabbinic literature extends the prohibition against theft to "stealing a person's heart" by inviting a person to be a guest when one does not wish to host the person. Partaking of a meal when the host does not have enough food to eat is also considered stealing.

In modern times such activities as plagiarism, copyright infringement, piracy of cable television broadcasts, etc., have been considered stealing.

ACTIVITIES

Primary

1. There are many good children's books which deal with the theme of stealing. Draw from the titles listed below and also check with the synagogue, school, and public libraries for additional titles. Each student can read a different book and then present an oral report. Remind students to include information on the theft, personal consequences for the perpetrator and victim, and what they learned from the story.

   References: *Gittel and the Bell* by Robert Goldshlag Cooks; *Onion Sundaes* by David Adler; *Nasty, Stinky Sneakers* by Eva Bunting; *Jamaica's Find* by Juanita Havill.

2. Ask students to imagine that they are taking a walk and that they find a dollar bill on the ground. Ask: What should you do? If you keep it, is it stealing? How can one return lost property that has no identification? Explain to children that, in the case of larger sums, they can call the police. If they find a coin or a dollar bill, suggest that they give it to *Tzedakah*.

3. Read *The Sign in Mendel's Window* by Mildred Phillips. Discuss the following questions: How did Mendel and Molly plan to make extra money? Who came to rent out half the shop? How did Tinker the Thinker plot to steal Mendel's money? How did Simka try and save Mendel? What did Molly do? How do Tinker the Thinker's actions violate the Mitzvah of Not Stealing? If he had been successful, what would have been the consequences for the residents of the town?

4. Have the students paint posters with an anti-theft theme. These may be hung in the synagogue or given to local shops and businesses.

5. Related to the Mitzvah of Not Stealing are those Mitzvot that deal with lost property. Read the "Lost and Found" ads from the classified section of your local newspaper. Pick out any unusual items mentioned and discuss the rewards that are offered. Talk about things the students have lost or found, and what the circumstances were.

Have the students write their own classified ads describing items in the lost and found box at your school. Circulate the ads among the other classes.

6. Write an acrostic that is an admonition against stealing. Begin each line with the letters of the phrase "Do Not Steal." Work on this as a class.

Intermediate

1. Assign students to find reports in the media which illustrate the seven categories of theft (see Overview above). Mount the articles on posterboard and list the penalty according to the Jewish tradition.

   Reference: *The Torah: A Modern Commentary* edited by W. Gunther Plaut, p. 584.

2. While television often glamorizes the criminal life style, viewers seldom see the results when criminals are caught. Arrange a tour of the local police station to show the consequences of criminal activity.

3. According to Jewish tradition, insincerely hosting someone is a form of stealing (*Mechilta* to Exodus 22:3). Have the students conduct a survey asking parents and friends for responses to situations such as those below:
   a. Your Bar/Bat Mitzvah is coming up. You wish to invite only people you know. Your parents want to invite business and work associates to pay back for invitations they have received. Should people you don't know be invited? (Remember, your parents are paying the bills.)
   b. Rachel always invites you to her birthday party. You don't really like her. Should you invite her to your birthday party anyway?

4. One of the Rabbinic categories of theft prohibits the use of false measures. Most states and provinces have an agency whose responsibility it is to enforce honest weights and measures for businesses. Invite a representative from such an agency to make a presentation to your class. Include a question period.

5. In Jewish tradition it is a Mitzvah to return lost property to its owner. Tell your students to imagine that they have each lost a prized posses-

sion. Have them write classified ads describing the article and asking for its return. Sugggest that they consider offering a reward.

6. Extend activity #5 by having students stand up and announce their lost article, as was done in ancient Jerusalem.

Secondary

1. While not a Jewish work, *Les Miserables* by Victor Hugo sets up the dilemma of a poor man who steals bread to feed his hungry children. Read excerpts from this novel to your class and brainstorm possible solutions to the poor man's dilemma. What could he have done instead of stealing bread? Is it ever permissible to break the Mitzvah of Not Stealing?

2. Many communities have established restitution as a part of the convicted criminal's responsibility. Invite a judge or district attorney to explain how this is done. Compare these to restitutions according to the Jewish tradition.

   Reference: *The Torah: A Modern Commentary* edited by W. Gunther Plaut, p. 584.

3. Ask students what prevents them from stealing. Discuss innovative ways of deterring crime. Write a letter to legislators and city council members suggesting these methods.

4. Have students write a play or skit that includes the ancient practice of announcing lost and found items from a high rock outside the city of Jerusalem.

5. In many university towns, there are groups which sell term papers. Divide the class into two groups. One group speaks in support of such a practice, claiming it is not stealing; the other group speaks against it, arguing that it is stealing.

6. Extend activity #5 by holding a secret ballot. Each student writes on a piece of paper whether or not he or she would buy a term paper to submit as his/her own and the reasons for the response. Place all ballots in a paper bag, shake and pass around for each student to draw one out and read it aloud. Discuss.

ALL-SCHOOL PROGRAMS

1. Work with the local police department to set up neighborhood watch programs.

2. A life of crime often begins when young people are offered little chance in life. Contact various social service agencies in your community to present a panel discussion on this issue. Choose a course of action in which the synagogue community can become involved in order to prevent youth from turning to stealing.

3. Kidnapping is one form of stealing. In our society it is necessary to train our children to take many precautions. Invite an expert to conduct a safety awareness program with your students. The local police department might be the best place to start.

RESOURCES
For the Teacher

Amsel, Nachum. *The Jewish Encyclopedia of Moral and Ethical Issues.* Northvalue, NJ: Jason Aronson Inc., 1994, pp. 107-111.

Birnbaum, Philip. *Maimonides' Mishneh Torah (Yad Hazakah).* Rockaway Beach, NY: Hebrew Publishing Co., 1944, pp. 213-225.

"Honest Scales." In *Lively Legends — Jewish Values: An Early Childhood Teaching Guide* by Miriam P. Feinberg and Rena Rotenberg. Denver: A.R.E. Publishing, Inc., 1993.

"Little Becomes Much." In *Lively Legends — Jewish Values: An Early Childhood Teaching Guide* by Miriam P. Feinberg and Rena Rotenberg. Denver: A.R.E. Publishing, Inc., 1993.

Plaut, W. Gunther, ed. *The Torah: A Modern Commentary.* New York: UAHC Press, 1981, pp. 584.

"The Precious Jewel." In *Lively Legends — Jewish Values: An Early Childhood Teaching Guide* by Miriam P. Feinberg and Rena Rotenberg. Denver: A.R.E. Publishing, Inc., 1993.

Stern, Jay B. *Syllabus for the Teaching of Mitzvah.* New York: United Synagogue Commission on Jewish Education, 1986, pp. 103-105.

"Theft and Robbery." In *Encyclopaedia Judaica.* Jerusalem: Keter Publishing House Jerusalem, Ltd., 1972, vol. 15, cols. 1094-1098.

For the Students

Adler, David. *Onion Sundaes*. New York: Random House, 1994. (Grades 2-4)

Baum, Eli. *Mitzvot Bein Adam Lachaveiro*. New York: KTAV Publishing House, Inc., 1980, pp. 17-10. (Grades 3-6)

Byalick, Marcia. *It's a Matter of Trust*. Orlando, FL: Harcourt Brace and Co., 1995. (Grades 7-9)

Bunting, Eva. *Nasty, Stinky Sneakers*. New York: HarperCollins Children's Books, 1994. (Grades 4-7)

Cone, Molly. *Who Knows Ten?* New York: UAHC Press, 1965, pp. 66-74. (Grades K-3)

Cooks, Roberta Goldshlag. *Gittel and the Bell*. Rockville, MD: Kar-Ben Copies, Inc., 1987. (Grades K-3)

Feinstein, Morley. *The Jewish Law Review Vol. 1*. Los Angeles: Torah Aura Productions, 1987, pp. 27-40. (Grades 6 and up)

Fox, Marci. *The Ten Commandments*. Instant Lesson. Los Angeles: Torah Aura Productions. (Grades K-2)

Getzel. *Manny the Thief*. Brooklyn, NY: Mesorah Publications, Ltd., 1992. (Grades K-2)

Havill, Juanita. *Jamaica's Find*. Boston: Houghton Mifflin Co., 1986. (PK-3)

Karkowsky, Nancy. *The Ten Commandments*. West Orange, NJ: Behrman House, 1988. (Grades 3-4)

Kaye, Joan S.; Jan Rabinowitch; and Naomi F. Towvim. *Why Be Good? Sensitivities and Ethics in Rabbinic Literature*. Boston: Bureau of Jewish Education of Greater Boston, 1985, pp. 47-56. (Grades 7 and up)

Neusner, Jacob. *Learn Mishnah*. West Orange, NJ: Behrman House, 1978, pp. 41-62. (Grades 5-8)

Phillips, Mildred. *The Sign in Mendel's Window*. New York: Macmillan Publishing Co., Inc. 1985. (Grades K-3)

Ten Times Ten. Instant Lesson. Los Angeles: Torah Aura Productions. (Grades 6-adult)

Topek, Susan. *Ten Good Rules*. Rockville, MD: Kar-Ben Copies, Inc., 1992. (Grades PK-1)

Audiovisual

Clayfeet. A 27 minute video about a boy who steals a copy of a test. Media Guild. (Grades 7-12)

The Hideout. A 15 minute trigger video in which a boy, anxious to play with the older children, steals boards for a club hideout from a neighbor. Churchill Media. (Grades 1-6)

Only Benjy Knows: Should He Tell? A 4 minute trigger film on video in which Benjy notices two friends shoplifting. Encyclopedia Brittanica. (Grades K-5)

UNIT 29

Not Taking Revenge
לֹא תִקֹּם

OVERVIEW

In performing many of the Mitzvot, we are said to be imitating God. Just as God visited the sick (Abraham after his circumcision), we are to visit the sick. Just as God is forgiving after the incident of the golden calf, so we should be forgiving. However, in at least one instance, we are told not to imitate God. There are many biblical examples of divine vengeance, yet human beings are prohibited from taking revenge. (Maimonides bases this negative Mitzvah on Leviticus 19:18.)

For example, when Cain complains to God that someone might kill him, God replies: "I promise, if anyone kills Cain, sevenfold vengeance shall be taken on the killer" (Genesis 4:15). At another time, God commands Moses to "avenge the Israelite people on the Midianites" (Numbers 31:2) because they instigated the immoralities at Baal-peor (see Numbers 25:16-17).

According to a *midrash*, the reason that God, but not human beings, can take vengeance is that "wrath controls a human being, whereas God controls divine wrath" (*Genesis Rabbah* 49:8).

The Rabbis explain vengeance as follows: "If A says to B: 'Lend me your sickle' and B refuses, and on the next day B says to A: 'Lend me your hatchet,' and A replies: 'I will not lend it to you, just as you refused to lend me your sickle,' that is vengeance" (*Sifra* to Leviticus 19:18).

While the Mitzvah forbidding one from taking revenge applies to personal matters, it does not apply to the seeking of redress through the courts. "Where a person has a legitimate case against another, it does not constitute revenge to summon the other to a court of law" (Nachmanides to Leviticus 19:18). However, one is not to take the law into one's own hands. Indeed, the Israelites are told that when they enter the land, they are to establish cities of refuge to which someone who accidentally killed another could flee and be safe from the one seeking vengeance for the death (Numbers 35:9-15).

The Talmud cites one exception to the Mitzvah of Not Taking Revenge: "A wise student who does not avenge himself and retains anger like a serpent, is not really a wise student" (*Yoma* 23a). Because an offense against another person, as in the case above, is an offense against the Torah, vengeance is permitted, although the Rabbis severely limited it. This situation does, however, point out the reality that one who does not take revenge is more likely than one who does to retain one's anger. (See remarks below on bearing a grudge.)

The biblical passage which prescribes the punishment of "an eye for an eye and a tooth for a tooth" (Exodus 21:24) is often mistakenly interpreted as an endorsement of vengeance. The purpose of this passage was to limit the compensatory action taken against a person at a time when it was not uncommon to seek revenge out of proportion to the original action. It is not clear whether this concept was practiced literally in the biblical period. By the Rabbinic period, however, this passage was interpreted to refer to monetary compensation in proportion to one's action.

Why should one not take revenge? A biblical commentator suggests that a person should ask oneself: "Just because this one is petty and malicious, should I follow suit? Rather, let me behave graciously toward the person, who will realize it, and thus increase harmony and love" (*Biur* to Leviticus 19:18). The *Palestinian Talmud* (*Nedarim* 9:4, 41c) offers this reasoning: If you cut your hand while cutting meat, you don't cut the hand which did the damage. In other words, we should regard all humankind as one body; harming one part is harming oneself.

Closely related to this Mitzvah is the Mitzvah not to bear a grudge. The Rabbis illustrated bearing a grudge with a story that is a twist on the sickle/hatchet story above. "A says to B: 'Lend me your sickle' and B refuses. The next day B says to A: 'Lend me your hatchet.' A replies: 'Here it is; I am not like you who would not lend me your sickle.'" (*Sifra* to Leviticus 19:18).

Maimonides explains the relationship between bearing a grudge and vengeance as follows: "As long as one nurses a grievance and keeps it in mind, the person may come to take vengeance" (*Yad Hazakah, Deot* 7:8).

Moses Chayim Luzzatto explains the challenge of these Mitzvot: "Revenge is sweeter to him than honey; he cannot rest until he has taken his revenge. If, therefore, he has the power to relinquish that to which his nature impels him; if he can forgive; if he will forbear hating anyone who provokes him to hatred, if he will neither exact vengeance when he has the opportunity to do so, nor bear a grudge against anyone; if he can forget and obliterate from his mind a wrong done to him as though it had never been committed; then he is indeed strong and mighty" (*Path of the Upright*, pp. 91-93).

ACTIVITIES

Primary

1. Ask students for examples of when they behaved improperly toward a friend or relative by taking revenge or by bearing a grudge. Solicit suggestions from students of how they might behave so as not to be guilty of taking vengeance or bearing a grudge.

2. Utilize pantomime to help students experience anger, vengeance, hurt, envy, sadness, happiness, and joy. Ask: How did your faces and bodies feel after each pantomime? Which did you prefer? Have you ever thought about how others feel when they are wronged by you? How do you want those around you to feel? How do you want to feel?

3. Read the story of Purim to your students. Identify the major characters and their qualities. Ask the students which character was seeking vengeance and why. Ask if the Jews took revenge.

   References: *A Purim Album* by Raymond A. Zwerin and Audrey Friedman Marcus; *Purim* by Miriam Nerlove.

4. Read the following situation to the class. Then read the four possible reactions. Discuss each one and decide which is the best outcome according to Jewish law. (For younger children you may want to illustrate the four reactions on posters or on the chalkboard.)

   Sarah had a brand new toy stroller for her dolls. Her little brother Alan wanted a turn with the stroller. Sarah and Alan started to argue, and Alan grabbed the stroller away from Sarah. The stroller cracked and broke.

   a. Sarah started screaming and crying and hit Alan.
   b. Alan said he was sorry, but if Sarah had shared the toy, it wouldn't have broken, so it was all her fault.
   c. Sarah and Alan looked at the broken stroller and each said they were sorry. They found some glue and repaired the stroller.
   d. Sarah took one look at what Alan had done and ran into his bedroom. She took a toy airplane and broke it in half. Sarah told her brother he deserved this, because he had broken her toy.

5. Ask students to imagine that they are angry with someone. What do they do? List the responses on the board. Ask if their responses are correct according to Jewish law. If not, ask what they could choose to do instead. Follow up by asking the same/similar questions for a situation when someone is angry at them.

6. Bring a large heavy object to class and announce that the object is a "Grudge." Explain what it means to "hold a grudge." Begin by holding the Grudge and saying, "I hold a grudge when I _____." You may need to give two or three examples before the children understand the concept. Ask for volunteers to make a similar statement. Hand them the Grudge before they make their statement. Continue until each student who wishes has had a chance to contribute. Repeat the activity, but this time each student places the Grudge on the ground and says, "I don't hold a grudge because _____."

Intermediate

1. Pose this question to your students: Why shouldn't a person seek revenge? Ask them what might happen if everyone sought revenge for wrongs committed against them.

2. Ask students to complete the following statements:
   a. The Torah instructs us not to bear a grudge or to take vengeance because _____.
   b. I might bear a grudge if _____.
   c. I might want to seek vengeance if _____.

3. Explain the examples describing vengeance and bearing a grudge in the Overview above. Then have students rewrite them using contemporary examples.

4. Cain and Abel were not a happy pair of brothers. Cain became so angered when God accepted Abel's sacrifice that he took vengeance and killed Abel. Read chapter 3 of Genesis. Create an add-on story to fill in the gaps in Cain and Abel's relationship. Gather the students in a circle. Each one takes a turn creating a part of the story speaking for two or three minutes. Tape the storytelling, replay it later, and discuss.

5. Read to the class a story about the Golem, such as *Golem: A Giant Made of Mud* by Mark Podwal or *The Golem: A Version* by Barbara Rogasky. Discuss: Was the Jewish community seeking vengeance or was the Rabbi simply trying to protect the Jews? Why did the Golem have to return to dust? What happens when the wrong people become powerful?

6. After briefly summarizing the material in the Overview section above, hold a slogan writing contest. Students create slogans which urge people not to bear a grudge or seek vengeance (e.g., "I can't bear to bear a grudge," or "Revenge results from reckless reasoning"). If desired, allow students to illustrate their slogans on poster board.

Secondary

1. Ask students to describe the difference between revenge and taking someone to court because they have wronged you. Play devil's advocate on this issue. You may want to invite an attorney or judge to help facilitate the discussion and provide additional information.

2. Read the following *midrash* from *Sefer Chasidim* (Frankfurt edition), paragraph 100 to the class:

The Man Who Honored His Father
There was once a man who honored his father. His father said, "Just as you honor me when I am alive, I hope you will continue to honor me after I die. I order you to control your temper and restrain your anger for one evening."
When the man's father died, the son went

away, leaving his wife. Unbeknownst to him, the wife was pregnant and she bore a son. Years later the man returned and went to his house. He heard a man's voice and through the window he saw a man kissing his wife. He was about to burst in and kill them, when he remembered his father's words.

Then he heard his wife say, "Your father has been gone so long. If he only knew he had a son, I'm sure he would come back to find a wife for you."

When the man heard this, he said, "Open the door, my lovely wife. Blessed is God who stayed my anger and blessed is my father who told me not to be angry for one evening."

Ask students if, like the man in the story, any of them have been quick to show anger and seek revenge. Did they come to regret their actions? Why or why not?

3. Extend activity #2. Instruct students to write their own version of "Restrain Your Anger for One Night" using a contemporary situation. They may wish to base the story on an incident in their own lives.

4. Is it possible that vengeance can ever lead to a positive outcome? Ask your students to research the groups Mothers Against Drunk Driving (M.A.D.D.) and Students Against Drunk Driving (S.A.D.D.) or a victim's assistance program. Invite a representative from one of these organizations to speak to your class.

5. Discuss the difference between not forgetting the Holocaust and bearing a grudge against the German people.

6. The biblical phrase "an eye for an eye, a tooth for a tooth" is often mistakenly cited as a justification for taking revenge. In Jewish tradition, however, it is interpreted quite differently. Read Exodus 21:22-25. Ask students what they think it means. Suggest that they offer examples. Most likely they will focus on literal retaliation. Ask if there is any other way to understand the verse. If there are no suggestions, point out that in Jewish teachings, the verse does not refer to retaliation, but instead places a limit on the monetary compensation that a person could receive for a bodily injury.

Reference: *The Torah: A Modern Commentary* edited by W. Gunther Plaut, pp. 571-572.

ALL-SCHOOL PROGRAMS

1. *Selichot* (which means forgiveness) is a service which occurs prior to the High Holy Days. Its purpose is to prepare the participants for the penitential period of Rosh Hashanah and Yom Kippur. In a sense, it is a warm-up or preview for the upcoming holidays. Plan a *Selichot* Service as an all-school assembly just prior to the High Holy Days. While not a standard worship service, there are a few guidelines to follow. If the service takes place on a Saturday evening, begin with *Havdalah*. Use meditations and readings relating to the themes of prayer, God, and the carrying out of good deeds. Use songs and readings which reflect the desire to return to God and to right the wrongs we have committed. The "*Al Chet*" and "*Avinu Malkeynu*" from the High Holy Day liturgy are appropriate. The service traditionally concludes with the sounding of a *tekiah gedolah* on the shofar.

   This service will help put the students into the frame of mind to redress any wrongs they have committed. Meditations and readings reflecting the themes of bearing a grudge and seeking revenge would fit very well into this observance. Ask the Rabbi and Cantor to help organize the service. Also, students should be encouraged to compose and read original work, poems, and prayers.

   Reference: *Selihot Service* by Ben Zion Bokser; *Gates of Forgiveness* (Central Conference of American Rabbis).

2. The teachers and/or aides present the following short skit at an assembly:

   Some students are sitting together when another student runs up and says he has the answers for the test that is to be given next period. All except one of the students are excited about getting the answers. This one student expresses reservations, and says the others shouldn't cheat.

   In the next scene, the students are in class and the teacher announces that the test is postponed because someone informed her that the answers were circulating around the school. The students glare at the student who had opposed cheating and say such things as, "We'll get you later."

   Break up into groups of students of mixed grade levels. Each group is to create a skit to complete the story, and then present its skit to the other groups.

3. To demonstrate the difference between vengeance and justice, hold a mock Nazi War Crime Trial. The defendant is accused of collaborating with the Nazis during the Holocaust. The defense argues that Judaism teaches that one should not bear a grudge or seek revenge. The prosecution argues that there is a difference between these Mitzvot and bringing someone to justice. Older students might play various roles (lawyers, witnesses, etc.). One witness can be the Rabbi (or someone playing a Rabbi) who can clearly point out that these Mitzvot should not prevent a criminal from being brought to justice. Let the rest of the students serve as the jury, which should vote at the end of the trial.

RESOURCES

For the Teacher

Bloch, Abraham. *A Book of Jewish Ethical Concepts.* New York: KTAV Publishing House, Inc., 1984, pp. 155-160.

Gates of Forgiveness. New York: Central Conference of American Rabbis, 1980.

Plaut, W. Gunther, ed. *The Torah: A Modern Commentary.* New York: UAHC Press, 1981, pp. 571-572.

"Vengeance." In *Encyclopaedia Judaica.* Jerusalem: Keter Publishing House Jerusalem Ltd., 1972, vol. 16, cols. 93-94.

For the Students

Abrams, Judith Z. *Selichot: A Family Service.* Rockville, MD: Kar-Ben Copies, Inc., 1991. (Grades PK and up)

Nerlove, Miriam. *Purim*. New York: Albert Whitman, 1992. (Grades PK-2)

Podwal, Mark. *Golem: A Giant Made of Mud.* New York: Greenwillow Books, 1995. (Grades 4-6)

Rogansky, Barbara. *The Golem: A Version.* New York: Holiday House, 1996. (Grades 4-6)

Zwerin, Raymond A., and Audrey Friedman Marcus. *A Purim Album.* New York: UAHC Press, 1981. (Grades PK-3)

UNIT 30

Not Placing a Stumbling Block
לֹא תִתֵּן מִכְשֹׁל

OVERVIEW

"You shall not curse the deaf nor place a stumbling block before the blind. You shall fear your God. I am the Lord" (Leviticus 19:14). On the surface this verse appears to be directed against taking advantage of an individual's physical handicap. However, Rabbinic sources interpret this verse quite differently. The prohibition against cursing the deaf is interpreted to mean that one should not curse any Jew (*Sifra* to Leviticus 19:14) and the prohibition against placing a stumbling block before the blind is interpreted as referring not to one who is physically blind, but to one who is "blind" concerning a particular matter (*Sifra* to Leviticus 19:14).

The Rabbis offer numerous examples of forbidden behaviors that are included within the rubric of this Mitzvah. "If one is blind in a matter and asks you for advice, do not give advice that is not appropriate" (*Sifra* to Leviticus 19:14). If someone asks you if a certain woman is qualified to marry a *Kohan* (a priestly descendent, one who cannot marry a divorcee or a Jew-by-Choice), you should not say yes if she is not qualified (*Sifra* to Leviticus 19:14). A person is not to offer drink to a Nazirite (who has vowed to abstain), since the Nazirite might be blinded by desire and accept it (*Pesachim* 22b).

This Mitzvah also forbids one from hitting one's adult child, since doing so might provoke the child to strike back and thereby commit a serious transgression (*Moed Katan* 17a). Goading a person into anger which might lead to the commission of a sin is also forbidden by this Mitzvah.

Maimonides points out that it is forbidden to sell a heathen or a robber weapons of war which might be used in violating a Mitzvah, although it is permitted to sell them defensive weapons, such as shields (*Mishneh Torah*, *Hilchot Rotzeach* 12:14).

If one loans money to a fellow Jew at interest, both the borrower and the lender are guilty of violating the prohibition against placing a stumbling block before the blind.

Here is also found the basis for the requirement that graves be clearly marked so that *Kohanim* can avoid contact with the dead as required by Jewish tradition. If one is aware that a grave is unmarked, one must mark it. From this we learn that even a completely passive person, one who is divorced from society, is not absolved from bearing responsibility for what is transpiring in the world at large — for the iniquity, violence, and evil there. By not protesting — not "marking the graves" and danger spots — one becomes responsible for any harm arising therefrom, and for violating the prohibition: "Thou shalt not put a stumbling block before the blind . . . ." (*Studies in Vayikra (Leviticus)* by Leibowitz, p. 178).

The phrase "You shall fear your God" appears in the Torah, according to commentators, whenever the performance of a Mitzvah is entrusted to the conscience of the individual, and cannot be dealt with by an earthly court. As in this case, if one offers bad advice, only he or she knows whether or not it was given intentionally.

While the Jewish teachings focus upon the figurative implications of not cursing the deaf or putting stumbling blocks before the blind, the literal meaning of these Mitzvot is also important. The Jewish and non-Jewish community alike have a responsibility to meet the needs of those whose physical hearing or sight is impaired, as well as those who have other handicaps — physical, intellectual, or emotional. Rising to meet such responsibilities on both a local and national level will be an ongoing challenge in the years ahead.

ACTIVITIES

Primary

1. One interpretation of placing a stumbling block is to deceive a person deliberately. To help the students understand how someone can be tricked, invite a magician to come to your class. The magician must be willing to share some of the tricks of his/her trade. He or she should demonstrate a few tricks and then show the students how they are done. If a magician is not available, become one yourself with the help of books about magic and some magic tricks purchased at a toy store.

2. Very often deaf people are excluded from synagogue worship because there is no sign

language interpreter available. This is their "stumbling block" to participating in the Jewish community. Young children are fascinated by sign language and are quite capable of learning to sign. Teach your students some basic Jewish signs, as well as the signs for the *Sh'ma*.

Reference: *The Second Jewish Catalog* by Sharon Strassfeld and Michael Strassfeld, pp. 151-173.

3. Read the following to your students:

Nathan has two toy trucks. One of them is in good condition, while the other one is broken. Nathan put the broken one back together with glue. Joshua comes over to play with Nathan. While playing, Joshua admires Nathan's trucks and asks if he can buy one. Nathan thinks a moment and says sure. He hands Joshua the glued together truck and gets 50 cents in return. Nathan never mentions that it was broken and has been repaired.

Ask students if they think Nathan was fair. Should Joshua have asked the "history" of the toy? If the toy breaks again, who is responsible? Have the students imagine that they are Joshua, and then answer the question. Then have them answer from the point of view of Nathan. How did Nathan place a stumbling block before Joshua?

4. Focus on the literal meaning of the verse, "You shall not place a stumbling block before the blind." As an aid to doing so, write to the Jewish Braille Institute of America, 110 East 30th St., New York, NY 10016 and request a sample biblical passage written in braille. Use this to trigger a discussion about blindness. Ask students to list some of the things they do that a blind person cannot do in the same way. Discuss with students how blind people adapt to their circumstance. For example, a blind person cannot see the words to read them, but can learn braille or can listen to books on tape. Ask students how they can prevent placing a stumbling block before the blind.

5. The Mitzvah not to insult the deaf is related to the Mitzvah of Not Placing a Stumbling Block and has been interpreted to mean that one shouldn't insult anyone (see Overview above).

Distribute two paper plates to each child. Ask each to draw a happy face on one plate and a sad face on the other. Tell the class that you are going to read several statements which someone might say to them. If the statement makes them feel happy, they are to raise the plate with the happy face. If the statement makes them feel sad, they are to raise the plate with the sad face. The following are some suggested statements:
a. Your clothes are ugly.
b. I like your smile.
c. You jump rope really well.
d. You read slowly.
e. Did you do poorly on another test?
f. I'm glad you are my friend.
After reading the statements, discuss with your students why they should not insult others.

6. View and discuss one of the films from the *Like You Like Me Series*. This series for kindergarten and first grade consists of ten animated short films about handicapped children.

Intermediate

1. Using the literal interpretation of the verse about a stumbling block, take students on a modified trust walk. Before the class arrives, rearrange your classroom. Greet the students at the door. Instruct them to choose a partner. One partner in each pair is to shut his/her eyes while the other partner acts as a guide. Have the pairs make their way through the classroom. If time permits have the partners switch roles and do the walk again. Afterward, discuss the difficulties of each role. Then determine which of the guide's actions helped them and which hindered them. In your discussions consider what life is like for a person who is blind. What stumbling blocks do they face?

2. For handicapped individuals, lack of access to a synagogue is a stumbling block. Invite an expert in services for the handicapped to make a presentation to your class. Then, with your guest, take a walking tour of your synagogue to determine its accessibility.

3. Another way to determine the accessibility of your synagogue is to have the students assume handicaps. Make arrangements for the loan of a wheelchair, crutches, and a walker. Also, to simulate blindness, some students should be

blindfolded. Pair each "disabled" student with one who is not. Have the pairs negotiate around the synagogue for 20 to 30 minutes. Remind them to try the doorways, the restrooms, the sanctuary, and the classrooms. Reassemble the class and discuss what happened. Generate a list of recommendations to the synagogue's Building Committee or the Board of Directors. Follow up to see what happens with the recommendations.

4. Share the following story with your students:

The Greedy Carpenter

There once was an excellent carpenter who designed and built beautiful homes, but he had one fault — greed. In the construction of his homes, he used cheap materials, but billed for expensive ones, pocketing the extra money. After many years of work, the mayor asked the carpenter to build an especially fine home. Following his usual practice, the carpenter created a breathtaking home from shoddy material. At its completion the mayor held a banquet at which he presented the home to the carpenter for his many years of building fine homes for the community.

Discuss the following questions: Who did the carpenter hurt by his business practice? Identify the stumbling block. Identify who was blind. How were the homes like the carpenter who built them? Do you think the carpenter got what he deserved? Why?

5. Read the story *Alexander and the Terrible, Horrible, No Good, Very Bad Day* by Judith Viorst. Ask your students if Alexander created his own stumbling blocks. How could he have prevented at least some of these? Ask if any of your students create their own stumbling blocks. What have they or the adults in their lives tried to do about them?

6. In the Overview above, mention was made of the requirement to mark graves and danger spots. Not doing so is to break the commandment of Not Placing a Stumbling Block before the blind. Give each student a pad of paper and a pencil. Their assignment for one week is to observe and record how our society marks the danger spots. Also, if they see a danger spot unmarked, they should record that and warn a

responsible adult about the situation. After one week, compare notes and discuss.

Secondary

1. Read the following *midrash* (*Kalilah ve Dimnah* II, 364, in *Mimekor Yisrael*, vol. 3, p. 1316) to the class:

A Dose of Medicine

In the land of Scinde, there was a wise doctor who died. Another man came to the area who said he was a doctor, but he was really not. Now, the king had a daughter who was pregnant and was having severe birth pains. They asked the advice of a wise physician who was blind. He said to give her a particular medicine which would cure her. But the king wanted another opinion, so he sent advisors to ask the new "doctor." This man really didn't know anything about healing, but nonetheless he mixed together some of the dead physician's medicine, mixed it together, and brought this to the king. "Here is the remedy, the best available," he said to the king. The king was very pleased and gave him 200 pieces of silver. But when he gave his daughter the medicine, she died.

The king ordered that the false doctor should take his own medicine, and thus he also died as a result of his deceitfulness.

The Mitzvah of Not Placing a Stumbling Block before the blind includes the giving of bad advice. Ask for examples of how bad advice might be a stumbling block. Have students write original *midrashim* about the giving of bad advice and its consequences.

2. Share the following from *Tanchuma Buber*, *Metzora* 26b with the class:

The Rabbis taught: We should not put opportunity to sin even before an honest man, much less before a thief, for the sages say this is like putting fire next to tow (very flammable unworked thread or fibers).

Ask students to give examples of placing temptation, i.e., a stumbling block, before the already tempted, i.e., blind. Also, ask: Have you ever been tempted by an acquaintance or situation? Did anything prevent you from succumbing to the temptation? Why or why not?

3. Individuals involved in confidence games or schemes to outwit someone are individuals who make a practice of placing a stumbling block before the blind. The police, consumer advocates, and the Better Business Bureau are three different sources for information on how these con artists operate. Invite a representative from one of these groups to make a presentation to your class, or several of them to take part in a panel discussion. Find out from these professionals how students can protect themselves and others from confidence games.

4. Explain to students that if a Jew lends another Jew money at interest, both are guilty of putting a stumbling block before the blind. Have students work in pairs and look up the following biblical verses: Exodus 22:24-26 and Deuteronomy 24:6, 10-13. Additionally, read the commentary on these verses in *The Torah: A Modern Commentary* edited by W. Gunther Plaut. Discuss how taking exorbitant interest is like placing a stumbling block. Who is hurt by such high interest on a loan?

5. Extend activity #4 by studying about Hebrew Free Loan Associations. Many communities have such a fund. If there is one in your community, interview its administrator. Or interview a Rabbi on this subject. Or contact the Jewish Free Loan Association, 6505 Wilshire Blvd., Suite 515, Los Angeles, CA 90048. Have the students send out a questionnaire to several Hebrew Free Loan Associations inquiring about their history, how they operate, who is eligible for loans, etc. Share and discuss the information as it comes in. Create an informational display of these materials.

   Reference: *A Credit to Their Community: Jewish Loan Societies in the United States, 1880-1945* by Shelly Tennenbaum.

6. Being uninformed about a matter can be a stumbling block. Hold a drug or cult awareness program for your high school students. Invite professionals in the field to conduct this program.

7. On some commercial airlines, the seating in certain exit rows is controlled. Handicapped people, elderly individuals, and people with small children are not permitted to sit in these rows since, in case of emergency, they would not be able to follow the crew's instructions to open the emergency doors. Recently, an official of the National Federation of the Blind refused a request to move from a seat the airline had mistakenly assigned him in an emergency exit row. Police were called in and the man was forcibly removed from the plane. Following the incident activists gathered to protest the arrest. Later, in a statement to the press, the man said, "We will continue to protest the brutal and discriminatory actions of the airlines against us until they are forced to treat us properly and with respect." Are the airlines placing a stumbling block before the blind, or is the safety of all the passengers the main consideration here? Have students write letters to the airlines and the National Federation of the Blind expressing their views on this situation.

ALL-SCHOOL PROGRAMS

1. In the Overview and Activities sections of this unit, there is much material that can be worked into short skits. Assign each class to present its own interpretation of Not Placing a Stumbling Block before the blind. If only one class is studying this material, have them present one or more skits for the rest of the school.

2. Show the film *Nicky: One of My Best Friends* as part of an assembly program. This film shows the reactions of students to the mainstreaming of a blind and partially paralyzed classmate. Follow up with a discussion about whether students with handicaps should go to a special school or should be mainstreamed. Which is better for the handicapped child, and why? Which is better for the other students, and why? Is it putting a stumbling block in front of the handicapped child to expect him or her to perform well in a regular school class? Or is it the other way around — that the stumbling block for the handicapped child is the special class itself?

3. Station teachers or aides at various places around a large room. Each is to act like a carnival barker, attempting to deceive the students. For example, one might be selling a miracle medicine that (supposedly) makes a person younger, another is selling shares in a (fake) gold mine, and still another is selling appliances (that don't really work) cheaply. Allow students to roam freely around the room for a short period of time. Then gather them together and discuss what they have experienced. Consider such questions as: In what ways were you being

deceived? How can one prevent being a victim of such practices? How were the "barkers" placing stumbling blocks before you?

RESOURCES

For the Teacher

Leibowitz, Nehama. *Studies in Vayikra (Leviticus)*. Jerusalem: The World Zionist Organization, 1980, pp. 173-178.

Maimonides, Moses. *The Commandments*. New York: The Soncino Press, 1967, vol. 2, pp. 277-188, 291-293.

Strassfeld, Sharon, and Michael Strassfeld, comps. and eds. *The Second Jewish Catalog*. Philadelphia: The Jewish Publication Society of America, 1976.

Tennenbaum, Shelly. *A Credit to Their Community: Jewish Loan Societies in the United States, 1880-1945*. Detroit: Wayne State University Press, 1993.

For the Students

Stern, Sara. *A Smile for Sammy*. Brooklyn, NY: Tamar/Mesorah, 1993. (Grades 3-6)

Viorst, Judith. *Alexander and the Terrible, Horrible, No Good, Very Bad Day*. New York: Macmillan Publishing Co., Inc., 1972. (Grades PK-2)

Audiovisual

Blind Sunday. A 31 minute film about a self-reliant, blind high school student and a newfound friend. University Film and Video. (Grades 7 and up)

A Rock in the Road. An 8 minute non-verbal story about three travelers, each of whom stumbles over a rock. Two put the rock back. The third removes the rock. Phoenix Films. (Grades 1-5)

Helen Keller in Her Story. A 45 minute inspirational film about the famous blind, deaf, and mute Keller, who overcame her handicaps. University Film and Video. (Grades 7 and up)

Invisible Children. A 24 minutes video in which human-like puppets, including some with disabilities, tour the country. Promotes awareness and acceptance. Learning Corporation of America. (Grades 3-10)

Like You Like Me Series. Ten animated 6 minute films about handicapped children. Encyclopedia Brittanica. (Grades K-3)

Nicky: One of My Best Friends. This 15 minute film shows the reactions of a group of students to the mainstreaming of a blind and partially paralyzed classmate. CRM Films. (Grades 4 and up)

People You'd Like To Know Series. Ten 10 minute films created to help able-bodied students, teachers, and others learn about the problems of the handicapped and how to help them adjust to school, home, and social situations. University Film and Video. (Grades 4 and up)

OVERVIEW

The following verse, which is the basis for the Mitzvah known as *Bal Tashchit* (don't be destructive or wasteful), is among the guidelines found in the Torah for waging war. "When in your war against a city you have to beseige it to capture it, you must not destroy its trees, wielding the ax against them. You may eat of them, but you must not cut them down. Are trees of the field human to withdraw before you into the besieged city?" (Deuteronomy 20:19).

In a sense, this verse provides a limitation to God's command to the first human beings to "fill the earth and master it" (Genesis 1:28). The Rabbis of the *Talmud* extended the principle of the verse from Deuteronomy to include many types of wastefulness. For example, they cautioned against allowing a lamp to burn too quickly, thus wasting fuel (*Shabbat* 67b). The killing of animals for no gainful purpose was also prohibited (*Chullin* 7b).

While rending one's garment upon hearing of a death was a Mitzvah, to tear it excessively was considered a violation of the precept *Bal Tashchit* (*Baba Kama* 91b). A person who tears one's clothes or breaks furniture in anger is compared to an idolater (*Shabbat* 105b). In yet another passage we are taught that one who could get by eating corn, but insisted on eating wheat (a rarer item), or one who could drink mead, but drank wine, also infringed on the prohibition of *Bal Tashchit*.

Other Rabbinic passages forbid the drawing off of sap for the sake of destruction, the spoilation of fruit, and the throwing of bread (which might ruin it). Maimonides codified these extensions to the original biblical law, stating that all needless destruction is included under the prohibition *Bal Tashchit* (*Yad Hazakah*, *Melachim* 6:10).

The theological basis for this Mitzvah is expressed by the Psalmist who wrote: "The earth is the Lord's and all that it holds, the world and its inhabitants" (*Psalms* 24:1). Everything ultimately belongs to God. We are merely caretakers. Our possessions are given to us in trust on the condition that we make wise use of them. This attitude differs significantly from the notion of private property, which gives one the right to do virtually anything with one's possessions. Jewish tradition extends this principle to one's body and, therefore, prohibits needless cutting of the flesh, the making of tattoos, and the taking of one's own life.

In modern times many Jews have been involved with ecology by recycling, conserving energy, and preserving the environment, all of which come under the rubric of *Bal Tashchit*.

ACTIVITIES

Primary

1. Plant a biblical garden. After researching the flora of ancient Israel, choose seedlings or seeds of those plants and create a small garden patch with your class. Depending on the climate and the time of year, you may need to plant your garden indoors. Teach the students how to weed, water, and cultivate their plants. Discuss how farmers take care of the world. Relate this caring to *Bal Tashchit*.

2. Plan a field trip to a recycling center. Questions to consider: What is recycling? Why should we do it? How can we go about recycling? How is recycling related to *Bal Tashchit*?

3. Discuss the following:
   a. What things have your parents given you for which you are responsible?
   b. How do you take care of these things?
   c. What could happen if you are not careful or responsible?
   d. How are we acting Jewishly when we take good care of our belongings?

4. After picking up litter on the grounds of the synagogue or school, turn the trash into a sculpture. You might include "litter" that nature has left behind, such as seed pods, dried leaves, twigs, etc. Discuss how this activity is similar to recycling.

5. *Bal Tashchit* teaches us not to be wasteful. Discuss ways that children are wasteful and how they might change some of their habits.

6. Read *The Giving Tree* by Shel Silverstein. Issues to discuss: When the boy was young, what did he and the tree do? As he got older, what happened? Was the boy/man fair to the tree? Did the boy take advantage of what the tree had to offer? What happened at the end of the story? Relate the story to the Mitzvah of *Bal Tashchit*, not being destructive of the environment. Use the information provided in the Overview above.

Intermediate

1. Lead a "circle of knowledge" during which each participant contributes a thought or an idea in response to the question, "What is a caretaker?" Explain to students how being a caretaker fulfills the Mitzvah of *Bal Tashchit*.

2. To stress the importance of the Mitzvah of *Bal Tashchit*, have each student create a "cause button" advertising some aspect of this Mitzvah. Some examples: Save the Whales; Be Astute, Don't Pollute; It's Our World — Don't Litter.

3. Nature itself does not always seem to obey the concept of *Bal Tashchit*. List ways in which nature is destructive — e.g., tornadoes, hurricanes, avalanches, earthquakes, volcanic eruptions, etc. Direct the students to research whether there may ultimately be positive results from some of these natural occurrences.

4. In conjunction with activity #3, have students create a collage of pictures about naturally occurring events.

5. Create a list of rules and guidelines with the students which encourage their family and friends not to be destructive or wasteful (e.g., turn off faucets tightly, don't track mud on the carpeting, turn off lights and TV when you leave the room, etc.). Call the list "Fulfilling the Mitzvah of *Bal Tashchit*."

6. Ask each student to bring in one item of trash (or teacher can provide a few). Brainstorm ways each of these items may be reused. For example, a small empty can might be decorated and used as a pencil holder.

Secondary

1. As a class read the book *Psalmist with a Camera* by Gail Rubin. Discuss what the author valued

most in her life. How is her death at the hands of terrorists a breaking of the commandment *Bal Tashchit*?

2. Have the students create an educational campaign for the Jewish community on *Bal Tashchit*. They should stress the ancient Jewish obligation to preserve our environment.

3. Design a poster which illustrates the concept *Bal Tashchit*.

4. Dr. Rathje, an anthropologist at the University of Arizona, runs "The Garbage Project." The project studies what Americans throw away. Numerous articles have appeared about this project. To find out more about this, visit a public library and research articles pertaining to this topic using *The Reader's Guide to Periodic Literature*. Have students survey what their parents, neighbors, and friends throw away. Talk about how our trash demonstrates that we are a wasteful society. How can we put the brakes on our "throw away" society and live more consistently by the Mitzvah of *Bal Tashchit*?

5. Discuss the ways in which the government is a caretaker of our environment. What would happen if we therefore just sit back and let the government fulfill the Mitzvah of *Bal Tashchit* for us?

6. In the Overview for *Bal Tashchit*, several prohibitions fall under the heading *Bal Tashchit*. In a brainstorming session with the group, generate as many ideas as you can which would fall under this heading. You might write it up as a flow chart, or web, as in the illustration on the following page.

7. *Bal Tashchit* includes the preservation of human life. Invite a guest speaker from a suicide prevention clinic or hot line.

8. Divide the class into groups of three or four students. Give each group a paper bag containing six to ten items of trash. Each group is to create a "useful" item or an *object d'art*.

9. Read chapter 10, "The Value of Life," pages 449-451, in *Voices of Wisdom: Jewish Ideals and Ethics for Everyday Living* by Francine Klagsbrun.

Preserve endangered species

Protect Natural Resources — **Bal Tashchit**

Reforestation

Taking Care of one's body

Visiting Doctor and Dentist

Seeking Counseling

Prohibition against suicide

Taking Care of one's possessions

Cleaning one's room

Doing Laundry

After reading the first three paragraphs, reenact the scenario with three Rabbis, the parents, doctors, etc. Try to resolve the dilemma. Afterward, read the conclusion of the story and compare it to your scenarios. Relate both scenarios to *Bal Tashchit*.

ALL-SCHOOL ACTIVITIES

1. Establish a synagogue recycling center. A local recycling center can usually help provide you with containers and might even pick up large quantities of paper, glass, or aluminum cans. Organize publicity both within the synagogue and in the local community which focuses on the Mitzvah of *Bal Tashchit*. (This project could also be a fund-raiser.)

2. *Bal Tashchit* includes the prohibition against taking one's life. Organize a forum on teen-age suicide prevention. Include mental health professionals, clergy, physicians, etc.

3. Arrange for an energy audit of the synagogue by your local utility company. Implement as many recommendations as possible and develop an educational campaign to inform members and visitors about how they can help save energy and about the meaning and responsibilities of *Bal Tashchit*.

4. Have a synagogue clean-up and plant project in springtime. In the publicity educate the congregation about the Mitzvah of *Bal Tashchit*.

5. Invite a guest speaker to talk about the environment at an assembly program. Some suggestions are: an ecologist, a forest ranger, a game warden, a professional recycler. Use your imagination to expand this list of possible speakers. You might consider creating a panel of presenters to speak on the environment as it relates to the Mitzvah of *Bal Tashchit*. Include a Jewish educator on the panel.

RESOURCES

For the Teacher

"The Best Blessing." In *Lively Legends — Jewish Values: An Early Childhood Teaching Guide* by Miriam P. Feinberg and Rena Rotenberg. Denver: A.R.E. Publishing, Inc., 1993.

Bloch, Abraham P. *A Book of Jewish Ethical Concepts*. Hoboken, NJ: KTAV Publishing House, Inc., 1984, pp. 246-247.

Glustrom, Simon. *The Language of Judaism*. Northvale, NJ: Jason Aronson, 1994, pp. 18-19.

Goldman, Gavriel. *Listen to the Trees: Jews and the Earth Teacher Guide*. New York: UAHC Press, 1996.

"Honi Ha-Meagel Sleeps for Seventy Years." In *Lively Legends — Jewish Values: An Early Childhood Teaching Guide* by Miriam P. Feinberg and Rena Rotenberg. Denver: A.R.E. Publishing, Inc., 1993.

"King Solomon and the Bee." In *Lively Legends — Jewish Values: An Early Childhood Teaching Guide* by Miriam P. Feinberg and Rena Rotenberg. Denver: A.R.E. Publishing, Inc., 1993.

Kirschen, Ya'akov. *Trees . . . The Green Testament.* New York: Vital Media Enterprises, 1993.

Klagsbrun, Francine. *Voices of Wisdom: Jewish Ideals and Ethics for Everyday Living.* Middle Village, NY: Jonathan David Publishing Co., 1986.

Leibowitz, Nachama. *Studies in Devarim (Deuteronomy).* Jerusalem: The World Zionist Organization, 1980, pp. 195-200.

Ross, Lillian. *The Judaic Roots of Ecology.* Miami: Central Agency for Jewish Eduation, 1986.

Stein, David E., ed. *A Garden of Choice Fruits: 200 Classic Jewish Quotes on Human Beings and the Environment.* New York: Shomrei Adamah, 1991.

Strassfeld, Sharon, and Michael Strassfeld, comps. and eds. *The Third Jewish Catalog: Creating Community.* Philadelphia: The Jewish Publication Society of America, 1980, pp. 306-315.

For the Students

Artson, Bradley Shavit. *It's a Mitzvah: Step-by-Step to Jewish Living.* West Orange, NJ: Behrman House and New York: The Rabbinical Assembly, 1995, pp. 50-61. (Grades 8-adult)

Baylor, Byrd. *Guess Who My Favorite Person Is?* New York: Charles Scribner's Sons, 1977. (Grades 3-6)

Bernstein, Ellen, and Dan Fink. *Let the Earth Teach You Torah.* Wyncote, PA: Shomrei Adamah, 1992. (Grades 7 and up)

Cherry, Lynne. *The Great Kapok Tree: A Tale of the Amazon Rain Forest.* Orlando, FL: Harcourt Brace and Co., 1990. (Grades K-3)

Cone, Molly. *Listen to the Trees: Jews and the Earth.* New York: UAHC Press, 1996. (Grades 4-6)

A Day in the Life of a Verse. Four page student folders. Los Angeles: Torah Aura Productions, 1985. (Grades 6 and up)

Elkington, John, et al. *Going Green: A Kid's Handbook to Saving the Planet.* New York: Viking Children's Books, 1990. (Grades 2 and up)

Ginot, Shai. *Echoes of a Landscape.* Hewitt, NJ: Gefen Books, 1993. (Grades 7 and up)

Gordon, Sol. *When Living Hurts.* New York: UAHC Press, 1985. (Grades 7 and up)

Grishaver, Joel Lurie, and Beth Huppin. *Tzedakah, Gemilut Chasadim and Ahavah.* Denver: A.R.E. Publishing, Inc., 1983, pp. 77-80. (Grades 7 and up)

Isaacs, Ronald H., and Kerry M. Olitzky. *Doing Mitzvot: Mitzvah Projects for Bar/Bat Mitzvah.* Hoboken, NJ: KTAV Publishing House, Inc., 1994, pp. 75-86. (Grades 6-8)

Pasachoff, Naomi. *Basic Judaism for Young People: God.* West Orange, NJ: Behrman House, 1987, pp. 21-26. (Grades 4-7)

Silverstein, Shel. *The Giving Tree.* New York: HarperCollins Children's Books, 1964. (Grades K and up)

Wahl, Jan. *Once When the World Was Green.* Berkeley, CA: Tricycle Press, 1996. (Grades 2-5)

Audiovisual

"Andy Lipkis: Tree Person." This 5 minute segment from the slide-tape show *Profiles in Courage* is about a person who works for the betterment of society. Torah Aura Productions. (Grades 4 and up)

Daisies and Ducklings. Audiocassette by Fran Avni containing cheerful songs about animals and the environment. Lemonstone Records. Available from A.R.E. Publishing, Inc.

The Giving Tree. A 10 minute animated film of the Shel Silverstein book of the same name. Barr Films Entertainment. (Grades 1-6)

Let's Clean Up Our Act: Songs for the Earth. Audiocassette. American Melody. (Grades PK-2)

UNIT 32

Preventing Accidents
מַעֲקֶה

OVERVIEW

It might be said that the Torah contains the first building code. "When you build a new house, you shall make a parapet for your roof, so that you do not bring blood guilt on your house if anyone should fall from it" (Deuteronomy 22:8). A parapet is a wall or a guard railing used on a bridge, a balcony, or a roof.

In ancient times house roofs were flat and it was common for people to sleep and walk on them. According to a *midrash*, the parapet could not be less than ten handbreadths high (approximately 4-6 inches) and must be able to prevent a person who leans on it from falling (*Sifre Deuteronomy* 229). The Rabbis, however, gave this passage a much broader interpretation: "By this injunction we are commanded to remove all obstacles and sources of dangers from all places in which we live" (Maimonides, *The Commandments*, vol. 1, p. 197).

Parapets are also to be built around cisterns and trenches so that no one will fall into them. Dangerous structures are to be repaired. One is "forbidden to leave obstacles or hindrances on public or private property, so as not to cause fatal accidents" (*ibid.*, vol. 2, p. 277). A person is not to keep a vicious dog or a shaky ladder in one's house.

This Mitzvah not only requires one to remove any obstacles which might endanger another's life, but, according to Maimonides, it also imposes upon everyone the obligation to safeguard one's own life (*Yad Hazakah, Rotzeach* 11:8). Life is a gift from God and we are caretakers of our lives and of the lives of others. Therefore, one is not permitted to have the attitude that it is no one else's business if one risks his or her own life.

A person who creates a hazardous situation is responsible for any injury or harm that may occur. "When a person opens or digs a pit and does not cover it, and an ox or an ass falls into it, the one responsible for the pit must make restitution by paying the price (of the animal) to its owner, but may keep the dead animal (Exodus 21:33-34).

Maimonides discusses who is responsible when a person puts a jug in a public place and another person trips on it and breaks it. Not only is the person who broke it not responsible for the breakage, he

asserts, but if the person was injured, the owner of the jug is responsible for the injury (*Yad Hazakah, Nizkei Mamon* 3:5). Furthermore, selling weapons of war, chains, wild animals, or anything else which constitutes a public hazard is forbidden (*Yad Hazakah, Rozeach* 12:12).

ACTIVITIES

Primary

1. Take a tour of the religious school and have the students list safe and unsafe conditions. Brainstorm ways of correcting the unsafe conditions. Decide which things the students can fix and which need adult help to correct. Relate this to the Mitzvah of Preventing Accidents.

2. Invite a fire and safety inspector to discuss fire and safety in the home. Consider inviting parents to this session. Ask children how preventing fires and always thinking about safety relates to the Mitzvah of Preventing Accidents.

3. If you have a doll house in your classroom, set up (prior to class time) several unsafe conditions, such as toys left in the front yard, a ladder left out, cleaning products within reach of young children, etc. After the students have examined the situation, ask them to describe all the violations. You could do this in a game format, the winner being the one to correctly identify all the unsafe conditions. Relate safety in the home to the Mitzvah of *Ma'akeh*.

4. Brainstorm a list of rules for the playground that will prevent accidents from happening (e.g., no pushing, do not pick up broken glass, etc.).

5. Hold a safety poster contest. Suggest themes to the class, such as traffic safety, home safety, or personal safety. Provide students with a variety of art materials and poster boards. Arrange to display some or all of the posters.

6. Show students a series of pictures depicting unsafe conditions. For each picture ask, "What is

wrong with this picture?" Discuss the students' responses.

Intermediate

1. Organize a jingle contest. In 25 words or less, students describe how to promote safety. Suggest that they include something about the Mitzvah of Preventing Accidents.

2. Several secular educational companies publish excellent material on safety. If there is a teacher supply store in your area, check for appropriate materials. To locate such a store, look under the categories "School Supplies" or "Educational Stores" in the Yellow Pages. (An excellent series of safety posters is published by Constructive Playthings, 1227 E. 119th St., Grandview, MO 64030.) With the students make your own similar materials that focus on the Mitzvah of Preventing Accidents. Share them with a younger class.

3. Hold a "bicycle rodeo." Invite students to bring bicycles or other riding toys. Set up a riding course that includes stop signs, yield signs, turns, and other obstacles. Ask a police officer to explain the importance of bicycle safety. Then relate bicycle safety to the Mitzvah of *Ma'akeh.*

4. According to the *Talmud,* the Mitzvah of *Ma'akeh* prohibits a person from keeping a vicious dog. From time to time, there are reported cases of dogs or other animals attacking their owners or other individuals. Invite a speaker from the Humane Society or the SPCA to discuss this problem.

5. Have each student observe a street or an intersection for 15-20 minutes. Have the observer record traffic violations and other unsafe activities of both drivers and pedestrians. Compare the lists. Compose letters identifying a hazardous condition and a possible solution. Send the letters to the appropriate authorities, such as the city manager, department of public works, or the police department. Write the letters from a Jewish perspective, explaining the commandment to prevent accidents.

6. In an enclosed space or room, provide riding toys, bicycles, and playground equipment. Bring the students to the area, and without directions

or guidelines, let them play for 5-10 minutes. Then stop play and hold an evaluation session. Ask: Did each participant play safely? Did anything go wrong? Is it possible to use a toy correctly, but still create an unsafe situation?

After discussing these questions, point out that even long ago when the Torah was given, there were safety rules. Display a poster with the commandment: "When you build a new house, you shall make a parapet for your roof . . ." Using information in the Overview above, explain what a parapet is and how the Rabbis developed more laws concerning safety based on this biblical quote.

Secondary

1. Organize a public relations campaign for automobile safety from the perspective of Jewish tradition. Write articles for the synagogue bulletin. Put on skits for other classes and perhaps at services. Make posters to be placed around the building, etc.

2. Create a safety patrol to monitor the synagogue or school parking area before and after classes.

3. Arrange a mock trial with the following scenario: In retrieving a ball from the Jewish Community Center roof, a student accidentally falls and sprains his/her ankle. The child's parents claim that the Jewish Community Center is responsible and should pay all medical costs. Put Center board members, played by students, on trial. The prosecution should use material from Jewish tradition contained in the Overview above. The defense should base their case on the feeling that the student should not have been up there in the first place.

4. The Jewish tradition extends the Mitzvah of Preventing Accidents to prohibit one from risking one's own life. Write a series of *Responsa* regarding whether or not one is permitted, according to Jewish tradition, to be one of the following: sky diver, lifeguard, stunt man, police officer, fire fighter, mountain climber, air traffic controller, boxer, etc. Consider mental stress, as well as physical risks. Consider, too, whether proper training can sufficiently reduce safety risks.

5. With the class identify a specific unsafe condition at your school or synagogue and decide how to

correct it. With the approval of the Director of Education or the Board of Directors, correct the unsafe condition.

6. As a part the Mitzvah of Preventing Accidents we are commanded not to sell weapons of war. Hold a class debate on whether or not Israel should sell weapons to other countries.

ALL-SCHOOL PROGRAMS

1. Have the Director of Education prepare an emergency exit plan. Give copies to each teacher and post the emergency escape routes in every room. Before a fire drill, the teachers explain these procedures to the students. (Younger students can practice leaving the building before the actual drill.) After the drill bring all classes together in an assembly to emphasize the importance of the emergency exit plan and to tie it into the Mitzvah of Preventing Accidents. You may want to invite a fire inspector to observe the drill, speak to the students, and give advice on how to improve the procedures.

2. Assign to each class or group of students a Jewish holiday. Each class prepares a skit dealing with an aspect of accident prevention or safety pertaining to the holiday. Some examples of potentially dangerous holiday situations: Using a sharp knife to slice apples on Rosh Hashanah, frying *latkes* in hot grease on Chanukah, wearing masks or restrictive clothing on Purim, etc. Each class presents its skit to the whole school.

3. Invite the parents of religious school students to participate in the following activity:

    Each family is given a large sheet of paper and a pencil. Ask them to draw the floor plan of their home. The leader of the activity then presents accident scenarios which each family is to solve. Some of these scenarios relate to the floor plan and some do not. Add or delete scenarios as you wish.
    a. It is the middle of the night and the smoke alarm goes off. What do you do?

    b. A fire has spread out of control from the fireplace (or kitchen). What is the escape route for each family member?
    c. Your baby sister has just started crawling. Make a list of things to do to "baby-proof" your home.

RESOURCES

For the Teacher

Birnbaum, Philip, ed. *Maimonides' Mishneh Torah (Yad Hazakah).* Rockaway Beach, NY: Hebrew Publishing Co., 1961, pp. 108-110.

Ganzfried, Solomon. *Code of Jewish Law: Kitzur Shulhan Arukh.* rev. ed. Hyman E. Goldin, trans. Rockaway, NY: Hebrew Publishing Co., 1991, vol. 1, ch. 33, pp. 108-110.

Maimonides, Moses. *The Commandments.* New York: The Soncino Press, 1967, vol. 1, p. 197; vol. 2, p. 277.

For the Students

Baum, Eli. *Mitzvot Bein Adam Lachaveiro.* Hoboken, NJ: KTAV Publishing House, Inc., 1980, pp. 27-29. (Grades 3-6)

Berman, Melanie, and Joel Lurie Grishaver. *My Weekly Sidrah.* Los Angeles: Torah Aura Productions, 1986, pp. 172-173. (Grades 3-6)

Neusner, Jacob. *Learn Mishnah.* West Orange, NJ: Behrman House, 1978, pp. 17-28. (Grades 5-8)

———. *Learn Talmud.* West Orange, NJ: Behrman House, 1979, pp. 18-42. (Grades 6-9)

Tucker, Gordon. "Jewish Business Ethics." In *Jewish Ethics: A Study Guide.* Joseph Lowin, ed. New York: Hadassah The Women's Zionist Organization of America, Inc., 1986, pp. 37-40. (Grades 7 and up)

Audiovisual

Safety First — I'm No Fool with Safety. A series of 8-10 minute animated films featuring Disney characters dealing with various aspects of safety. Walt Disney Educational Media Co. (Grades K-3)

UNIT 33

OVERVIEW

No fewer than nine positive *mitzvot* relate to God. Jews are commanded to believe in God, to believe in the unity of God, to fear God, to worship God, to cleave to God, to swear only by God's name, to walk in God's ways, and to sanctify God's name. A brief explication of each follows.

We do not find in the Bible an explicit command to believe in God. Rather, this Mitzvah is derived from the first of the Ten Commandments: "I the Lord am your God who brought you out of the land of Egypt, out of the house of bondage" (Exodus 20:2). According to Maimonides this statement means that one must believe that there is a God who is the creator of everything in existence (*The Commandments*, vol. 1, p. 1). Furthermore, it is forbidden to believe in or to consider any other as being God (*The Commandments*, vol. 2, p. 1). This prohibition is derived from the second of the Ten Commandments: "You shall have no other gods besides Me" (Exodus 20:3). For the Jew, these commandments are the underpinnings of faith.

The primary proclamation of belief, which also affirms God's unity, is the *Sh'ma*: "Hear, O Israel, the Lord is our God, the Lord is One" (Deuteronomy 6:4). To say that God is One is to say that God cannot be divided or fragmented. It naturally follows that God cannot be a physical being, since any physical being could be divided. Biblical references to God which contain anthropomorphisms are to be interpreted figuratively. The reason such phrases are used is that "the Torah speaks the language of human beings" (*Berachot* 31b). The unity of God is also the basis for the concept of all peoples being interrelated.

The commandment to love God (Deuteronomy 6:6) means that we should "dwell upon and contemplate [God's] commandments, [God's] injunctions, and [God's] works, so that we may arrive at a conception of [God], and in conceiving [of God] attain absolute joy" (Maimonides, *The Commandments*, vol. 1, p. 3). At the same time, we are to fear God (Deuteronomy 6:13, 10:20) — a commandment which serves as the basis for the belief of divine reward and punishment.

The Torah commands four times that we serve God (Exodus 23:25, Deuteronomy 6:13, 11:13, 13:5). A *midrash* interprets these passages to refer to the act of praying (*Sifre* to Deuteronomy 11:13), which should be done with the proper *kavanah* (spiritual attention and devotion).

The Torah also commands that we cleave to God (Deuteronomy 10:20 and 11:22), which is explained as meaning that we should associate with wise persons and their disciples (*Sifre* to Deuteronomy 11:22).

The command to swear only by God's name (Deuteronomy 6:13 and 10:20, and see chapter 16 in this book, "Keeping One's Word") means that when we are required to confirm or deny something on oath, we are to do so only by God's name.

To walk in God's ways (Deuteronomy 10:12, 28:9) means to emulate, in like manner, the qualities of God. "Just as God is called merciful, so you shall be merciful; just as God is called gracious, so you shall be gracious; just as God is called righteous, so you shall be righteous; just as God is called kind, so you shall be kind" (*Sifre* to Deuteronomy 10:12). We are also to clothe the naked, as God clothed Adam and Eve; to visit the sick, as God visited Abraham after the circumcision; to comfort mourners, as God comforted Isaac after his father died; and to bury the dead, as God buried Moses (*Sotah* 14a).

The commandment to sanctify God's name (Leviticus 22:32) is interpreted to mean that we must proclaim our religion to the world, and even be willing to die for it if necessary. The term for martyrdom is *Kiddush HaShem* — literally, sanctification of the divine name — an act for which there are specific guidelines in Jewish tradition.

God is not an abstract concept. Rather, God's existence is a given in the Bible and in Rabbinic literature. God created the universe and sustains it, and God directs the unfolding of Jewish history. When the Temple was destroyed, the prophets knew that it was God's punishment of the people for their transgressions, for the God of Israel can never be defeated.

Throughout history Jews have had an intimate relationship with God: talking to God, praising God, even cursing God. The Holocaust, however, opened the door to a significant theological question. How could God allow such evil to happen to the Jewish people? Jewish and non-Jewish thinkers alike view this as one of the key existential questions of our day.

ACTIVITIES

Primary

1. We are commanded to walk in God's ways. A commentary on Deuteronomy explains that this means we are to be like God. Just as God is merciful, we should be merciful. Just as God is righteous, we should be righteous. And just as God is kind, we should be kind. Brainstorm with students actions and deeds that reflect these three attributes of God.

2. When we teach about God, we have to teach by implication, using metaphors and allegories. While God is intangible, God nonetheless inspires in us a feeling of awe. Talk to the class about this feeling and about what inspires this feeling in you (the teacher). You might mention such things as a loud, booming thunderstorm; standing under a very tall tree and looking up; being outside in a big wind; standing at the top of a big hill, etc. Elicit from the students words, images, and sounds that fill them with awe. Follow up by teaching the song "Eli, Eli," based on a poem by Hannah Senesh.

   Reference: *Songs and Hymns: A Musical Supplement to Gates of Prayer*, p. 26.

3. The Torah commands us to love God. Maimonides explains that we should think about God's works and, from those, begin to understand God. Once we understand God, he continues, we will be joyful. Ask students to give examples of God's works. Share with them the story of creation from Genesis 1:1-2:3. Show the animated film *Clay*. Then divide the class into small groups, assigning each group one or two of the days of creation. Distribute clay in a variety of colors. Have children create a representation of the days assigned to them.

   When the project is complete, discuss the following questions: Was the work difficult? Why did you keep working if it was hard? How did you feel when it was finished? Do you think your work is complete, or is there more that you could do? Relate this discussion to *tikun olam*, the

righting or finishing of the world. This is the part that we play in creation.

4. In the book *Who Knows Ten?*, read the story "The Princess Who Saw God." Suggested questions for discussion: Why was the princess so selfish? How did the princess learn to be more caring? Who showed her? Did the princess actually see God? Do you think that through our actions we can be like God? If yes, give some examples.

5. Teach students to recite the *Shehecheyanu*. Describe this blessing as a way of saying thank-you to God for special times, occasions, and holidays. Ask the children to suggest times when saying this blessing would be appropriate. Create an illustrated mural depicting such times.

   Listen to and discuss the song "Thank You God" on the record *To See the World With Jewish Eyes*, Volume I.

6. Share with the class the following *midrash* from *Beresheet Rabbah* 38:13:

   Abraham and the Idols
   When Abraham was a young boy, his father Terach left him in charge of his idol shop. There were many idols, each made for a special purpose. Abraham did not believe that these idols had any special powers or abilities, but his father believed they did.

   One day when he was watching the shop, Abraham smashed all the idols except the largest. He put a big stick near the remaining idol.

   When Terach, Abraham's father, returned and saw the damage, he asked Abraham what had happened. Abraham replied that the largest idol had said that it was all-powerful and smashed all the other idols. Terach said that this was impossible. An idol is made of clay and could not possibly act in this way. Abraham replied that if they can't do that, how could they do any of the other things that people pray to them to do?

   Discuss Abraham's unique role as the first Jew. Ask the students: What did Abraham do when his father left him in charge of the idol shop? What was Abraham trying to teach his father? Was it a very brave thing that Abraham did? Would you have had the courage to do such a thing? Teach the class to recite the *Sh'ma* in Hebrew and English. Explain the meaning and intent of the *Sh'ma* (see the Overview above).

Intermediate

1. Distribute copies of the synagogue prayerbook to each student. Allow them 10 to 15 minutes to examine it and to choose a prayer which best describes their personal concept of God. Each student may then read his/her choice aloud and tell why it has personal meaning.

2. There are several incidents during which biblical characters had direct experience with God. Divide the class into small groups and assign each pair a different incident to portray in a skit. Discuss the skits. Citations for passages with such incidents follow:
   a. Genesis 3:1-24 (Garden of Eden)
   b. Genesis 4:1-16 (Cain and Abel)
   c. Genesis 6:9-22 (Noah)
   d. Genesis 18:16-33 (Sodom and Gemorrah)
   e. Exodus 3:1-22, 4:1-17 (Moses at the Burning Bush)
   f. Exodus 6:26-30, 7:1-9 (Moses and Aaron)
   g. Deuteronomy 3:23-28 (Moses)

3. There are several prayers that evoke clear images of ways we can think about God. Examine a daily and Shabbat *Siddur* (prayerbook) or a High Holy Day *Machzor*. Choose a prayer to recreate as a mosaic (either of paper or tile). Some suggested prayers: *Ma'ariv Aravim, Hashkiveynu,* morning blessings of thanksgiving.

4. We are commanded never to erase or destroy God's name. Any book which contains God's name must be buried or stored away. Such items are called *Shaymot*, meaning names. Have students investigate what your synagogue does with worn-out Bibles, prayerbooks, and other *Shaymot*. If your synagogue does not have a burial place for such, establish one with your class.

5. When God gave the Torah to the Jewish people, God wanted something in return. Read chapter 1, "Who Will Be My Surety?" in *Lessons From Our Living Past*, edited by Jules Harlow. Utilize the questions found at the end of the chapter.

6. One of the traditional Mitzvot relating to God is *Kiddush HaShem* (the sanctification of God). This term is used to refer to martyrdom. On a number of occasions in our history, Jews have been faced with the choice of breaking Jewish law and being allowed to live, or being faithful to Judaism and being put to death. One may, in fact, when faced with the threat of death, break any of the Mitzvot except for killing another person, idolatry, or adultery. Present this concept to the class. Discuss: Under certain circumstances would you be willing to give up your life for Judaism? Is there anything for which you would give up your life?

Secondary

1. To encourage students to talk about their personal beliefs in God, hand out sheets of paper. Ask each student to write out a brief personal statement about God. Tell them not to sign their names. The sheets are folded and placed in a paper bag. They are then mixed up. Each student pulls one out to read.

2. Explain to students that God is called both *Adonai* and *Elohim* in the Torah. Tradition teaches that the name *Adonai* is associated with God's merciful qualities, while the name *Elohim* refers to God's sense of justice. Both of these qualities are needed to sustain the world. Have the class create a diamante poem using *Adonai* for the first line and *Elohim* for the last line. The format follows:

   Line 1: one word subject: noun, opposite of word in last line.
   Line 2: two words: adjectives describing the subject in line one.
   Line 3: three words: participles (verbs ending in "ing" or "ed") about the subject in line one
   Line 4: four words: nouns about the subject in lines one and seven
   Line 5: three words: participles about the subject in line seven
   Line 6: two words: adjectives describing the subject in line seven
   Line 7: one word subject: noun, opposite of the word in the first line.

   Reference: For other forms of poetry, see *Poetry from A to Z* by Paul B. Janecko.

3. Pose these challenges to your students: Does God need our praises? Does God need us to pray? Tell your students to imagine that they are Rabbis and they are to write a 3-5 minute sermon based on these two questions. They may

take either a pro or con approach. Afterward, they may deliver these sermons to the class.

4. Our tradition teaches that the Torah speaks in the language of human beings. The Torah uses terms that we understand to describe God, even though those terms do not come close to portraying God accurately. Exodus 34:6-7 gave scholars an opportunity to derive thirteen attributes of God. Read these two verses with your students. (*The Torah: A Modern Commentary*, edited by W. Gunther Plaut, pp. 663-664 provides an excellent discussion of these two verses.) Point out that these verses are a part of the High Holy Day Liturgy. Discuss why these attributes are particularly appropriate for that time.

5. Share the following with your students. In the *V'ahavta* we are commanded to love God. We are not asked to love God, or suggested to love God, but commanded. Consider and discuss the following: If one is not sure of one's belief in God, how can one love God? Is it important to love God? Can one live as a Jew and not love God?

6. Different faiths vary in their attitudes and beliefs concerning how God works in our lives. Invite the Rabbi or Director of Education to class. Watch one of the television ministry shows. Discuss how the view of God portrayed differs from Jewish teachings.

ALL-SCHOOL PROGRAMS

1. Choose an older class (Grades 7-12) to put on the play "Oh God, My God!" from *Heroes, Heroines and Holidays: Plays for Jewish Youth* by Elaine Rembrandt. Discuss the performance in small groups.

2. Have each student in the school contribute to a list of praise words referring to God; include attributes and metaphors. Have students write these on opaque projection transparencies, placing the words so that additional overlays will create an incremental statement of praise. Ask student volunteers to find poems and prayers of praise. Arrange these words of praise in a pleasing order and select background music. Make a 10-15 minute tape of the students reading their prayers and poems with the music playing softly

in the background. Play the tape and show the transparencies, adding additional overlays as the readings progress. This can be a part of a school creative service, inserted after the *Barchu*, after the *Kedushah*, or in place of a sermon.

3. View the movie *Oh God!*, which is available on videotape. Break up into groups and discuss the portrayal of God. Does the film give a Jewish view of God? Explain.

RESOURCES

For the Teacher

Blumberg, Sherry H. "The Challenge of Teaching about God." In *The New Jewish Teachers Handbook*. Audrey Friedman Marcus and Raymond A. Zwerin, eds. Denver: A.R.E. Publishing, Inc., 1994.

Dorff, Elliot N. *Knowing God: Jewish Journeys to the Unknowable*. Northvale, NJ: Jason Aronson Inc., 1992.

Gellman, Marc, and Thomas Harman. *Where Does God Live? Questions and Answers for Parent and Children*. New York: Ballantine Books, 1991.

"God." In *Encyclopaedia Judaica*. Jerusalem: Keter Publishing House Jerusalem Ltd., 1972, vol. 7, cols. 641-674.

Goodman, Roberta Louis. "Faith Development: A Jewish View." In *The New Jewish Teachers Handbook*. Audrey Friedman Marcus and Raymond A. Zwerin, eds. Denver: A.R.E. Publishing, Inc., 1994.

Janeczko, Paul B., comp. *Poetry from A to Z: A Guide for Young Writers*. New York: Bradbury Press, 1994.

Maimonides, Moses. *The Commandments*. New York: Soncino Press, 1967, vol. 1, pp. 1-15; vol. 2, pp. 1-8.

Sonsino, Rifat, and Daniel B. Syme. *Finding God: Ten Jewish Responses*. New York: UAHC Press, 1986.

Songs and Hymns: A Musical Supplement to Gates of Prayer. New York: Central Conference of Cantors and Central Conference of American Rabbis, 1977.

Wolpe, David J. *The Healer of Shattered Hearts: A Jewish View of God*. New York: Henry Holt and Co., Inc., 1990.

———. *Teaching Your Children about God: A Rabbi Speaks to Concerned Parents*. New York: Henry Holt and Co., Inc., 1993.

For the Students

Bissell, Sherry, with Raymond A. Zwerin and Audrey Friedman Marcus. *God: The Eternal Challenge.* Denver: A.R.E. Publishing, Inc., 1980. (Grades 7 and up)

Bogot, Howard, and Daniel B. Syme. *I Learn about God.* New York: UAHC Press, 1982. (Grades K-2)

———. *Prayer Is Reaching.* New York: UAHC Press, 1982. (Grades K-2)

Caswell, Helen. *God's World Makes Me Feel So Little.* Nashville, TN: Abingdon Press, 1985. (Grades K-3)

Cone, Molly. *About God.* The Shema Story Books IV. New York: UAHC Press, 1973. (Grades K-3)

———. *Who Knows Ten?* New York: UAHC Press, 1965. (Grades K-3)

Groner, Judyth, and Madeline Wikler. *Thank You, God! A Jewish Child's Book of Prayers.* Rockville, MD: Kar-Ben Copies, Inc., 1993. (Grades PK-2)

Harlow, Jules, ed. *Lessons from Our Living Past.* West Orange, NJ: Behrman House, 1972. (Grades K-3)

Ingram, Robert D. *Who Taught Frogs To Hop? A Child's Book about God.* Minneapolis: Augsburg, 1990. (Grades PK-2)

Kerdeman, Deborah, and Lawence Kushner. *The Invisible Chariot: Introduction to Kabbalah and Jewish Spirituality.* Student Workbook and Leader Guide. Denver: A.R.E. Publishing, Inc., 1986. (Grades 9-adult)

Kushner, Lawrence. *The Book of Miracles: A Young Person's Guide to Jewish Spirituality.* New York: UAHC Press, 1987. (Grades 4-6)

Pasachoff, Naomi. *Basic Judaism for Young People: God.* West Orange, NJ: Behrman House, 1987, pp. 35-42. (Grades 4-7)

Prager, Janice, and Arlene Lepoff. *Why Be Different? A Look Into Judaism.* West Orange, NJ: Behrman House, Inc., 1986, pp. 7-28. (Grades 6-8)

Sasso, Sandy Eisenberg. *God's Paintbrush.* Woodstock, VT: Jewish Lights Publishing, 1992. (Grades K-4)

———. *In God's Name.* Woodstock, VT: Jewish Lights Publishing, 1994. (Grades K-5)

Snyder, Carol. *God Must Like Cookies, Too.* Philadelphia: The Jewish Publication Society of America, 1993. (Grades PK-3)

Sonsino, Rifat, and Daniel B. Syme. *Finding God: Ten Jewish Responses.* New York: UAHC Press, 1986. (Grades 9 and up)

Wood, Douglas. *Old Turtle.* Duluth, MN: Pfeifer-Hamilton Publishers, 1992. (Grades K-3)

Audiovisual

Clay. An 8 minute animated film in which clay is shaped to create a variety of life forms. University Film and Video. (Grades K-3)

Crimes and Misdemeanors. This serious full-length drama poses questions about the nature of good and evil and how each is rewarded or punished. For sophisticated audiences. Available at video stores. (Grades 10 and up)

I Asked for Wonder — Experiencing God. In this 57 minute video, several people who are studying about God talk about dealing with serious illness or pain, and also learn from theologians. Jewish Theological Seminary of America. (Grades 10 and up)

Oh God! and Oh God, Book II. These full-length films feature George Burns as God. Theology and philosophy are mixed with humor. Available at video stores. (Grades 7 and up)

Questions of Faith: What's God Got To Do with Evil? Leading religious thinkers, including Rabbi Harold Kushner, discuss the problem of evil in this half-hour video. EcuFilm. (Grades 9 and up)

Questions of Faith: Who Is God? Leading religious thinkers from different faiths discuss theological questions in this half-hour video. EcuFilm. (Grades 9 and up)

"Take God with You." On the audiocassette *Walk with Me* by Julie Silver. A Silver Girl Production. Available from A.R.E. Publishing, Inc.

"Thank You God." A prayerful song for little children on the sound recording *To See the World through Jewish Eyes, Volume 1.* UAHC Press. (Grades PK-K)

"You Are the One (Reb Nachman's Prayer)." On the audiocassette *Renewal of Spirit* by Debbie Friedman. Available from A.R.E. Publishing, Inc. (Grades 3 and up)

UNIT 34

Loving One's Neighbor

וְאָהַבְתָּ לְרֵעֲךָ כָּמוֹךָ

OVERVIEW

"You shall love your neighbor as yourself" (Leviticus 19:18). According to Rabbi Akiba, this is the most important principle of the Torah (*Sifra* to Leviticus 19:18). When a heathen challenged Hillel to teach him the entire Torah while standing on one foot, Hillel replied: "What is hateful to yourself do not do to your neighbor. That is the entire Torah; all the rest is commentary. Go and learn it" (*Shabbat* 31a).

Yet, as simple and straightforward as this Mitzvah appears, its extentions and ramifications are both complex and controversial. In his *Mishneh Torah*, Maimonides explains how this Mitzvah is the source of so many others: "It is a positive commandment of Rabbinic law to visit the sick, to console the mourner, to attend to the dead, to provide a dowry for the bride, to escort one's guest, and to perform all the rites of burial . . . to cheer the bride and groom and to afford them support in all their necessities . . . . Though all these commandments are a matter of Rabbinic law, they are nevertheless embraced in the verse 'You shall love your neighbor as yourself'" (*Hilchot Avel* 14:1).

This verse is valued by the Christian faith as well. In the Gospels Jesus says that this commandment is second in importance only to the commandment to love God (*Mark* 12:28). Paraphrasing the Leviticus text, Jesus is quoted as saying, "All that you would wish that men should do unto you, do also unto them" (*Matthew* 7:12). This statement has become known to Western civilization as the Golden Rule.

Part of the controversy surrounding this Mitzvah stems from its different formulations. Is Jesus' pro-active version significantly different from Hillel's version? Is Hillel being more realistic in asking only that we refrain from doing what we do not want done to ourselves? Are the differences more a matter of style or are they truly substantive? Another issue is whether or not it is possible to command someone to love someone else. Nachmanides, for instance, felt that this was not realistic. He interpreted the verse from Leviticus to mean that we should wish our neighbor the same well-being that we wish ourselves (Nachmanides to Leviticus 19:18).

Another difficulty concerns the interpretation of the word "neighbor." It might appear from the first part of the verse to refer to a fellow Jew; perhaps it was even taken for granted that one's neighbor was a Jew. However, another Mitzvah bids us to love the stranger, later interpreted to mean the proselyte (see Chapter 35 in this book), thus, the confusion as to whom the neighbor might really be.

This rather abstract value is addressed, though not entirely clarified, by various principles and stories found in Jewish sources.

The Talmud (*Baba Metzia* 62a) discusses the case of two men traveling in the desert. One of them has a jar with enough water to keep him alive until he reaches civilization. One sage, Ben Peruta, says that the water must be shared, so that both men will survive for a while, though both will eventually die. Rabbi Akiba, however, rules that the man holding the water is not obligated to share it. However, we read in the Talmud: "While one's own needs are to take precedence over those of one's neighbor, one should not insist on one's own needs always being met first" (*Baba Metzia* 33a). The issue of whether the man is permitted to share the water or to give it entirely to his companion is, unfortunately, not fully explored.

In another case, a man is faced with helping either an enemy struggling to load his animal or a friend struggling to unload his animal. While preference is normally given to unloading an animal (to relieve the animal's stress), in this case preference is given to the enemy because of the potential of turning an enemy into a friend.

As if to emphasize this point, we have the account of Rabbi Meir who, upset at some lawbreakers in his neighborhood, prayed that they should die. His wife, Beruria, challenged him: "Does the Psalm read 'Let sinners cease out of the earth' (Psalms 104:35)? Rather, read the verse: 'Let sins cease . . . .'" In other words, Rabbi Meir should not have prayed that the men would die, but rather that they should repent of their sins and live.

In modern times the theologian Martin Buber built his philosophy of I-Thou around this Mitzvah, teaching that we should treat others not as things or objects, but as beings much like ourselves.

157

ACTIVITIES

Primary

1. Write the following on the blackboard and read it to the class: "What is hateful to yourself do not do to your neighbor" (Hillel). Ask the class what the quotation means to them. Then ask for examples of the kind of behavior about which Hillel was talking. Have students apply the Mitzvah of Loving One's Neighbor in creating behavior guidelines for your class. Copy the new rules on a large chart with Hillel's saying at the top.

2. Ask students to write or dictate a list of ways we show that we love our neighbors. Take the student work and fold it into an illustrated accordion-style booklet.

3. One of the ways that we learn to love our neighbors and care about each other is to share our private lives with those we know. Create a class videotape. With a video camera, visit each child in his/her home. Film the child and his/her family, asking a few interview-style questions. Have the child describe a special room or place in his/her home or backyard or neighborhood. When all the filming is complete, have a film screening party.

4. Get to know your Jewish neighbors. If there is another synagogue in your community or one in a nearby town, investigate whether a class in their religious school would like to become pen pals with your class. (Choose a class with students the same age as yours.) If desired, have classes meet and share a holidy party or other outing.

5. Ask the students: "Who is your neighbor?" Guide the discussion so that students expand their concept of neighbor to include: all members of their community, all Jews, and all human beings.

6. Unroll a long length of plain white paper providing enough space for each class member to have a 16" to 20" section. Make a mural with the theme "Love Your Neighbor." In large letters at the center of the mural, copy out the commandment. Then have each student paint his or her interpretation of this Mitzvah.

7. Read and discuss *My Special Friend* by Floreva G. Cohen. This tells the story of a friendship between two young boys, one of whom has Down's Syndrome. Questions to consider: What are some of the special things that Doron and Jonathan do together? Do you know anyone like Jonathan? How do you feel about being friends with someone like Jonathan? How does the boys' relationship reflect the Mitzvah of Loving One's Neighbor?

Intermediate

1. One aspect of the Mitzvah of Loving One's Neighbor is about turning an enemy into a friend. View the film *My Bodyguard,* which is about a student who, when he is being picked on, chooses the school bully to protect him. Discuss it in light of the Talmudic story about turning an enemy into a friend (see Overview above).

2. Have your students reenact the story of the heathen who challenges Shammai and Hillel to teach him the entire Torah while standing on one foot. For the complete story, see *Shabbat* 31a. Perform the story for another class or the whole school.

3. Have each student or group of students write short stories using Hillel's maxim, "What is hateful to yourself do not do to your neighbor" as the title and theme.

4. Supply the class with a variety of recent newspapers, magazines, scissors, glue, and a large sheet of paper or poster board. Have the students look for examples of the Mitzvah to love one's neighbor and create a collage with their clippings.

5. This exercise will help students evaluate their personal attitudes and beliefs regarding the issues surrounding Loving One's Neighbor. Read each of the statements below to the class. In response to each one, students place themselves on a values continuum. The continuum may be drawn as a line on the chalkboard or made with masking tape on the floor. Label one end of the continuum "Strongly agree," and the other end

"Strongly disagree." Place a range of opinions in between, such as "Somewhat agree," "Undecided," and "Somewhat disagree." Statements for reactions:

a. Rich people are smarter than poor people.

b. Boys are better at sports than girls.

c. Able-bodied people feel uncomfortable around handicapped people.

d. If someone hits you, you should hit back.

e. Each racial group (Black, Hispanic, Asian, white, etc.) should live in its own separate neighborhood.

Discuss responses, asking students to defend their positions and to identify factors that might change these attitudes. Relate the discussion to the Mitzvah of *V'ahavta L'rayacha Kamocha*.

6. This activity, which uses unshelled walnuts as a metaphor for human beings, will demonstrate the unique qualities and special attributes of every individual.

Bring a bag of unshelled walnuts to class. Give one nut to each student. Be sure students do not in any way mark or label the walnuts. Have each examine a walnut, noting creases, wrinkles, cracks, and other distinguishing marks. Collect all the walnuts in a bowl and mix them up. Each student then tries to find his/her walnut.

Discussion questions: Do all the walnuts look alike? Why or why not? What are some examples of unique characteristics of walnuts? Of people? Has anyone in the class ever thought that people of a particular ethnic group all look alike or behave alike? Is this possible? Do non-Jews view Jews as all alike in some ways? Why? What can be done to help people see the uniqueness of every human being?

Secondary

1. Invite a Priest, a Minister, and a Rabbi to discuss the verse from Leviticus 19:18 — "You shall love your neighbor as yourself" and Jesus' paraphrase "All that you would wish that men should do unto you do also unto them" (*Matthew* 7:12). Utilize the questions raised in the Overview above as a basis for the discussion.

2. As mentioned in the Overview section, the Talmud recounts the case of two men traveling in the desert, only one of whom has a jar of water. Pair up members of the class, distributing a copy of the tale. Each pair will present its own ending

to the situation. Once all the presentations have been made, write up the endings and create a class commentary to this Talmudic story.

3. Many community organizations are based on the principle of loving one's neighbor. A few examples are: The Salvation Army, a soup kitchen or shelter, Mazon, HIAS, The Joint Distribution Committee, the Red Cross, and the Magen David Adom, etc. Sometimes a secular or Jewish newspaper, the Chamber of Commerce, or a community ombudsman has access to a complete listing of these organizations. Have your students collect materials and information about these groups, then set up an information table at the synagogue for the benefit of members.

4. Give students an opportunity to fulfill the Mitzvah of Loving One's Neighbor by participating in a community service project. Brainstorm a variety of options from which to choose (e.g., working in a food pantry, tutoring younger children, doing chores for an elderly or handicapped individual, reading to a blind or visually impaired person).

5. Invite a group of students of a different racial, ethnic, or religious background to participate in an organized discussion on interpersonal issues.

a. Pair students with a partner from the other group. Assign one student to be partner A and the other partner B. During a two or three minute conversation, the partners introduce themselves to each other, telling something about their interests and hobbies, where they were born, what school they attend, favorite friends, most interesting experience, etc. Then have each partner introduce the other to the group as a whole.

b. Set up two concentric circles of chairs, each with the same number. Students seated in the inner circle face out and those in the outer circle face in. Direct the students from the synagogue to sit in the outer circle and the guests to sit in the inner circle. (If there are more students from one group, some of them should sit in the other group's circle. Have them switch periodically with others in their group. If there is an odd number of students, a teacher or aide can participate.)

c. The group leader announces an issue which each pair of students discusses. After discussion the group leader elicits comments to be shared with the whole group. Before announcing the next issue, the students in one of the circles move one chair to the left or right so that they have a new partner for the next issue. Repeat the process. Some suggested issues for discussion: Who are some of your heroes/heroines, and why? What are some areas of conflict between you and your parents(s)? People are poor because they are lazy. How do you feel when someone makes a slur against your racial, ethnic, or religious group? How do you feel when someone makes a slur against another group? One thing I do not like about being Jewish, Black, etc., is _____.

6. View and discuss the film *Eye of the Storm*, which records a unique two-day experiment done by a third grade teacher in a midwestern community. During the experiment the teacher made an arbitrary division of her class into superior and inferior groups based solely on eye color. Attitudes, behavior, and classroom performance were seriously affected as the children were subjected to segregation and discrimination. Consider questions such as these: How did the teacher divide the students? How did each group react to its status? How would you have reacted if you had been a member of the group that was favored? Of the group that was discriminated against? Which group is more likely to practice the Mitzvah of Loving One's Neighbor?

ALL-SCHOOL PROGRAMS

1. Hold a photography show with the theme "Love Your Neighbor." Have cameras available for the students to check out and use. When the pictures are taken and developed, mount and display them, inviting the synagogue membership to the showing. Note: For young children simple Instamatics are the easiest to use.

2. Hold an all-school "sing down." The sing down works as follows: Divide the students into several groups of mixed ages. Each group in turn thinks up a song with a particular word in it, in this case the word love, or its Hebrew equivalent, *ahavah*. The group must sing the song until they come to this word. After each group has sung a song, the first group begins again. When a group is not able to come up with a song for its turn, it is eliminated. The last remaining group is declared the winner.

3. At an assembly for Grades K-6, show the film *The Toymaker*. In the film two hand puppets, one striped and one spotted, are friends until they discover that they are different. Break up into groups by class and discuss such questions as the following: Have you ever been friends with someone who was, in any way, different? Did their being different stop you from being friends? Has anyone stopped being friends with you when they realized you were Jewish? How do physical differences affect friendships?

RESOURCES

For the Teacher

Bloch, Abraham P. *A Book of Jewish Ethical Concepts.* New York: KTAV Publishing House, Inc., 1984, pp. 197-200.

Jacobs, Louis. *The Book of Jewish Belief.* West Orange, NJ: Behrman House, 1984, pp. 166-173.

Layman, Robert. *My Child Is Different.* New York: United Synagogue Commission on Jewish Education, n.d.

Leibowitz, Nehama. *Studies in Vayikra (Leviticus).* Jerusalem: The World Zionist Organization, 1980, pp. 194-198.

Maimonides, Moses. *The Commandments.* New York: The Soncino Press, 1967, vol. 1, pp. 220-221.

Plaut, W. Gunther, ed. *The Torah: A Modern Commentary.* New York: UAHC Press, 1981, pp. 892-893.

For the Students

Cohen, Floreva G. *My Special Friend.* New York: Board of Jewish Education of Greater New York, 1986. (Grades K-2)

DuVall, Lynn. *Respecting Our Differences: A Guide to Getting Along in a Changing World.* Minneapolis: Free Spirit Publishing, 1994. (Grades 7 and up)

Isaacs, Ronald H., and Kerry M. Olitzky. *Doing Mitzvot: Mitzvah Projects for Bar/Bat Mitzvah.* Hoboken, NJ: KTAV Publishing House, Inc., 1994, pp. 124-134. (Grades 6-8)

Audiovisual

Behind the Mask. An 8 minute film which explores the uniqueness of each individual and the similarities that unite all people. Anti-Defamation League. (Grades K-6)

Ben Adam L'chaveiro. A 15 minute film set in a Jewish summer camp about the relationships among campers. USC Film Library. (Grades 5-8)

The Courage To Care. A 30 minute video about non-Jews who helped protect and rescue Jews during the Holocaust. Anti-Defamation League. (Grades 7 and up)

Eye of the Storm. A 25 minute film which records a two-day experiment during which a teacher separated her class into "superior" and "inferior" groups, based solely on eye color. Anti-Defamation League. (Grades 5 and up)

My Bodyguard. A 96 minute video about a student who is being picked on, and who chooses the school bully to protect him. Available from video stores. (Grades 7 and up)

To Jew Is Not a Verb. In a 15 minute video, David is accused of "jewing" another boy while trading baseball cards. A lesson about stereotyping results. Beacon. (Grades 4-9)

The Toymaker. A 15 minute film about two hand puppets, one striped and the other spotted, who are friends until they discover that they are different. University Film and Video. (Grades PK-4)

"V'ahavta L'reyacha Kamocha." On the audio-cassette *Only This* by Mah Tovu. BeeZee Productions. Available from A.R.E. Publishing, Inc. (Grades 3 and up)

UNIT 35

Loving the Proselyte
אַהֲבַת הַגֵּר

OVERVIEW

The Jewish attitude toward the convert is derived from the verse "You shall love the *ger*" (Deuteronomy 10:19). In the Bible *ger* (pronounced *geyr*) means a stranger, one who is born elsewhere, but is residing in Israel. In the Rabbinic period, however, the word *ger* came to mean a person who had adopted the Jewish religion and had become a part of the Jewish people. Maimonides draws on this interpretation to codify the Mitzvah: "You shall love the convert." He points out that while a Jew-by-Choice is included in the Mitzvah of loving one's neighbor as oneself because converts adopted the faith of Israel, God called for more love for them by adding a special commandment in their behalf (Maimonides, *The Commandments*, vol. 1, p. 222).

The only clear biblical reference to an individual adopting the Jewish religion is Ruth, who refuses to abandon her widowed mother-in-law, saying: "Don't urge me to leave you or to turn back from following you. For where you go, I will go, and where you live, I will live. Your people will be my people, and your God will be my God. Where you die, I will die, and there will I be buried. Thus and more the Lord shall do to me if anything but death separates me from you" (Ruth 1:16-17).

Rabbinic literature contains conflicting views about converts. On the one hand, a convert is considered dearer to God than all of Israel who stood at Mt. Sinai. "Had the Israelites not witnessed the lightening, thunder, quaking mountain, and sounding trumpets, they would not have accepted the Torah. But the convert, who did not see or hear any of these things, came and surrendered himself to God and took the yoke of heaven upon himself" (*Tanchuma Buber, Lech Lecha* 6, 32a). On the other hand, another *midrash* warns: "Do not trust a convert even to the twenty-fourth generation, because the inherent evil is still within him" (*Ruth Zutra* 1:12). Still another *midrash* strikes a balance, saying that one should repel a potential convert with the (weaker) left hand and draw [him/her] near with the (stronger) right hand (*Mechilta, Amalek* 3).

In fact, the general practice of Rabbis since Rabbinic times has been to refuse a person seeking conversion to Judaism three times in order to determine his or her sincerity.

While there is concern about the motive of a person who wants to become Jewish, the Rabbis generally displayed a positive attitude toward converts. The difficult conditions under which many Jewish communities existed during the Middle Ages, however, led some Rabbis to refuse to accept any converts. In certain places, under both Christian and Moslem rule, conversion to Judaism was prohibited, and the convert, and anyone who aided him or her, was put to death. Nevertheless, Jewish tradition is supportive of a positive attitude toward those who did become Jewish.

The Rambam was especially positive toward converts. A proselyte asked if he was permitted to recite the words "Our God and God of our fathers" in the *Amidah* and the words "You have brought us out of the land of Egypt" in *Ezrat Avoteynu*. Rambam answered: "In the same way that every Jew by birth says prayers and blessings, you, too, may pray and bless . . . . Do not consider your origin as inferior. While we are the descendants of Abraham, Isaac, and Jacob, you derive from God through whose word the world was created" (*A Maimonides Reader* by Isadore Twersky, pp. 475ff). In keeping with this sentiment, according to Jewish law, one is not supposed to mention that someone is a convert, lest the person be embarrassed about his or her origins. Caution regarding the acceptance of converts was common in most Jewish communities into the first part of the twentieth century. In recent years, a more open approach has been taken, especially within the liberal Jewish community.

One of the major proposals of the outreach program of Reform Judaism initiated in 1978 is to welcome with open arms those who wish to accept Judaism. Although there remain serious disagreements among the movements with regard to the requirements for conversion, there is general agreement that a sincere convert should be welcomed and encouraged by the Jewish community.

ACTIVITIES

Primary

1. Explain the Mitzvah of loving the convert. Have each student draw a picture of his or her favorite Jewish holiday to share with someone who is becoming Jewish. Include holiday symbols, foods, and practices.

2. Make *Shalach Manot* for Purim and send them to persons who have become Jewish during the past year. The *Shalach Manot* might include *hamentaschen*, nuts, dried fruit, and pennies.

3. Invite prospective and/or recent Jews-by-Choice to a class and share a cooking experience, preparing a Jewish food such as *challah*, *latkes*, *hamentaschen*, or *matzah* balls.

4. Discuss how the students feel when they enter a new situation (a new school, club or group). What are some things that help them to feel comfortable in these new situations? Which of these can be done to welcome newcomers to the synagogue?

5. Invite a Jew-by-Choice to the class to teach an age-appropriate lesson. The person can briefly describe the process of becoming Jewish and why he or she chose Judaism.

6. Read and discuss the following version of Ruth 1:1-16:

The Story of Ruth

Once there was a Jewish woman named Naomi who lived in Moab. Each of her two sons married a non-Jewish woman. The names of the wives were Orpah and Ruth.

When her sons died, Naomi decided to return to Israel and let her daughters-in-law get on with their lives. Naomi told Orpah and Ruth to stay in Moab, where they would have a good chance of getting married again and having a family.

But they loved her so much they didn't want to leave her.

Finally, Orpah agreed to stay behind. She kissed Naomi goodbye. But Ruth refused to leave Naomi, and said to her "Do not tell me to leave you. I will go wherever you go. I will live wherever you live. Your people will be my people, and your God will be my God."

So Naomi allowed Ruth to stay with her and the two of them went to Israel.

Some suggested questions: Why does Naomi tell Orpah and Ruth to stay in Moab? How do they respond at first? What does Ruth tell Naomi? Explain to the students that this statement indicates that Ruth wants to be Jewish.

Intermediate

1. As a class, prepare a presentation on a topic that has been studied during the year and present it to an "Introduction to Judaism" class. Be prepared to answer questions.

2. Interview a person who has become Jewish. Prior to the interview have each student prepare appropriate questions to ask. Each can write a short report after the interview is completed. Share the reports in class.

3. Generate a list of reasons why someone might become Jewish. Ask the students what they like best about being Jewish. Discuss whether or not a non-Jew might also like those same things.

4. Point out to students that Jews-by-Choice are to be regarded in the same manner as born Jews. In fact, Jewish tradition teaches that we are not to mention that a person is a convert. Create guidelines for how Jews should treat Jews-by-Choice. Share the guidelines with the congregation by publishing them in the bulletin.

5. Ask each student to pretend that he/she has recently decided to become Jewish. Have each write a diary entry or a letter to a friend or relative telling about this decision.

6. Read and discuss the following story from *Bamidbar Rabbah* 8:2:

The Flock of Goats and the Stag

Once there was a king who had a flock of goats. One day, a stag joined the flock and grazed with them. When the flock rested, the stag rested.

When the king learned about this he said: "When the stag is in the field, let him have a nice shepherd; don't let anyone harm him. When the stag comes in with the flock, give him something to drink."

The shepherds were surprised. They said: "Master, you have so many goats and you don't warn us about them. Every day, you warn us about the stag."

The king replied: "The goats have no choice. They always graze in the field all day and come in each night to sleep in the stable. Stags, however, usually sleep in the wilderness. They aren't used to entering the living places of human beings. Shall we not consider it a merit for this stag who has left behind a vast wilderness, and has come to be with us?"

Similarly, shouldn't we be grateful to the convert who leaves a family, a home, and a people, and comes to us? Therefore, God provided extra protection for a convert, as it is written "You shall love the convert" (Deuteronomy 10:19).

Some suggested questions: Why does the king treat the stag differently from the goats? What is so special about the stag? How is a Jew-by-Choice similar to the stag?

Secondary

1. Arrange for class members to assist those studying Judaism by tutoring Hebrew, sitting with them during services, or inviting them to their homes for a Shabbat or festival meal.

2. Research and report on the lives of important Jews-by-Choice. Among those you may wish to include are: Jethro; Rahab; Ruth; Onkelos; Aquila; Bulan, King of the Khazars; Obadiah the Norman; Setsuzo Kotsuji; Sammy Davis, Jr.; and Lydia Kukoff.

3. Watch the videotape *Choosing Judaism*. Among the questions to discuss: What are some of the problems faced by Jews-by-Choice? What can the students do to help ease their difficulties?

4. Read the following "letter" to the class:

Shalom!
I am a member of a synagogue in a large city. Recently we have had a lot of new members join who are Jewish-by-Choice. They seem to know as much or more about Judaism than most born Jews, but I am very concerned about their

impact on the congregation. They have only been Jewish a short time and don't really know what it means. What should we do?

Each student should answer this letter as if he/she were a Jewish advice columnist. Share the responses.

5. Plan a worship service on the theme of conversion. Use some of the quotations from the Overview section, as well as from other appropriate sources. Ask a Jew-by-Choice to give the sermon.

6. Ask the students to role play a person telling a group of Jews that he/she is planning on becoming Jewish. Reactions should range from enthusiastic acceptance to disbelief ("Why would anyone want to be a Jew?"). Other reactions might be: "Converts make the best Jews"; "It's tough to be a Jew"; "If you need anything, we'll be glad to help."

7. Create a packet of materials to be given to a person interested in becoming Jewish. Among the items to include: A Jewish calendar, a bibliography of basic Judaism, a guide to local Jewish institutions and places of interest, and information about conversion.

ALL-SCHOOL PROGRAMS

1. Organize a host-family program for your congregation. Members of the congregation serve as hosts (or extended family) for a person becoming Jewish.

2. Have students design and implement a campaign to sensitize the congregation to the needs of Jews-by-Choice. Such a campaign might include writing a regular column in the newsletter, beginning adult education programs, designing flyers to be sent home from school, creating posters for the synagogue, etc.

3. Establish a videotape library of interviews with Jews-by-Choice. Older students can design a questionnaire, then find and interview Jews-by-Choice. Questions can include relevant subjects, such as personal background, reasons for becoming Jewish, reaction of family, etc. Intermediate students can catalog the videotapes and promote them to teachers, congregants, and the com-

munity through articles and flyers. Primary students can create a bulletin board about this new videotape library.

4. At an assembly have one class give a lecture or put on a play about one of the famous Jews-by-Choice. (For a list of some of these individuals, see Secondary activity #2 above.)

RESOURCES

For the Teacher

Dubner, Stephen J. "Choosing My Religion." *New York Times Magazine,* March 31, 1996.

Eichhorn, David Max, ed. *Conversion to Judaism: A History and Analysis.* Hoboken, NJ: KTAV Publishing House, Inc., 1965.

Epstein, Lawrence. *Conversion to Judaism: A Guidebook.* Northvale, NJ: Jason Aronson, 1994.

Epstein, Lawrence, ed. *A Light Unto the Nations: Readings on Conversion to Judaism.* Northvale, NJ: Jason Aronson, 1995.

Huberman, Steven. *New Jews: The Dynamics of Religious Conversion.* New York: UAHC Press, 1979.

Isaacs, Ronald H. *Becoming Jewish: A Handbook for Conversion.* Hoboken, NJ: KTAV Publishing House, Inc., in press.

Orenstein, Debra, ed. *Lifecycles: Jewish Women on Life Passages & Personal Milestones.* Vol. 1. Woodstock, VT: Jewish Lights Publishing, 1994, pp. 231-254.

"Proselytes." In *Encyclopaedia Judaica.* Jerusalem: Keter Publishing House Jerusalem Ltd., 1972, vol. 13, cols. 1182-1184.

Rosenbloom, Joseph R. *Conversion to Judaism: From the Biblical Period to the Present.* Ann Arbor, MI: Books on Demand, n.d.

Strassfeld, Sharon, and Michael Strassfeld, comps. and eds. *The Third Jewish Catalog.* Philadelphia: The Jewish Publication Society of America, 1980, pp. 258-268.

Why Choose Judaism: New Dimensions of Jewish Outreach. New York: UAHC Press, 1985.

For the Students

Baum, Eli. *Mitzvot Bein Adam Lachaveiro.* Hoboken, NJ: KTAV Publishing House, Inc., 1980, pp. 62-64. (Grades 3-6)

Newman, Shirley. *An Introduction to Kings, Later Prophets and Writings.* West Orange, NJ: Behrman House, 1981, pp. 140-146. (Grades 6-9)

Portnoy, Mindy Avra. *Mommy Never Went to Hebrew School.* Rockville, MD: Kar-Ben Copies, Inc., 1989. (Grades PK-3)

Audiovisual

Choosing Judaism. A 30 minute video in which four Jews-by-choice reveal their personal reasons for choosing Judaism. UAHC Press. (Grades 10 and up)

Intermarriage: When Love Meets Tradition. This 33 minute video focuses on five young interfaith couples and explores such challenges as acceptance, finding common values, raising children, etc. (Grades 10 and up)

Prager, Dennis. *Why Jews Must Seek Converts.* A 90 minute discussion on the topic, available on video or audiocassette. Ultimate Issues. (Grades 10-adult)

UNIT 36

OVERVIEW

Kibud Av Va'Aym, honoring one's father and mother, is the only Mitzvah of the Ten Commandments, and one of the few Mitzvot in the Torah, with a promise attached to it. "Honor your father and mother, that you may long endure [and that you may fare well] on the land that the Lord your God is giving you" (Exodus 20:12). Words in brackets are included in the repetition of the Ten Commandments in Deuteronomy 5:16. The inclusion of the promise implies that the Mitzvah is extraordinarily important. It is among the Mitzvot for which one is rewarded in both this world and in the world to come (*Peah* 1:1). Saadia Gaon, who taught in the tenth century, considered this commandment to be the most important of the Ten Commandments.

The first four of the Ten Commandments are clearly human obligations toward God, while the last five are human obligations toward other human beings. Honoring one's parents serves as a transition between the two groups because, by honoring one's parents, one honors God. As Rabbi Gunther Plaut explains: "Parents are God's representatives and partners in the rearing of their children, and children who fail to respect this special position are offending against God as well" (*The Torah: A Modern Commentary*, edited by W. Gunther Plaut, p. 556).

The Talmud quotes God speaking of one who honors one's parents: "I ascribe merit to them as though I had dwelt among them and they had honored me" (*Kiddushin* 30b).

According to a *midrash*, honoring one's parents includes "providing them with food and drink, clothes and warmth, and guiding their footsteps [when they are old and frail]" (*Sifra* to Leviticus 19:3). In general, studying Torah and doing good deeds are considered ideal ways to honor one's parents. In addition, one is to perform the Mitzvah joyously.

Furthermore, if a child sees a parent transgressing Jewish law, the child should not say, "You have transgressed a law of Torah." Rather, the child should ask, "Is it not written in the Torah thus?" However, if a parent orders a child to transgress a law such as profaning the Sabbath, the child is to disobey because God's law is highest. Also, if a child wishes to leave home in order to study Torah, the child may do so even over the parents' objections.

Complementing the Mitzvah to honor one's parents is the commandment to revere one's parents. This is taught in the verse, "A person shall revere his mother and his father" (Leviticus 19:3). The Hebrew word *yarey* is difficult to translate. It can mean to fear, to respect, to show awe, or to revere.

Why in Leviticus 19 is the mother listed first, while the father is listed first in the Ten Commandments? Because it is more natural to honor one's mother, the father is listed first in the Ten Commandments, where the verb "honor" is used. Similarly, it is more natural to revere one's father, so the mother is listed first in Leviticus 19:3, where the verb "revere" is used.

According to a *midrash*, to revere one's parents means one should not sit in their chair, speak in their place, or contradict their words (*Sifra* to Leviticus 19:3). Two negative Mitzvot forbid a person from cursing (Exodus 21:17) and striking parents. Although the Torah does not explicitly forbid either of these actions, the Mitzvot are derived from the Torah's prohibition against cursing (Exodus 21:17) or striking (Exodus 21:15) another Jew. In both cases, the Torah specifies the penalty as death, although it is unlikely that such punishment was ever carried out.

Kibud Av Va'Aym applies to stepparents and anyone else with parenting responsibilities.

ACTIVITIES

Primary

1. Discuss with students what is special about their parents? How do the students honor their parents? What responsibilities do they have toward them?

2. In the secular world, we observe Mother's Day and Father's Day as special days to celebrate mothers and fathers. Have the students list ways they celebrate these occasions. Next, have them

create a list of ways they can honor their parents on a daily basis.

3. Have the students generate all the possible replies to the question, "What makes a parent?"

4. Make a family scrapbook. Remember that there are many different types of families (i.e., single parent, step families, foster families). Help students realize that everyone's family is unique and special. The scrapbooks can be made of construction paper stapled together with hand drawn pictures or more elaborately made with photos and "store-bought" scrapbooks. Students should present these as gifts to their parent(s) as a way of fulfilling the Mitzvah of *Kibud Av Va'Aym*.

5. Learn the Hebrew words for mother (*ema*) and father (*aba*). Sing the song "*Ema-Aba*" from *Especially Wonderful Days* by Steve Reuben. As a part of the unit on this Mitzvah, invite parents to class to hear this song presented.

6. Read and discuss the story "A Big Red Tomato" from *Who Knows Ten?* by Molly Cone. Consider the following questions: How does Mr. Benjamin treat his parents? How does the other man treat his parents? Why does Mr. Benjamin receive the baby? If you were Mr. Day, would you have given the baby to Mr. Benjamin? Who does a better job of fulfilling the Mitzvah of *Kibud Av Va'Aym*?

7. With your students create a description of the ideal parent. Evaluate the list. Did students list things that their own parents could agree to? Are there items on the list that describe their own parents? How would a description of an ideal parent written by their parents be the same as their descriptions? How would such a description be different?

Intermediate

1. Divide the class into groups of three or more students each. Assign each group a different biblical family: Abraham, Sarah, and Isaac; Isaac, Rebekah, Jacob and Esau; Adam, Eve, Cain, and Abel; Noah and his family; Jacob, Leah, Rachel, and their children.

   Students should read the appropriate biblical passages in order to create short skits. The

material in the passages should depict either honor or dishonor being shown parents. At the conclusion of each skit, the students should evaluate the situation and discuss how honor or dishonor was shown.

2. Have students write an original story entitled "What My Parent(s) Mean To Me" or "Special Times With My Mom/Dad." Illustrate these if desired.

3. Ask students to write a letter nominating their parent(s) as "Parent(s) of the Year," with reasons why they deserve this honor.

4. Discuss with the students: Do you have to help around the house? For what chores are you responsible? What happens if you don't follow through with your jobs? How is taking part in family chores a way of honoring father and mother?

5. Ask each student to list four concerns he/she would have as a parent (e.g., the health of children, safety, influence of television, etc.). Each student should then interview his/her parent(s), asking each to list four concerns they have as parents. Also, ask parents how they would like their children to show them honor. Discuss the similarities and differences in the responses.

6. Instruct students to draw a comic strip which illustrates one way that they honor their parents.

Secondary

1. View and discuss the film *Lies My Father Told Me*. In what ways does the boy honor and dishonor his father? In what ways does the boy's father honor and dishonor his father-in-law?

2. View and discuss the film *Fiddler on the Roof*. What is the relationship between Tevye and his daughters? How is he like a father to Mottel the tailor? Are parental relationships still like this? How have things changed? Did children seem to honor their parents more during Tevye's time than now? How has modern society contributed to a change in our relationships with our parents?

3. During the mid-1980s, there was a flurry of cases in which teen-agers turned their parents in to the

authorities for illegal drug use. Poll the students to see whether they would report their parents for similar unlawful behavior. Discuss the pros and cons for turning in parents. Elicit from the students alternative courses of action, such as talking to their school counselors, Rabbi, other relatives, or support groups. You may wish to point out that the Nazis and other repressive regimes encouraged children to report their parents for doing or saying things against the government.

4. According to Jewish tradition, if a parent orders a child to transgress a Mitzvah, the child should disobey. Also, if a child wants to leave home to study Torah, the child may do so even over parental objection. Have the students describe situations in which they think it is legitimate to disobey their parents. Examples might include: if they want to live in Israel, but their parents don't want them to; if they want to be a conscientious objector, etc.

5. Compare the Mitzvot to honor one's parents and to fear/revere one's parents. Have students look up the meanings of these words in the dictionary. (Students familiar with Hebrew could look up the Hebrew words *yarey* and *kavod*.) Also point out that there is no commandment to love one's parents. Discuss.

6. Describe this scenario to your students: Miriam is a thirteen-year-old daughter of parents who smoke. She does not like the smell of the smoke; it makes her eyes water. She has also learned that people who smoke are much more likely to contract lung cancer. Have the students role play Miriam confronting her parents while trying not to break the Mitzvah of Honoring Parents.

ALL-SCHOOL PROGRAMS

1. Plan a Parent/Child Day geared toward improving communication. Among the activities to choose from, depending upon the age of the participants, are the following:
   a. Listen to the song "Cat's in the Cradle" by Harry Chapin. Provide each participant with a copy of the lyrics. Have parents and children share their reactions to this song.
   b. Have parents write a letter to their child(ren) describing what it was like when they were growing up, how their life as a teen-ager

compares to life now, how they got along (or didn't get along) with their parents. Parents might opt to tape this on cassette. Provide for sharing time of this material.
   c. Make anonymous wishes. Have children and parents write up wishes they have for each other, leaving them unsigned. Toss all of the wishes together in a basket, bag, or other container. Have each participant draw out a wish and read it aloud. There will be no dearth of material to discuss. Utilize social workers, youth group staff, teachers, Director of Education, and Rabbi to develop additional ideas utilizing this theme of communication.

2. Plan a Mother's Day/Father's Day worship service and brunch. Students may find appropriate readings from Jewish tradition, as well as write their own selections.

3. Sponsor a family camp-out at a local park or campground with the theme *Kibud Av Va'Aym*. Utilize some of the activities described in this chapter. The program could run over Shabbat. This would provide a way for families to get away from it all and to spend time together. Allow time for celebrating Shabbat, hikes, resting, meals, etc.

RESOURCES

For the Teacher

Jacobs, Louis. *The Book of Jewish Practice*. West Orange, NJ: Behrman House, 1987, pp. 54-59.

Maimonides, Moses. *The Commandments*. New York: The Soncino Press, 1967, vol. 1, pp. 226-228.

"Parents, Honor of." In *Encyclopaedia Judaica*. Jerusalem: Keter Publishing House Jerusalem, Ltd., 1972, vol. 13, cols. 100-101.

Plaut, W. Gunther, ed. *The Torah: A Modern Commentary*. New York: UAHC Press, 1981, pp. 553-560.

For the Students

Artson, Bradley Shavit. *It's a Mitzvah: Step-by-Step to Jewish Living*. West Orange, NJ: Behrman House and New York: The Rabbinical Assembly, 1995, pp. 96-117. (Grades 8-adult)

Baum, Eli. *Mitzvot Bein Adam Lachaveiro*. Hoboken, NJ: KTAV Publishing House, Inc., 1980, pp. 12-14. (Grades 4-6)

Cone, Molly. *Who Knows Ten?* New York: UAHC

Press, 1965, pp. 39-46. (Grades K-3)

Fox, Marci. *The Ten Commandments.* Instant Lesson. Los Angeles: Torah Aura Productions. (Grades K-2)

Gersh, Harry. *Midrash: Rabbinic Lore.* West Orange, NJ: Behrman House, 1985, pp. 57-58. (Grades 9 and up)

Isaacs, Ronald H., and Kerry M. Olitzky. *Doing Mitzvot: Mitzvah Projects for Bar/Bat Mitzvah.* Hoboken, NJ: KTAV Publishing House, Inc., 1994, pp. 51-62. (Grades 6-8)

Karkowsky, Nancy. *The Ten Commandments.* West Orange, NJ: Behrman House, Inc., 1988. (Grades 3-4)

Kaye, Joan S.; Jan Rabinowitch; and Naomi F. Towvim. *Why Be Good? Sensitivities and Ethics in Rabbinic Literature.* Boston: Bureau of Jewish Eduation of Greater Boston, 1985, pp. 13-24. (Grades 7 and up)

Rosenberg, Amye. *Mitzvot.* West Orange, NJ: Behrman House, 1984, pp. 3-5. (Grades K-2)

Shalom Bayit Game. Boston: Bureau of Jewish Education of Greater Boston. (Grades 7 and up)

Ten Times Ten. Instant Lesson. Los Angeles: Torah Aura Productions. (Grades 6-adult)

Topek, Susan. *Ten Good Rules.* Rockville, MD: Kar-Ben Copies, Inc., 1992. (Grades PK-1)

Audiovisual

The Bent Tree. A short animated film, available in 4 or 8 minute versions, which tells of a child's longings and a mother's responsibilities. Films Incorporated. (All grades)

Bloomers. A 30 minute film about the relationship between a daughter and mother who need each other's support. Churchill Media. (Grades 4 and up)

"Ema-Aba." On the audiocassette *Especially Wonderful Days* by Steve Reuben. A sing along song in Hebrew. A.R.E. Publishing, Inc. (Grades K-6)

Fiddler on the Roof. The popular 169 minute feature film on video, based on the stories of Sholem Aleichem. Facets Multimedia, Inc. and local video stores. (Grades 5 and up)

Lies My Father Told Me. A 102 minute film about the relationship between a young Jewish boy, his assimilated father, and traditional grandfather. Modern Sound Pictures, Inc. (Grades 10 and up)

When Parents Grow Old. A 15 minute trigger film edited from the movie *I Never Sang for My Father.* A young man on the verge of marriage must decide where his responsibility lies to his suddenly widowed father whose health is failing. Board of Jewish Education of Greater New York. (Grades 7 and up)

General Bibliography

For the Teacher

Berkovits, Eliezer. *Not in Heaven: The Nature and Function of Halakha.* New York: KTAV Publishing House, Inc., 1983.

Birnbaum, Philip. *Maimonides' Mishneh Torah (Yad Hazakah).* Rockaway Beach, NY: Hebrew Publishing Co, 1944.

"Commandments, The 613," and "Commandments, Reasons for." In *Encyclopaedia Judaica.* Jerusalem: Keter Publishing House Jerusalem Ltd., vol. 5, cols. 760-792.

Ganzfried, Solomon. *Code of Jewish Law: Kitzur Shulhan Arukh.* Rockaway Beach, NY: Hebrew Publishing Co., 1961.

Isaacs, Ronald H., and Kerry M. Olitzky. *Sacred Celebrations. A Jewish Holiday Handbook.* Hoboken, NJ: KTAV Publishing House, Inc., 1994.

Jacobs, Louis. *The Book of Jewish Belief.* West Orange, NJ: Behrman House, 1984.

Klein, Isaac. *A Guide to Jewish Religious Practice.* New York: The Jewish Theological Seminary of America, 1979.

Knobel, Peter S. *Gates of the Seasons: A Guide to the Jewish Year.* New York: Central Conference of American Rabbis, 1983.

Kolatch, Alfred. *The Jewish Book of Why.* Middle Village, NY: Jonathan David Publishing Co., 1981.

Leibowitz, Nehama. *Studies in Devarim (Deuteronomy).* Jerusalem: The World Zionist Organization, 1980.

Maimonides, Moses. *The Commandments.* New York: The Soncino Press, 1967.

Maslin, Simeon J., ed. *Gates of Mitzvah.* New York: Central Conference of American Rabbis, 1979.

Schechter, Solomon. *Aspects of Rabbinic Theology.* Woodstock, VT: Jewish Lights Publishing, 1993.

Stern, Chaim, ed. *On the Doorposts of Your House.* New York: Central Conference of American Rabbis, 1994.

Strassfeld, Michael. *The Jewish Holidays: A Guide and Commentary.* New York: Harper and Row Publishers, 1988.

Telushkin, Joseph. *Jewish Literacy.* New York: William Morrow and Co., Inc., 1991.

———. *Jewish Wisdom.* New York: William Morrow and Co., Inc., 1994.

For the Students

Drucker, Malka. *The Family Treasury of Jewish Holidays.* Waltham, MA: Little, Brown & Co., 1994. (All ages)

Feldman, Sarah. *Mitzvot.* New York: Behrman House, 1996. (Grades K-2)

Fox, Marci. *Making the World Better.* Instant Lesson. Los Angeles: Torah Aura Productions. (Grades K-2)

Gold-Vukson, Marji, *Jewish Holiday Copy Pak™* K-3. Denver: A.R.E. Publishing, Inc. 1993. (Grades K-3)

Gold-Vukson, Marji, *Jewish Holiday Copy Pak™* 4-6. Denver: A.R.E. Publishing, Inc. 1993. (Grades 4-6)

Neusner, Jacob. *Mitzvah.* West Orange, NJ: Behrman House, 1981. (Grades 6-8)

Rosenberg, Amye. *Mitzvot.* West Orange, NJ: Behrman House, 1984. (Grades K-1)

Siegel, Danny. *Tell Me a Mitzvah: Little and Big Ways To Repair the World.* Rockville, MD: Kar-Ben Copies, Inc., 1993. (Grades 2 and up)

Sulkes, Zena, and Al Sulkes, *Mitzvot Copy Pak™.* Denver: A.R.E. Publishing, Inc. 1989. (Grades 5-7)

Computer Program

Mitzvah Mania (for Windows). Chicago, IL: Davka Corporation, 1995. Participants attempt to "gobble up" all the Mitzvot on the screen. Contains six levels of play.

List of Distributors of Audiovisual Materials

Alden Films
Box 449
Clarksburg, NJ 08510

Altschul Group Corp.
11560 Sherman Ave. Suite 100
Evanston, IL 60201

American Melody
Box 270
Guilford, CT 06437

A.R.E. Publishing, Inc.
3945 S. Oneida St.
Denver, CO 80237

Anti-Defamation League
823 United Nations Plaza
New York, NY 10017

Arthur Cantor, Inc.
1501 Broadway, Suite 403
New York, NY 10036

Audio Brandon Films
34 MacQuesten Pkwy. N.
Mt. Vernon, NY 10550

Barr Films Entertainment
122801 Schabarum Ave.
Irvington, CA 91706

Beacon Films Inc.
1560 Sherman Ave.
Evanston, IL 60201

BFA Films & Video, Inc.
2349 Chaffee Dr.
St. Louis, MO 63146

Board of Jewish Education of Greater Boston
333 Nahanton St.
Newton, MA 02159

Board of Jewish Education of Greater New York
426 W. 58th St.
New York, NY 10019

Bureau of Jewish Education
6505 Wilshire Blvd.
Los Angeles, CA 90048

Churchill Media
6901 Woodley Ave.
Van Nuys, CA 91406

The Cinema Guild
1697 Broadway
New York, NY 10019

Coaliltion for the Advancement of Jewish Education
468 Park Ave. South, Room 904
New York, NY 10016

Committee on Congregational Standards of the
United Synagogue of America
155 Fifth Ave.
New York, NY 10010

Constructive Playthings
1227 E. 119th St.
Grandview, MO 64030

CRM Films
2215 Faraday Ave.
Carlsbad, CA 92008

Davka Corporation
7074 N. Western Ave.
Chicago, IL 60645

Direct Cinema
P.O. Box 10003
Santa Monica, CA 90410

EcuFilm
810 Twelfth Ave. South
Nashville, TN 37203

Encyclopedia Brittanica Education Corp.
310 S. Michigan Ave.
Chicago, IL 60604

Ergo Media Inc.
P.O. Box 2037
Teaneck, NJ 07666

Facets Multimedia, Inc.
1517 W. Fullerton Ave.
Chicago, IL 60614

Filmakers Library
124 E. 40th St.
New York, NY 10016

Filmfair Communications
1560 Sherman Ave., Suite 100
Evanston, IL 60201

Films for the Humanities and Sciences
FFH Video
Box 2053
Princeton, NJ 08543

Films, Inc.
5547 N. Ravenswood
Chicago, IL 60640

Franciscan Communications
1229 Santee St.
Los Angeles, CA 90015

Hanna-Barbera Productions
3400 Cahuenga Blvd.
Hollywood, CA 90068

Higher Authority Productions
9500 Collins Ave.
Bal Harbour, FL 33154

Institute for Creative Jewish Media
P.O. Box 426
West Simsbury, CT 06092

International Film Bureau
332 S. Michigan Ave.
Chicago, IL 60604

Jewish Theological Seminary
Department of Radio and Television
3080 Broadway
New York, NY 10002

Learning Corporation of America
1440 S. Sepulveda
Los Angeles, CA 91602

Lightyear Entertainment
350 Fifth Ave., Suite 5101
New York, NY 10018

McGraw-Hill
1221 Avenue of the Americas
New York, NY 10020

Media Guild
11722 Sorrento Valley Rd., Suite E
San Diego, CA 92121

Media Projects
5215 Homer St.
Dallas, TX 75206

Modern Sound Pictures
Box 710
East Lansing, MI 48826

Motion Picture Clearing House
189 Church St.
Toronto, Ont.
Canada M5B 1YF

Museum of Modern Art Circulating Film Library
11 W. 53rd St.
New York, NY 10019

National Center for Jewish Films
Brandeis University, Lown Bldg. 102
Waltham, MA 02254

New Day Films
22-D Hollywood Ave.
Ho-Ho-Kus, NJ 07423

New Legends
608 W. Upsal St.
Philadelphia, PA 19119

NFTY Resources
838 Fifth Ave.
New York, NY 10021

Orion Corporation
1888 Century Park East
Los Angeles, CA 90067

PBS
Division of Public Broadcasting Service
1320 Braddock Place
Alexandria, VA 22314

Phoenix Films
2349 Chaffee Dr.
St. Louis, MO 63146

Simon Wiesenthal Center
9760 W. Pico Blvd.
Los Angeles, CA 90035

Social Studies School Service
P.O. Box 802
Culver City, CA 90232

Swank Motion Pictures
211 S. Jefferson Ave.
St. Louis, MO 63103

Tara Publications
8 Music Fair Rd.
Owings Mill, MD 21117

Torah Aura Productions
4423 Fruitland Ave.
Los Angeles, CA 90058

Torah Umesorah Publications
160 Broadway
New York, NY 10038

Ultimate Issues
6020 Washington Blvd.
Culver City, CA 90232

Union of American Hebrew Congregations (UAHC)
838 Fifth Ave.
New York, NY 10021

UAHC TV & Film Institute
Division of Media and Communications
838 Fifth Ave.
New York, NY 10021

United Jewish Appeal
99 Park Ave.
New York, NY 10016

United Synagogue Commission on Jewish
Education
155 Fifth Avenue
New York, NY 10010

University Film and Video
University of Minnesota
1313 Fifth Street S.E., Suite 108
Minneapolis, MN 55414

USC Film Library
University Park, MC 2212
Los Angeles, CA 90089

Walt Disney Educational Media Co.
500 S. Buena Vista St.
Burbank, CA 91521

Women Make Films
462 Broadway
New York, NY 10013

Zerach Greenfield
77-42 164th St.
Flushing, NY 11366

OTHER TEACHER MANUALS FROM A.R.E.:

Bar/Bat Mitzvah Education: A Sourcebook, edited by Helen Leneman

Creative Movement for a Song: Activities for Young Children by JoAnne Tucker

Hands On! Teacher-made Games for Jewish Early Childhood Settings by Barbara Grundleger

Head Start on Holidays: Jewish Programs for Preschoolers and Their Parents by Roberta Louis Goodman and Andye Honigman Zell

Jewish History — Moments and Methods: An Activity Source Book for Teachers by Sorel Goldberg Loeb and Barbara Binder Kadden

Jewish Literature for Children: A Teaching Guide by Cheryl Silberberg Grossman and Suzy Engman

The Jewish Preschool Teachers Handbook (Revised Edition) by Sandy S. Furfine and Nancy Cohen Nowak

The Jewish Principals Handbook, edited by Audrey Friedman Marcus and Raymond A. Zwerin

Learning Together: A Sourcebook on Jewish Family Education by Janice P. Alper

Lively Legends — Jewish Values: An Early Childhood Teaching Guide by Miriam P. Feinberg and Rena Rotenberg

The New Jewish Teachers Handbook, edited by Audrey Friedman Marcus and Raymond A. Zwerin

Shirah B'Tiyul: A Musical Israel Curriculum by Lori L. Abramson and Joel K. Abramson

Teaching Tefilah: Insights and Activities on Jewish Prayer by Bruce Kadden and Barbara Binder Kadden

Teaching Torah: Insights and Activities by Sorel Goldberg Loeb and Barbara Binder Kadden

A Teachers Guide to Jewish Holidays by Robert Goodman

The Teacher Pleaser: 10,000 Instant Activities for the Jewish Classroom by Marji Gold-Vukson

Torah in Motion: Creating Dance Midrash by JoAnne Tucker and Susan Freeman

Torah Talk: An Early Childhood Teaching Guide by Yona Chubara, Miriam P. Feinberg, and Rena Rotenberg

To order, write, fax, or e-mail A.R.E. Publishing, Inc. 3945 South Oneida Street, Denver, Colorado 80237, (800) 346-7779; (303) 363-7779 (in Colorado); (303) 363-6069 (fax); AREpublish@aol.com (e-mail).